WIND GARDENS

From the tail of a bird
a seed fell,
into the desert of the
howling gales.
Black burned leaves,
branches twisted with
tortured
shrieks of winter blasts.
Roots baked dry.
Salt crystals sparkled
on scarred limbs.
I shall endure,
to flower and seed,
and am that beauty
sculptured by the wind.

W I N D
GARDENS

How to create beautiful gardens in exposed places

Jacob De Ruiter

Te Papa Press
Wellington
2001

Te Papa Press
Museum of New Zealand Te Papa Tongarewa

First edition published as Gardens in the Wind, 1991,
by GP Publications Ltd
This revised and enlarged edition first published 2001
Text and images © Jacob De Ruiter 2001

Te Papa™ is a trademark of the Museum of New Zealand Te Papa Tongarewa
Te Papa Press is an imprint of the Museum of New Zealand Te Papa Tongarewa

ISBN 0-909010-76-5

Design and layout by Walter Moala
Digital imaging by Jeremy Glyde and Michael Hall
Drawings and diagrams by Caroline Campbell
Edited by Jane Parkin with assistance from Lisa Wharton
Index by Janet Hughes
Printed in New Zealand by Brebner Print
Cover photograph by Michael Hall, Te Papa

Published by the Museum of New Zealand Te Papa Tongarewa,
PO Box 467, Wellington

Contents

Preface

There is always a reason for success or failure in gardens and man-made landscapes. It may be due to a lack of understanding of different environmental factors or a limited knowledge of plant selection. Often garden plantings are unbalanced: trees shade and block out views, or maintenance is endless, or gardens are too soon spent. The aim of this book is to offer an insight into these factors, and show how to deal with the elements of salt and inland winds and to re-create the harmony we enjoy in natural landscapes.

Although some people may feel the ideas here expressed could be challenged scientifically, my methods are based on practical experience and a passion for plant observation. Why certain plant species are found in particular habitats, and how they compete and survive, is of particular interest to me. I ask you to read this book with a mind open to the potential of a wide range of plant habitats, from the wild and wind-swept to the sheltered or frosted. *Wind Gardens* deals with most New Zealand habitats, so it is a practical guide for the Kiwi gardener. It will help you to develop your own garden.

After a formal training as an apprentice gardener and subsequently graduating from Lincoln University, I began a search for natural methods that would reduce continuous maintenance. I was then given the challenge by the former Director of Parks in Wellington, the late Ian Galloway, to colonise plants along the extremely wind-swept Cobham Drive. Thus I began the task of learning and developing new techniques for gardening in harsh places.

I have worked on re-vegetation projects and diverse domestic garden styles throughout New Zealand, successfully creating serene landscapes or flamboyant plant displays, sometimes in very difficult environments. These gardens are artistic and personal expressions of a range of styles.

I grow companionate native and exotic plants together so that gardens can become self-sustainable, and able to dominate weeds. By choosing plants which, with equal vigor of growth, can compete with weeds, I can create a low-maintenance garden that flowers throughout the year and expresses the changes of the seasons. I ensure that every plant has an appropriate place where it will flourish for the enjoyment of all. It is this harmony of self-sustainability that I seek from a garden and landscape.

I enjoy new challenges. Each new site has new opportunities. Having free-lanced for 25 years now, I enjoy the reward of my clients' satisfaction in my work. The trick is to create a landscape and to make that re-creation blend in, creating its own harmony so it looks as if it has always been there.

Coral Hyam, my loved partner, has been very patient and helpful with my persistence in writing this book. I am forever grateful that we work well together; one half complements the other.

I also thank Walter Moala, Anne French, Michael Hall, and Jane Parkin for their creative and patient contributions to this book – they have been great to work with. I hope that this publication will provide all the reading necessary for gardening in the wind.

Jacob De Ruiter
Wind Gardens
236 Houghton Bay Road
Houghton Bay
Wellington 6003, New Zealand
Telephone: 04 387 9541 Fax: 04 387 9441
Email: jacob@windgardens.com
Web: www.windgardens.com

Introduction

This book offers a natural approach to ornamental gardening in the wind, an approach that harmonises and absorbs the extremes of climate rather than opposes them. It is a practical guide based on the idea that nature provides us with models that we can observe and adapt to suit our purpose, creating an oasis of surprising beauty in a wind-ravaged place. Wind has many qualities which affect our ability to garden successfully. It restricts plant growth, erodes the soil, and prunes and dries the plants. Plants must either adapt to it or die.

Even though this book is not focused on vegetable gardening, the principles for obtaining shelter in exposed areas apply equally to vegetable as to landscape gardening.

This book is divided into four sections. The first outlines the key considerations to keep in mind when analysing a site, climate, soils and plants. The second section explains how to plan and build your site, and how to prepare it for planting and create wind deflection. It also suggests points to keep in mind when purchasing plants. The third section provides examples of gardens in windy places; and the final section alphabetically lists plant species that can be used in wind gardens, and describes their ability to withstand various kinds of wind conditions.

A landscaped garden is not just a collection of plants but an expression of nature's beauty. For some it may be formal; for others it may be wild and natural. Wherever the winds blow at their harshest, we experience a chilling feeling, and have a vision of a barren landscape scorched by the sun and battered by the elements. While having an inherent beauty, such places appear inhospitable and difficult to garden.

By forming microclimates by bending the wind using the tools of nature, such as earthen mounds and suitable plant species, as well as artificial protection, a different beauty can be nurtured. Certain protective plants can be encouraged to flourish, enabling more delicate ones to survive under their shelter.

Wind is the force of air movement between two different air pockets. If the air pressure of one is greater than the other, it causes air to suck and rush from the high-pressure to the low-pressure zone in order to equalise. The resulting gusts of wind affect the temperature and our sense of well-being.

Strong winds over sea water will lift into salt spray – an effect not often recognised by the human eye, but clearly seen from the burnt foliage of nearby vegetation. Climatic factors such as this differentiate coastal plants from inland plants.

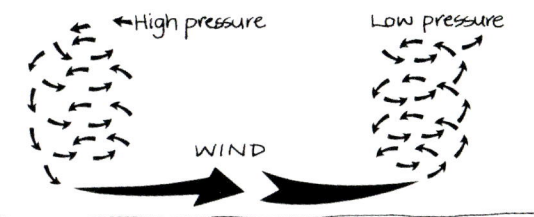

Wind will flow through the lowest path such as Cook Strait. Here the north-westerlies are funnelled, increasing in air preasure to form the famous gusty winds of Wellington.

Wind is the equalising of air pressure, where one mass of air is greater in pressure than the other.

Wind usually seeks the lowest path, and will follow this unless deflected around or above an obstruction. It often increases in pressure as it sweeps and falls down to enter a gap through which it can charge in a turbulent flurry. Its path can be blocked with solid objects or by planting, the latter being more effective as it filters the force of the wind. This force can be strong enough to suck up heavy objects, carry them over a considerable distance and drop them.

But wind has its moods. In the bush it can roll in gusts, and you can hear it roaring some distance away until, with a loud thud, it comes thumping down, pushing with force against any object in its way.

Clouds of stinging seawater can be carried some distance by the wind. Heavier droplets soon fall, but fine salty spray is blown well beyond the coastline. The stronger the burning force of the wind, the more severe the damage caused, especially when the temperature is cold. This damaging factor restricts the survival of many plant species.

Wind is forced to ascend as it pushes over hills and mountains. Its load of moisture condenses and forms rain, which is dumped as the air cools. Then, on the leeward side, the wind flows downhill, warming and drying on descent. The effect of this can be seen in the changes to vegetation patterns from Christchurch, on the east coast of the South Island, across to Hokitika on the west coast. The lush forest growth on the west side of the main divide and the contrasting open tussock landscape on the east are both caused by the prevailing west wind.

Despite all these qualities of the wind, the main visible evidence is the effect it has on plants: the pruned and deformed shapes of trees and shrubs, which are often brittle and woody specimens that are prevented from reaching their optimum growth.

Wind has a drying effect upon the soil as well as the plants. This is why most of the xerophytic plants (those able to tolerate dry conditions) are able to live in windy areas. Plants react to wind and dryness by having reduced leaves or a waxy film over their foliage; by growing small hairs and reducing their stomata (the pores through which they breathe); or by curling leaves, and growing into the shape the wind dictates.

Wind has many qualities that affect our ability to garden successfully. This book focuses on two wind types – salt winds and salt-free winds – and it is these characteristics that differentiate inland from coastal climates.

Designing the garden

Designing a landscape

A landscaped garden differs in essence from a natural garden because it is designed to satisfy human needs. Successful landscaping involves clarifying your intentions, identifying the natural advantages and limitations of your site, then working through a series of steps towards realising your plans. You may wish to achieve several things. List those needs you expect to fulfil when creating your garden. For example:

PRACTICAL NEEDS	ABSTRACT NEEDS
Erosion control	Privacy and tranquillity
Revegetation of bare ground	Security
Wind shelter	Meditation places
Reduced maintenance	A beautiful place
Food supply	Expression of a particular theme
Weed control	Enhanced quality of social
Source of income	gatherings

These needs may change as time passes. Nevertheless, they provide a focus for decisions about site layout and plant selection.

Cabbage trees planted closely in a cluster provide a dramatic, textured entrance to the Wellington College of Education, Karori.

Aesthetic elements

The sensory appeal of a garden should be planned, using principles that relate to the use of colour, texture, habits, line, and form. These elements are important in any landscaping venture.

A desirable garden will display these factors, and will reflect the practical needs as well as the sensuous highlights. When these qualities are absent a garden will lack appeal. There should be an effective relationship between the dwelling space and the garden. Aim to use form and decoration to create places that are enjoyable to be in, as well as to look at.

COLOUR

Plants all have differences in their visual appearance, and the artistic gardener must recognise these individual qualities.

Notice the effects that colours have. Reds and yellows advance; they stand out and greet you instantly. Blues and purples recede and are pleasant background

Wild flower mixes can be very successful along roadside verges. This example is in Carterton, Wairarapa.

colours. The blending of these colours into tones affects the feeling of a garden. But remember that greens are moderating colours; they are placid and absorb other contrasting colours.

TEXTURE

All elements in the garden have a surface appearance. Consider weather-blasted timber, cobbled paving stones, the glossy leaves of taupata or the sword-edged leaf of the feathery toetoe. There is an excellent range of texture combined with colour in the foliage of New Zealand native plants. The flax hybrids, for example, make a handsome display, contrasting texture with colour and form.

Bearded iris, seen here along a roadside garden in Crookston, Otago, have a strong impact.

Native grasses can be very desirable for windy banks along pathways. Their texture and colour look very effective with wind patterns swaying through them.

PLANT FORM

The shape of the plant is known as its form. This may be weeping, upright, prostrate or rounded. These forms can be looked upon in terms of their foliage colour, texture, flower colour, size, scent, and the time of year when their new growth occurs. Forms can be contrasted or grouped for various effects.

This border in the Christchurch Botanic Gardens is a superb example of what a perennial garden should be. It runs from east to west, so that the garden can capture a full day's sun. Taller plants are positioned to the rear, with smaller plants nearer the path. They are grouped together in correct positions to allow optimum growth of each species.

This perennial garden at the Auckland Botanic Gardens in Manurewa has an excellent arrangement of plant species suited to Auckland conditions. Note how the groupings have been carefully positioned to prevent overcrowding of small plants by taller ones.

PLANT HABITS

These can be observed with the change of seasons. Dormancy is a habit of many herbaceous perennials and annuals, which flower during the summer months and become absent during winter. Autumn colours are a habit of deciduous trees; and flowering bulbs are a feature of spring.

LINE AND FORM

The essence of line and form is that each marks the distinction between the constructions of humans and the creations of nature. In the wild there are few straight lines, so when you garden you are contriving to create a sense of the natural by emphasing curves with flowing, merging lines. You will need to become aware of these two kinds of line in the garden: the constructed – for example, pathways, buildings, fences, boundaries, and structures; and the natural outlines of individual species, clusters of plants, and the profiles of plants marked against the skyline.

Most gardens are rectangular in shape and have straight-lined boundaries which separate one property from another. You can overcome this rigid framework by softening the boundaries with tree plantings. Place the taller plants on the boundaries, with shorter species encroaching into the inner garden spaces. This will create two dominant flows of line. The first marks the profile of the boundary; the second marks the profile across your site.

Residential properties can be softened and sheltered by planting along the boundaries. This is often a cheaper and more satisfying solution than fencing.

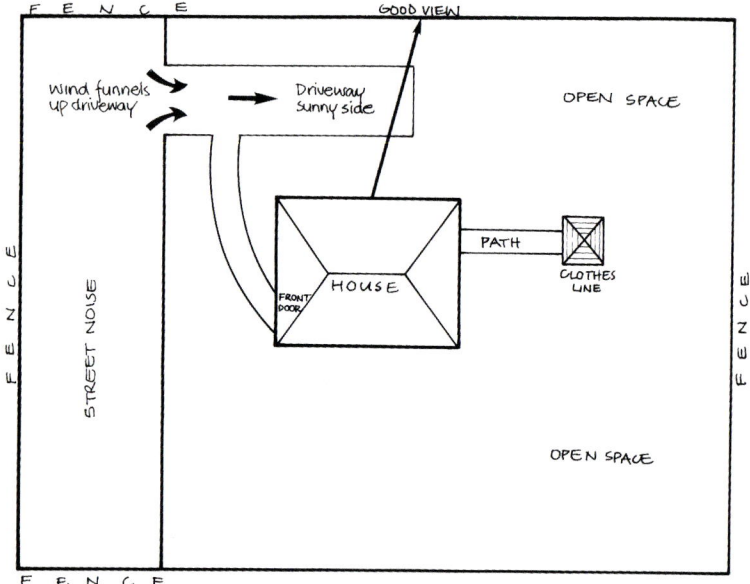

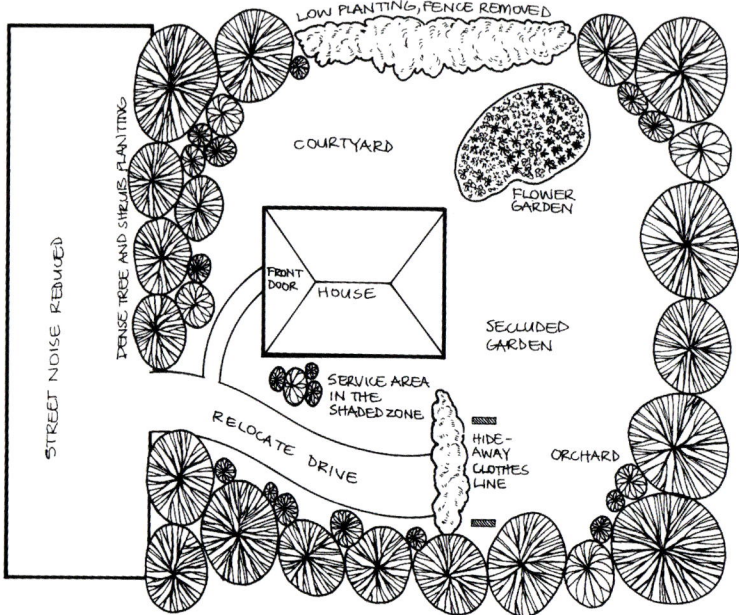

LINE DELINEATES FORM

The form or shape of plants is determined by their habit, modified by the climatic restraints within the area. As plants grow, their forms change. As time passes, this will affect the overall feel of the garden. You can accentuate form with your planting by creating either compact or taller shapes or by contrasting enclosure with open space. Try to merge the flow of these spaces to enhance the focus upon a beautiful vista and to emphasise the theme of your garden. Remember there are no straight lines in nature. If you curve the lines, perhaps to suggest the flow of water, you can begin to create a more restful, intriguing character.

CONCLUSION

You can contrast colours with light and shade, long grass with cut grass, and foliage depth with form and texture. These are all decorative tools that can be used to highlight and accentuate the garden's character and your awareness of seasonal change. They can also be introduced into the design, to produce a feeling of progression towards a climax. The art of aesthetic gardening requires a great deal of thought.

Before you begin, you will have an idea of the sort of garden you would like to have. However, decisions about the garden theme are best left until you have worked your way through the evaluation of existing features and an analysis of existing plants. Tranquil ponds surrounded by maidenhair ferns and delicate plants may not survive the ravages of a sou'wester fresh from the Tasman Sea.

Water and ponds always impart a peaceful, lush atmosphere.

Garden design

DESIGN BRIEF

A design brief is a statement of the development required for a site. When responding to a design brief, the designer must know what is wanted and how to manipulate the land, bearing in mind what the consequences will be. For example, do open spaces, which are required for play, hinder privacy and encourage draughty winds? Will crowded plantings cause shading or frost pockets, or hide views? What impact will the flower garden, recreational area, vegetable garden, shelter, fencing, and buildings have on the areas concerned? Always consider these visual elements and seek a harmony between natural elements and the design brief.

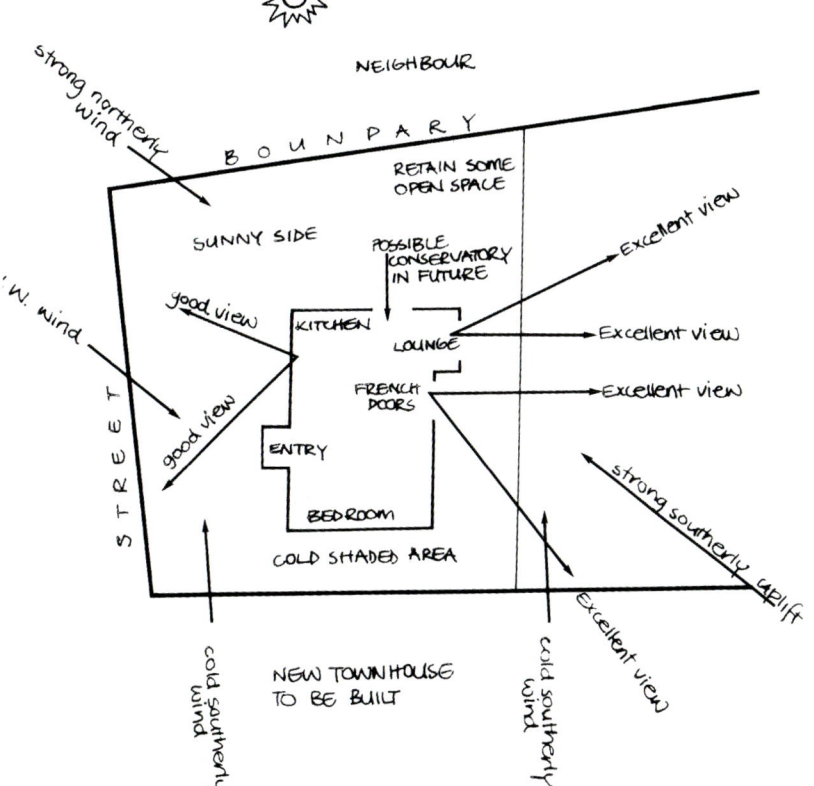

Requirements:
1 position garage on site
2 create a shelter for outdoor activities
3 establish vegetation – none at present
4 retain views

Problems:
1 no topsoil
2 no vegetation
3 severe wind
4 severe salt wind

Work within nature's elements, so that your landscaped garden can develop on an evolving path. When you ignore the natural influences, the consequences will be constant weeding, costly methods, wasted labour, and the death of new plants. If you are designing your own garden, ask yourself what function you require from your site. Is it a practical choice? What side-effects will there be? This analysis is very important, as the final form of the garden landscape will be influenced by its function.

DESIGN TECHNIQUES

Human skills modified by natural constraints create a landscape to satisfy human needs and desires. This social purpose or function will help determine the garden's form, shape, and layout – in other words, its design. Therefore, when designing a garden it is important to follow a set of procedural steps (and see also **Site planning**, p. 42).

- Keep in mind your original intention, but be prepared for changes.
- Analyse existing features on site, climate, soils, and shelter.
- Understand plant species, plant competition, balance, succession, and dominance.
- Draw a scaled site plan that records the results of your analysis. From this plan you can form design considerations. Anticipate future developments, such as new buildings, plant growth.
- Re-evaluate your intentions and themes.
- Purchase or propagate your selected plants.
- Consider site preparation, entrances, pathways, public, and private places, streams, ponds, excavation, topsoiling, circulation, roading, drainage, mounding, fencing, terraces, services, and dwelling areas.
- Consider care and maintenance.

Design principles

The basic principles of design are
- unity
- simplicity
- scale
- balance and proportion.

UNITY

A sense of unity is created when similar elements are repeated throughout the site. Unity can be created simply by the use of one colour, one stone type, or one particular textured wood.

Elements such as scent, colour, and texture, and effects such as surprise and enclosure are tools to highlight your design. Over-use of these tools can lead to a kaleidoscope of confusion.

All spaces must be integrated into an overall plan. The theme of the site is set at a point of entry, where the transition from public to private space occurs. It may be formal or informal, rugged and open, or sheltered and intimate. You can determine this at the entry point by having bold displays of flowers, barricades of walls or fences, stone arches or vistas that lead the eye.

A formal white theme can be stunning. In this courtyard, paths lead the eye to a piece of sculpture, enhancing the dramatic effect of the colour scheme.

SIMPLICITY

The golden rule is to keep things simple. Simplicity enhances unity, so avoid clutter and confusion. Your access must be direct, although it should flow to the destination concerned; it should be simple and in its natural function, with bold highlights to add to the experience of the garden theme.

Apply the rule of simplicity to plant types, visual forms, shape of passageways, views, and construction materials. Maintain the strength of your chosen theme by using a few key elements. For example, the line of vegetation and pathway should lead naturally to the main entrance; multiple entries, diverging pathways, blocked vision of the entrance, and competing visual attractions create confusion.

Screen off undesirable views and focus attention by using tall plants. Try to frame points of interest. These focal points can be distant vistas or closer highlights, such as a fountain, or a hide-away space sitting amongst decorative plantings. Keep focal points simple and strong, and don't clutter the line of sight with a confused variety. These glimpsed views should not detract from the main objective but should enhance the quality of the pathway to the main door. If it is not possible to obtain a line of sight from the street to the main door, create key focal points which, flowing through direct pathways, will lead you to the main entrance of the house. Perhaps a trellis, pergola, seat, boulder, lamp, tree or distinctive post can be used.

Integrate these focal points with the planting theme used on your site. As you move closer to your front door, enhance the sense of privacy with a more intensified, decorative display of colour.

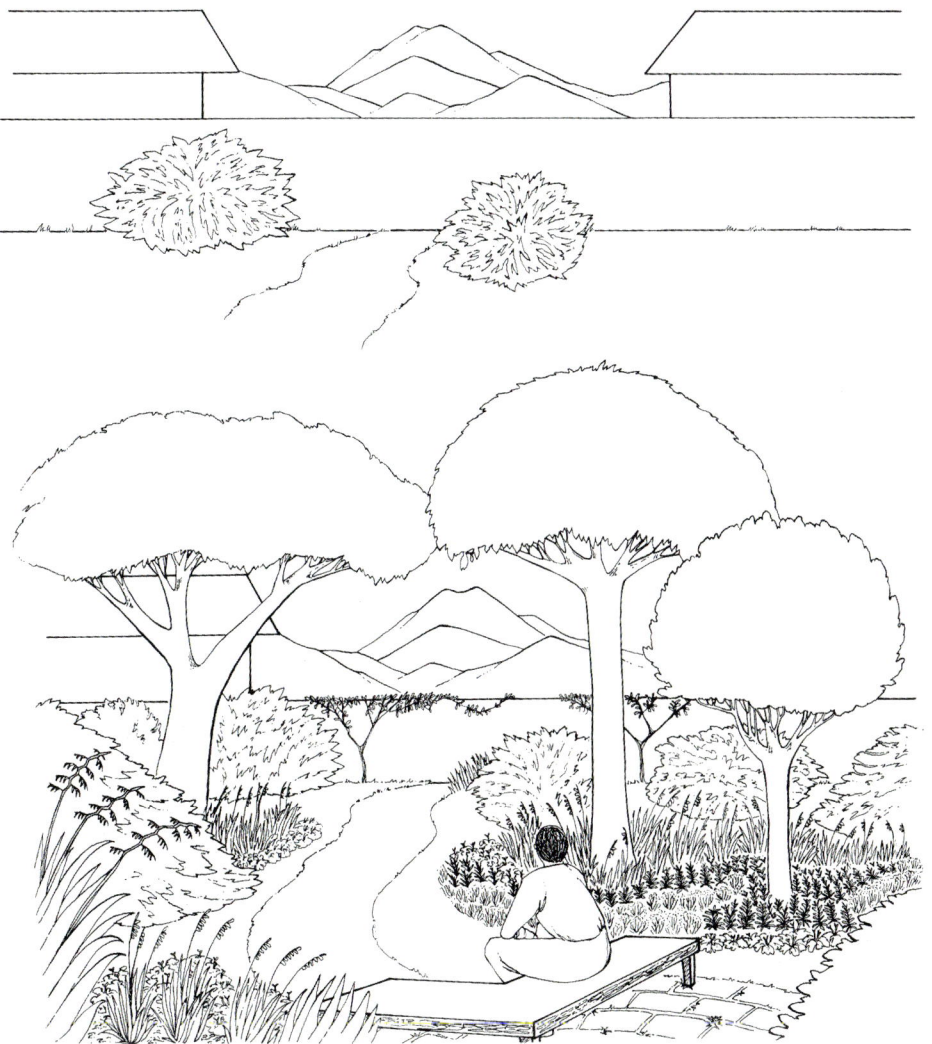

An open area between houses can be scaled pleasantly, by blocking the unsightly aspects and framing desirable views with selective planting of suitable trees.

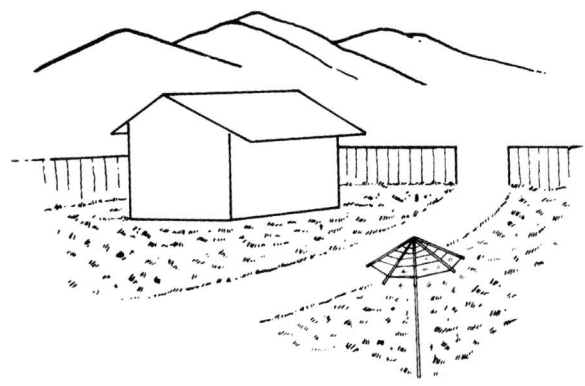

A bare backyard can be enhanced by planting clusters of trees and plants in areas that balance the scale of your property with the overall natural landscape. By planting trees in specific locations, the scale of the house is reduced in the visual landscape. A balance between the house and the natural landscape creates a softer, more harmonious view.

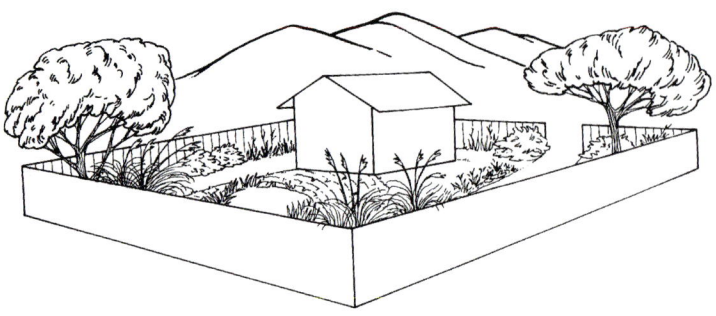

SCALE

Scale is important because it involves a consideration of the area of the site and the suitability of the design brief. Are you creating a garden on a child's scale, an adult's scale, or a public scale such as the open space of a football field? Bear in mind a child's perspective: distances for children are far greater than for adults. Contrast this with the feeling of vastness associated with a large open space. For example, in the Auckland Domain the museum sits on top of a small hill surrounded by large open spaces and big cluster plantings of oak trees. These are easily absorbed within the viewed landscape and create an almost grandiose feeling. This particular large-scale effect is purposely planned. Contrast this with the effect of an enclosed garden space, which has a feeling of protection and intimacy.

Different scales create quite different effects.

To create a sense of character, the required function of a site must match the scale. A sense of intimacy would be as inappropriate for the Auckland Domain as a sense of the grandiose would be in a patio garden. A small secluded sitting area invites passive activity rather than a game of cricket. The choice of an appropriate scale to suit the function will enhance the desire to pursue a particular activity.

Seclusion, privacy, and security are evoked by reducing the size of spaces with planting, fencing, and buildings. Removing vegetation, walls or buildings opens up space, creating a sense of exposure and vastness.

BALANCE AND PROPORTION

In a symmetrical garden, the two halves are balanced proportionately, as if in a mirrored reflection. This is known as symmetrical balance and gives a feeling of formality. Asymmetrical balance is where one side becomes more dominant than the other, suggesting informality.

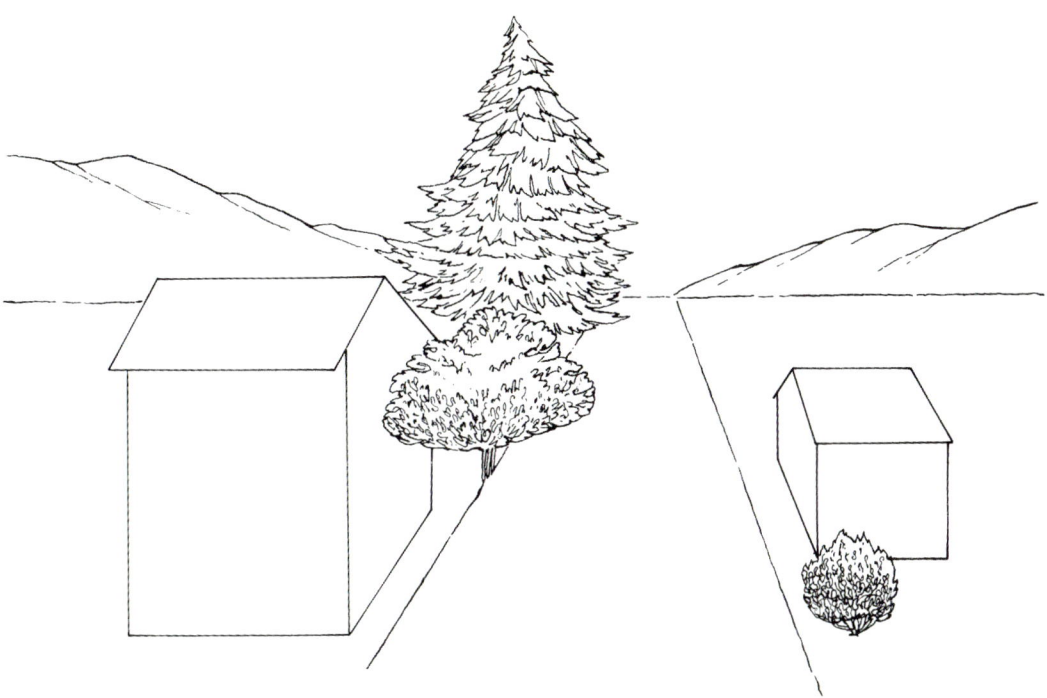

Asymmetric balance is found readily in the wild, where you find clusters of trees growing in one spot and not in another.

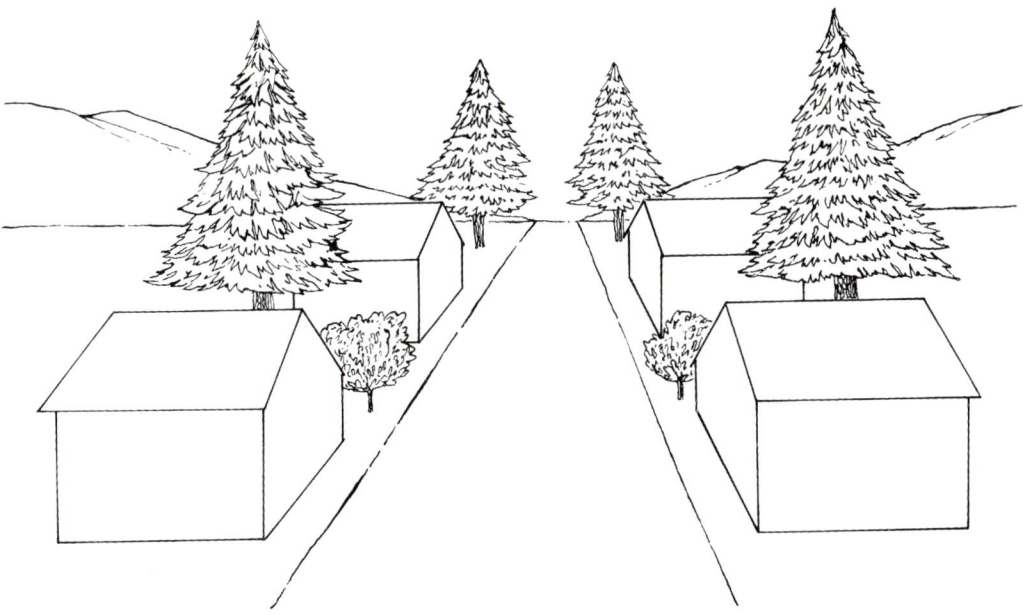

Symmetrical balance gives a feeling of formality and is an art form of its own. It is often used in courtyards.

When designing an open space, it is important to balance sides or corners with unifying elements, such as buildings or plantings of tall trees. These physical structures help reduce the space to a human scale, creating a link with the sky and earth.

CONCLUSION

When you are ready to decide on the final design plan, after your site and plant analysis, review these principles, and remember too that the site must be well planned to anticipate future changes such as rebuilding, new drains or subdivision of the property.

The careful designer will arrange each space according to its function. Service areas can be screened with planting or fencing. The access to the house will follow the most practical route. There should be spaces within the site that will lend themselves to other opportunities such as recreation and decoration. The site must conform to a plan so that each space will integrate with other spaces, flowing into the total design layout.

Themes

A theme is an idea suggested by the repetition of a particular element, the layout of the site, the selection of certain types of plants, or the selection of certain colours. A theme may be expressed in a very formal, structured way, as in classical Renaissance gardens, or in an informal way, as in gardens that attempt to copy nature.

(Above left) Cineraria and fuchsia smother a bank along a semi-shaded roadway at the Wellington Botanic Gardens.

(Above right) A shade garden near the gardeners' hut at the Wellington Botanic Gardens. Here rengarenga lilies flower in the shade under large beech trees, and make excellent groundcover.

Chionochloa flavescens makes a dramatic path edging in windy areas.

The Renaissance gardens of Mogul India and the water gardens of Italy conveyed the theme of progression from the insignificant to the grandiose. The highly formalised structures began with a trickle of water which slowly built up into a lake-encircled fountain. These gardens reflected the wealth, power, and control of the societies that built and appreciated them.

In contrast, the humanised naturalism of the Japanese garden expresses the partnership between nature and humanity, either modestly or on a grand scale. Another more naturalistic theme is the romantic concept of a wilderness, forever in flower and changing, like the art nouveau and early cottage gardens of the Victorian era in England. These gardens are full of colour and scent.

The theme of a wind garden can be created by suggesting a windswept rocky coastline: taupata, pohutukawa, and karo can be deformed into low, rock-hugging shapes; and tussocks and flaxes can emphasise the swaying of the wind. In contrast a theme of security can be suggested by the creation of havens which are sheltered, warm, intimate places on a small human scale.

The cliffs at Sumner in Christchurch are usually frost free, with salt winds and dry soils. This is an ideal habitat for xerophytic plants such as *Echium candicans*, and species of *sedum* and *mesembryanthemum*. The rock gardens that have naturalised here are a beautiful feature.

You can choose to restrict your choice of plants to native species, which will give an indigenous theme. Or you may wish to convey a sense of exotica by using xerophytic non-natives such as the Proteaceae, Graminaceae, and Compositae plant families. The strength of the theme will depend on the degree to which its elements are unified.

The contrasting rhythms of the four seasons can be expressed by choosing plants of a seasonal nature. Autumn colours are provided by asters, dahlias, and the fall of leaves from deciduous trees such as cherries and maples. The green lush season of winter, when plant form and texture come to light, can be seen in the brightening colours of ornamental conifers, Chinese bamboo, and hybrid flaxes. These lead into the continuous unfolding of successive colours displayed by spring-flowering plants such as arctotis, marguerite daisies, daffodils, stock, cornflowers, and wind flowers (anemone). These are followed by summer's petunias, begonias, and herbaceous annuals such as strawflowers.

CONCLUSION

A theme is an idea; in expressing it we create an effect, a sensation that can be felt from the very first moment you enter a site.

The first step is to identify the theme you wish to express, and to seek those elements in your site that most effectively convey this. Each site is unique. Only by recognising the natural advantages and enhancing them by phasing out the discomforting elements, such as wind chill, wind burn, and unsightly views, can you begin to create and enjoy a beauty that has been inspired by nature.

Site analysis

To evaluate a site, it is necessary to look at its positive and negative elements and to consider the features of the existing vegetation. No matter how large or small the area, there are always opportunities for improvement. Record notes from your analysis on the scaled site plan.

Positive elements

PLEASANT FEATURES

Look for those parts of the site that are sheltered, oriented towards the sun, warm, private, have atmosphere or character, suggest age or timelessness, and are worth preserving or could be enhanced.

DESIRABLE VIEWS

Consider the quality of the views. Identify visual delights within your site and pleasurable vistas beyond. Frame these vistas either by planting or by pruning existing vegetation to allow glimpses of a distant feature.

Note those views you wish to retain and those you wish to hide. **D** is the unpleasant feature, so it needs to be blocked out by planting.

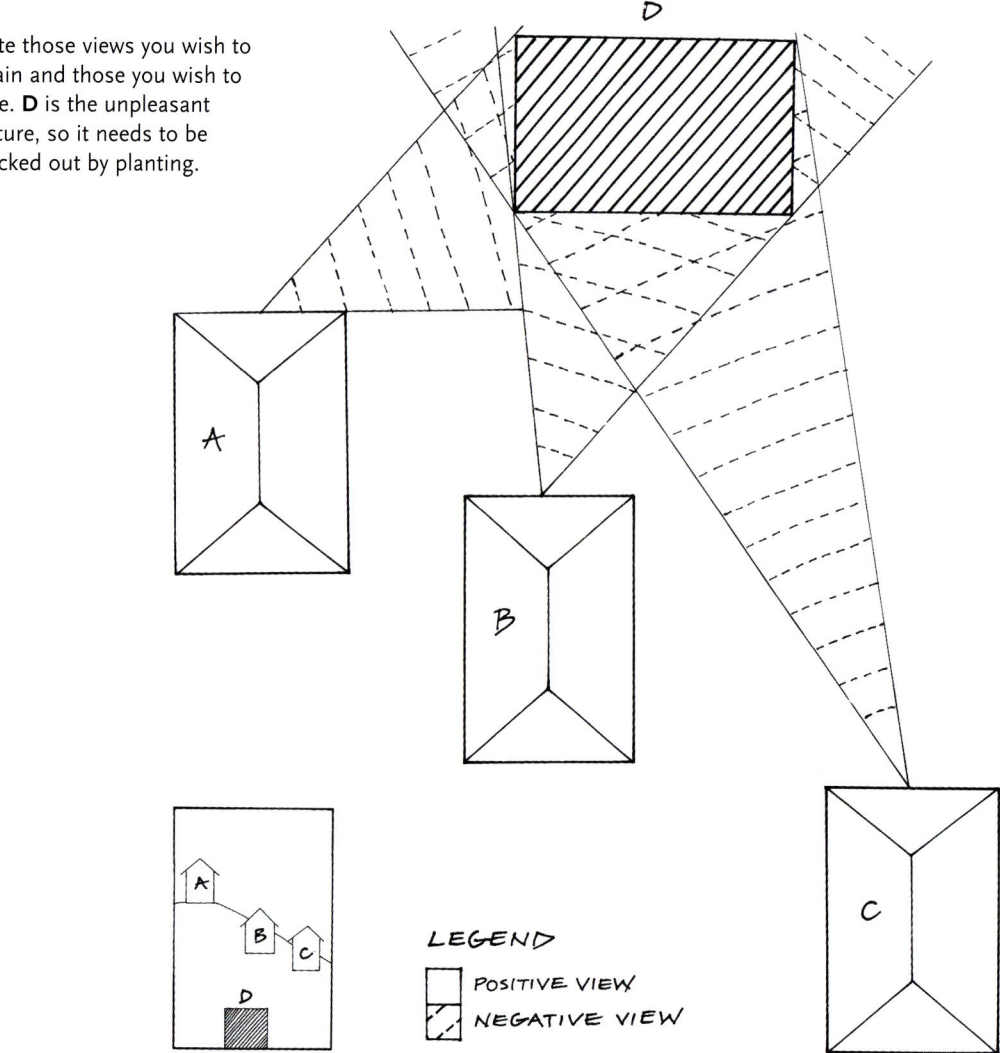

LEGEND

POSITIVE VIEW
NEGATIVE VIEW

ORIENTATION TO THE SUN

This influences the amount of heat absorbed and the amount of moisture retained – qualities that segregate the distribution of plant species. Observe and determine seasonal changes in the availability of sunlight, and select plants suited to sun, shade, or seasonal contrasts between summer and winter shade.

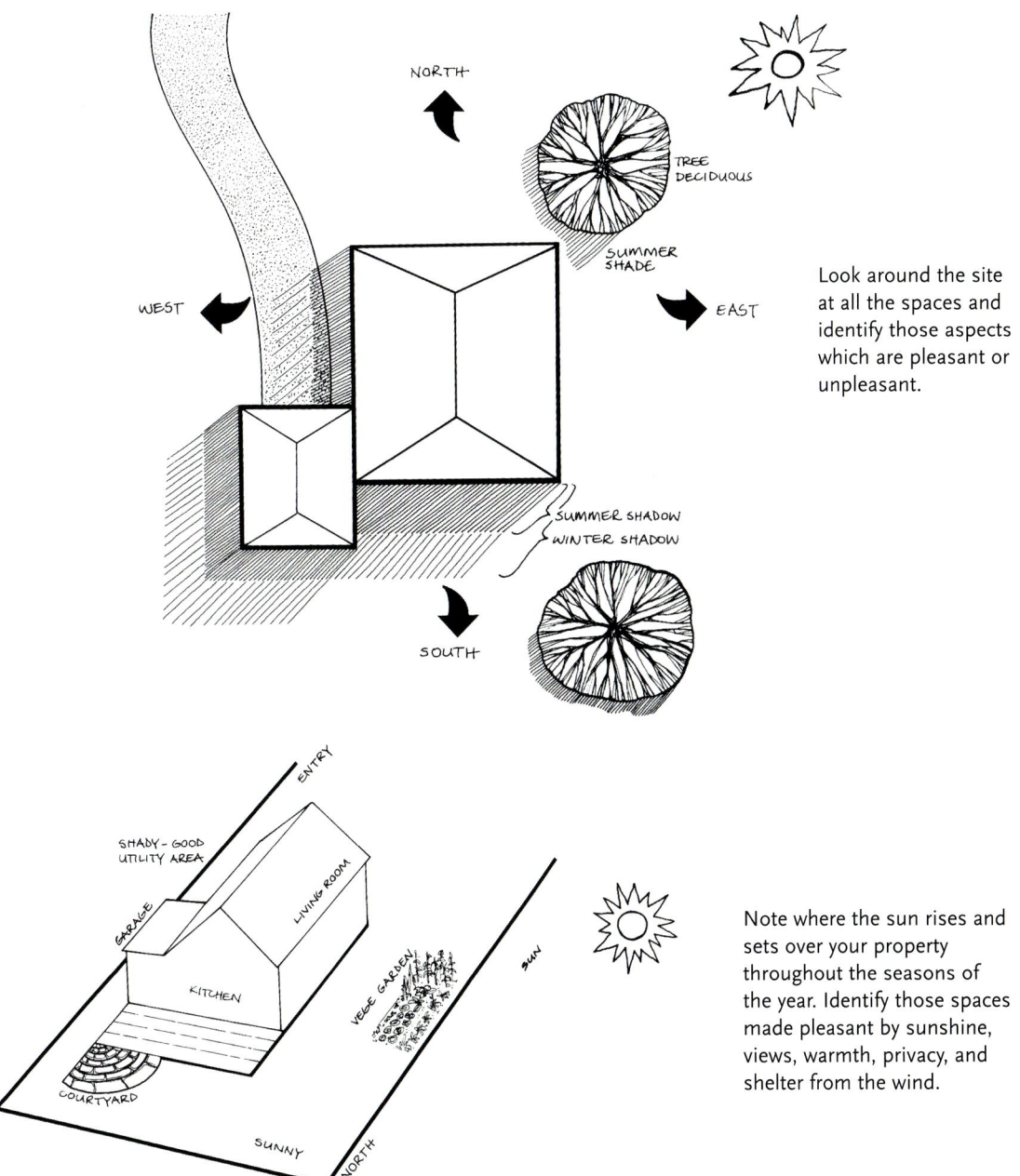

Look around the site at all the spaces and identify those aspects which are pleasant or unpleasant.

Note where the sun rises and sets over your property throughout the seasons of the year. Identify those spaces made pleasant by sunshine, views, warmth, privacy, and shelter from the wind.

WATER

When creating a wind garden it is important to minimise the amount of care and maintenance necessary. Identify water sources, such as springs, surface or underground streams, ponds, and tap water: these can be used to reduce the effects of summer droughts.

SOIL TYPE

What is the pH level of your soil? Is the soil sandy, loamy, or peaty? Sandy soils are infertile and hold little moisture, whereas peaty soils are fertile and generally acid. These aspects must be analysed for the type of vegetation the soil is able to support. You can make an estimation of the soil's structure by taking a sample, wetting it in your hand, then rubbing it with your fingers. If it adheres into a fine paste, you can be assured that the soil is poorly drained and has a clay consistency. If the sample breaks up into small particles, you can assume that the soil is of a good texture and allows drainage.

EXISTING SHELTER AND MICROCLIMATES

(Left) The bare trunks of trees with dense foliage above create a wind funnel and an increase in wind pressure.

(Right) Wind deflected by objects can be reduced by up to 50 per cent.

Note those areas of your site that are either exposed or sheltered under different weather conditions. Look for areas where wind is funneled by narrow passages, or deflected downwards by high walls. Look for calm places in the lee of fences or tall plants on the brow of hills or terraces. This contrast between exposed and sheltered places is marked by temperature variations and consequent changes in soil moisture, which certain plant species prefer to others. Increased shelter increases the temperature, thereby allowing a wider variety of vegetation suitable for planting.

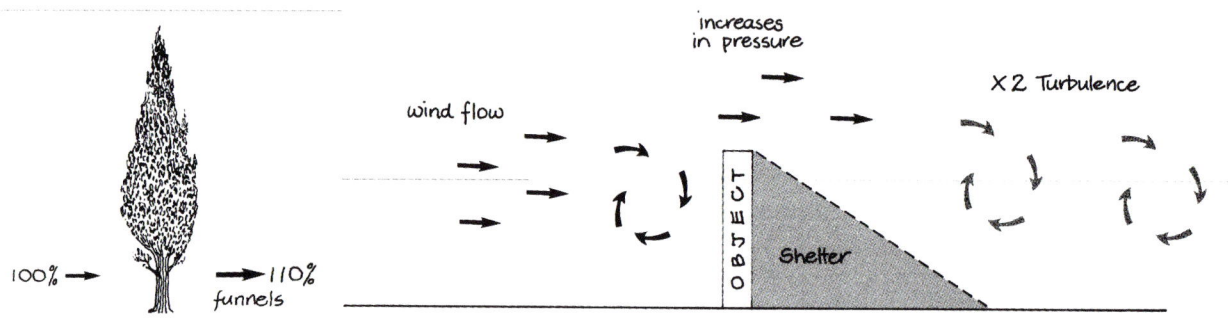

Wind will be sucked through under large trees wherever there are gaps. Old pine trees or macrocarpas can often create an uncomfortable windchilled environment, ceasing to give effective wind shelter.

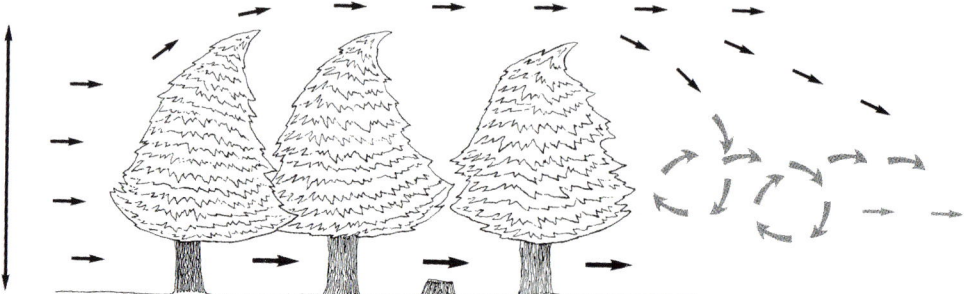

ESTABLISHED HEALTHY PLANTS

Existing plant specimens that appear to be of a good quality can be re-utilised within the new design of the site. These plants are valuable because of their size. Having several years of valuable growth behind them, they provide shelter for other plants. Observation of these plants will indicate specific features of the local climate within the site. For example, salt burn is revealed by the burnt, blackened foliage on the side facing the sea. Wind burn is evident if the plant leans away from the prevailing wind.

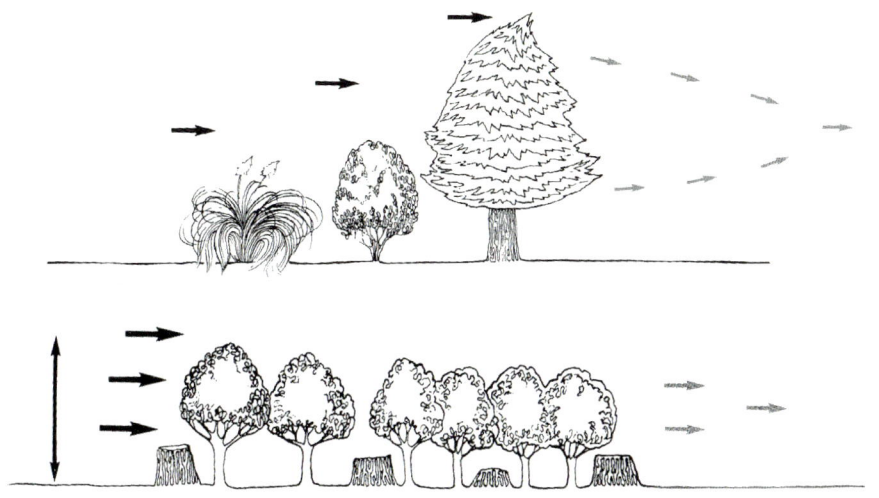

Cluster planting helps to diffuse wind pressure.

THE ABSENCE OF UNDESIRABLE WEEDS

Look at the surrounding areas for weeds that because of their strong competitive habits are able to smother similar sites to your own but have not taken a hold on your place. For example, a neighbour may have infestations of aggressive weeds, like fennel or convolvulus. Make sure that these do not infest your site in the future. Weed competition can be overcome by planting species of an equal or stronger habit: for example, toetoe will compete with gorse.

Negative elements

UNPLEASANT FEATURES

Identify those features that you feel are unsatisfactory: for example, an inappropriate sense of scale (overcrowded or too vast) or an area that is too exposed, too public, lonely, cold, or without character. If the scale is too vast, consider how your space can be subdivided by planting, so as to create a series of smaller functional spaces suitable for recreation, privacy or socialising. Cluttered spaces may require removal of unwanted rubbish to the nearest tip.

UNDESIRABLE VIEWS

What are the aspects that spoil the garden? There may be an intrusion from industry, traffic or unfriendly neighbours, or simply a lack of privacy. Such unpleasant features can be screened by fences, plants or buildings.

DAMAGE BY PEOPLE AND ANIMALS

Areas that people have used for their convenience, without any regard for the damage caused by eyesores such as oil spillages, tyre tracks, and trampled plants will need to be repaired. Work out your service areas, and localise vehicle maintenance and other construction activities. Reconsider the layout of pathways: if a path is not a natural passage between two points, people will always be tempted to take the obvious short cut. Animals which cause damage will require either training or restraining. You might even need to make a special enclosure for them, to stop them destroying the garden.

SHADING FROM THE SUN

In winter, look for frost pockets: areas that become cold and damp over the winter months. These are ideal for driveways, car parks, garages, and even to build upon; this utilises space positively, preserving the favourable sunny areas for outdoor living.

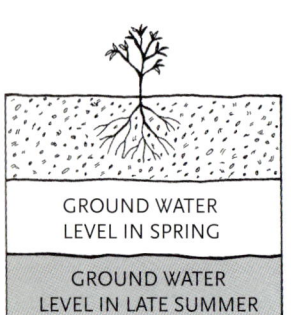

GROUND WATER
LEVEL IN SPRING

GROUND WATER
LEVEL IN LATE SUMMER

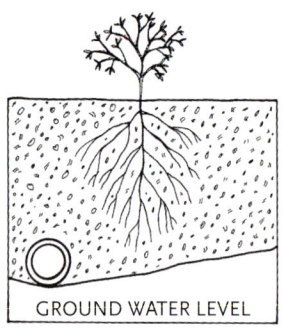

GROUND WATER LEVEL

Piping inserted into wet soils gives better drainage, leading to better root development of plants.

SEVERE EXPOSURE TO WIND AND SALT

This occurs where the wind is strongest and where salt wind burns most severely. Plants need to be protected by artificial or natural methods.

WATER-LOGGING

Areas that become too wet in the winter months will need drainage. Poorly drained stagnant soil will need to be aerated, either by proper drainage of collected water or by digging gritty sand into the soil. The gritty sand allows air to pass through the soil particles. Alternatively, replace the existing soil with new soil once the drainage has been improved.

Poorly-draining bogs are subject to seasonal change, and may be a suitable place to build a pond as a feature item. By excavating a shallow hole and lining it with a fine clay to hold the water, you can create an attractive place for fish and for water plants.

WATER STRESS

Summer droughts dehydrate plants, and constant watering is needed. Areas where this happens should be observed seasonally: they may be very boggy in winter and dry in summer. Select xerophytic species for year-round dry areas. Species such as flax, cabbage tree, and agapanthus can withstand both summer droughts and winter bogs.

POOR SOILS

Is the existing soil polluted, stony or infested with the seeds of noxious weeds such as couch grass or gorse? Is the soil a clay? Has the original topsoil been completely removed from the site, as often occurs in a new housing area? New, clean topsoil may be required to overcome these difficulties, or existing soil can be improved with compost or fertiliser.

DISEASES AND PESTS

Pests and diseases also affect plant habits. In Auckland, for example, the humidity causes a greater prevalence of fungal diseases. These are less common further south because of lower temperatures and less humidity.

In areas of lush growth, aphids and other sucking insects will also attack young shoots and cause certain species to become deformed.

Plants that suffer from water stress have a lower resistance to pests and diseases, and should be removed to accommodate stronger specimens.

Climate and microclimate

As you move about the surrounding landscape you will be able to feel those areas that are warm and those that are cooler. Plants grow better in some locations than in others because of topographical changes in the landscape. Mounds bend the wind and dense plantings filter the wind, but buildings and houses funnel the wind along each side. Observe the influences from different wind angles; acknowledge the places of most comfort; and plan to reduce wind pressure. Mounds, cluster plantings, and fencing or building structures located in the wind's path will eventually bend it on to a new path and thus create a new microclimate.

Optimum growth depends upon the suitability of a particular climate for any given plant species. The microclimatic effect of the larger landscape is repeated in the microcosm of a garden, where we find suntraps that receive more sun and are drier and warmer than other places that face away from the sun. The climatic requirements and tolerances of plants need understanding if you are to garden successfully.

Temperature is influenced by the uneven surface of a large landmass creating warmer and colder pockets. On open flat land, there are fewer microclimatic variations than where there is an uneven topography. In the surrounding landscape, areas that are warmer or cooler can be felt. Hilltops, for example, are usually exposed to all weather, and wind chill reduces the temperature.

Ground and air temperatures are affected by large masses of water like the ocean or inland lakes. Inland areas receive more frost than coastal areas because consistent sea temperatures warm the cool night air. In low inland areas, away from water masses, valleys become frost pockets as cold air drifts into hollows on clear cloudless nights. As water is slower to heat and cool than earth and air, it has a moderating effect and creates a microclimate for plants. On frosty mornings, cool air as fog or mist over a lake or ocean is warmed to a few degrees higher than the surrounding land by the mass of water. This also occurs where rivers and streams steam on cold mornings.

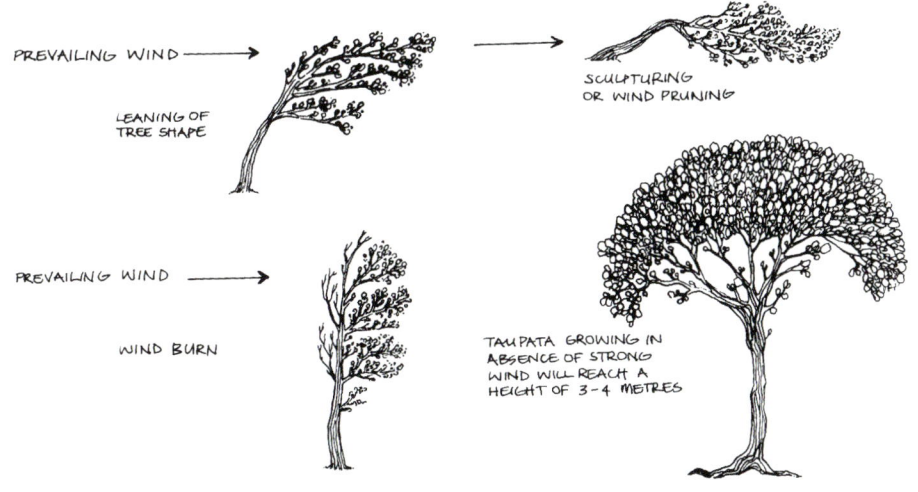

PREVAILING WIND

LEANING OF TREE SHAPE

SCULPTURING OR WIND PRUNING

PREVAILING WIND

WIND BURN

TAUPATA GROWING IN ABSENCE OF STRONG WIND WILL REACH A HEIGHT OF 3–4 METRES

The shape of tree growth is formed by the wind. Storms will burn young growth, often sculpturing the tree. To understand the local microclimate, the landscaper must learn to read the effects of wind on plant growth.

Here on the Wairarapa coast only certain native species such as muehlenbeckia will survive, sculpted from salt winds driven along the coast.

Plants reflect their environment by the way they grow. Their response is their own optimum growth. Microclimates can be recognised by the shape, height, and overall quality of a species in each different location. The type of plants growing in a defined habitat is dependent upon the climate, and each climatic factor is interrelated, working together with the others. Severity of climate restricts the optimum growth and the distribution of a plant species. Strong plants – those that prevail over any site – survive by competition and an ability to endure the elements. By observation of both the climatic effects and the interaction between species, it is possible to determine the appropriate plant balance: a sensitive relationship, with limitations within which the successful gardener must work.

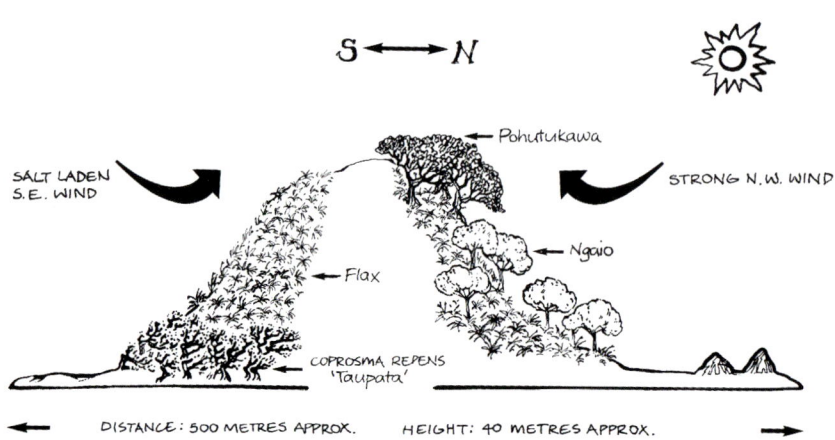

Sometimes certain plant species grow in localised areas where usually they would not be found. For example, nikau palms, frequently regarded as a sub-tropical species, grow profusely on the South Island's West Coast at a latitude associated with temperate zones. The Tasman Sea maintains a moderating influence on lower-altitude coastal plains in this area, producing a warmer yearly temp-erature range than that found elsewhere at similar latitudes.

Taputeranga Island, Island Bay, Wellington, shows how insolation affects the dispersal of native plant species. Orientation to the sun has an effect upon plant species variation and can be clearly seen along the south coast of Wellington. Flax (*Phormium cookianum*) predominates on shady south-facing cliffs, while the drier north-facing slopes receive more sunshine and are dominated by gorse and rejuvenating native bush.

In Auckland, citrus, hibiscus, canna lilies, and kikuyu grass all grow very well. These are seldom found in colder areas. In Wellington, frost-tender plants, such as pohutukawa, puka, and ngaio, will thrive; and further south the frosted regions of Otago are known for their deciduous plants, which define the distinct seasons. In the northern regions, plants are easily swamped by the competitive growth caused by the warmer climate. The same species of plant will grow at a slower rate in colder regions.

When the climate of an area is modified by local influences, a microclimate is created. Microclimates exist within a broad range of spaces. For example, the broad leaves of puka, whau, or rangiora will create microclimatic variations in temperature as well as in the availability of light and moisture around the plants. Clusters of plants will also create microclimatic variations, as will specific site variations in slope, aspect, orientation to prevailing wind, and proximity to lakes or the sea. Microclimatic variations affect the competitive advantages of one plant over another, and of clusters of one species over clusters of another.

INSOLATION AND SUN ANGLES – SUMMER AND WINTER

Insolation is the amount of solar energy received at the earth's surface. The amount of heat absorbed is dependent on the topography and the sun angle. In other words, the greater the slant of the angle of sunlight to the earth's surface, the cooler the temperature. The uneven surface of the landscape thus creates warmer and colder pockets. This explains why plants are naturally found clustered in localised environments: the heat absorbed into the land affects the temperature and, consequently, the moisture available.

Sun angles in summer differ greatly from sun angles in winter. The further south in latitude, the longer the winter shadows become, owing to the curvature of the earth. Here a hillside that faces directly south, for example, receives summer sun, but mid-winter sun angles cast long shadows completely over the site. Sometimes these wintry shadows last for three or four months, and these slopes are considerably colder and frostier than those that face north and receive sunshine. Likewise, east-facing sites that receive the morning sun usually have a different collection of plants from those drier sites that face west and bask in long hot sunny afternoons, where drought-tolerant species are found. These temperature changes affect complete ranges of plants. Evergreens are more susceptible to shadows than deciduous species.

Grasslands, without foliage cover, tend to lose heat more than bush does, because of the quick cooling of dew that settles on the grass.

Certain plant species are sometimes found growing in localised areas where you would not generally expect to find them. For example, at Walter Peak Station on Lake Wakatipu, near Queenstown, a large kauri tree thrives. Normally these natives are found in the northern districts of New Zealand, where they flourish in the warmer climate. However, in the station's homestead garden there is a sheltered little haven near the lake's edge. The garden faces directly north, where maximum insolation is received. The temperature of the lake is above freezing during the winter months, and this helps to influence the immediate air temperature along the water's edge. These factors enable the kauri to survive freezing conditions. In this particular habitat, the re-radiated warmth of the lake keeps the night air warmer at the lakeside than in areas beyond, water being slower to cool than air. With the garden's orientation to the north, it is able to attain further warmth during the day from insolation, whereas other gardens in nearby Queenstown can remain frozen for days.

Some plants prefer drier situations than do others. The warmer/drier and the cooler/wetter areas represent two extremes that affect the competition between plant species. The dependency on available water, or on heat from the sun, influences the distribution patterns of plant species. On the cliffs of Banks Peninsula near Sumner there are garden escapees which have naturalised in a dry rocky habitat. These species include *Aeonium arboreum*), shrubby stonecrop (*Sedium praeltum*), marguerite daisy (*Argyranthemum frutescens*) and pride of Madeira (*Echium candicans*). Here these plants favour a habitat of dry rocky outcrops that face into the warm morning sunshine after frosted nights.

ORIENTATION

Orientation influences the growth habits of plants because the sun's angle affects the insolation. This in turn affects soil moisture, transpiration, and evaporation, and is reflected within the landscape by variations in growth and distribution of local plant species.

Orientation and its effect on plant habits needs to be considered when selecting plants appropriate to a particular site, as the extra warmth can exhaust some plant species during summer.

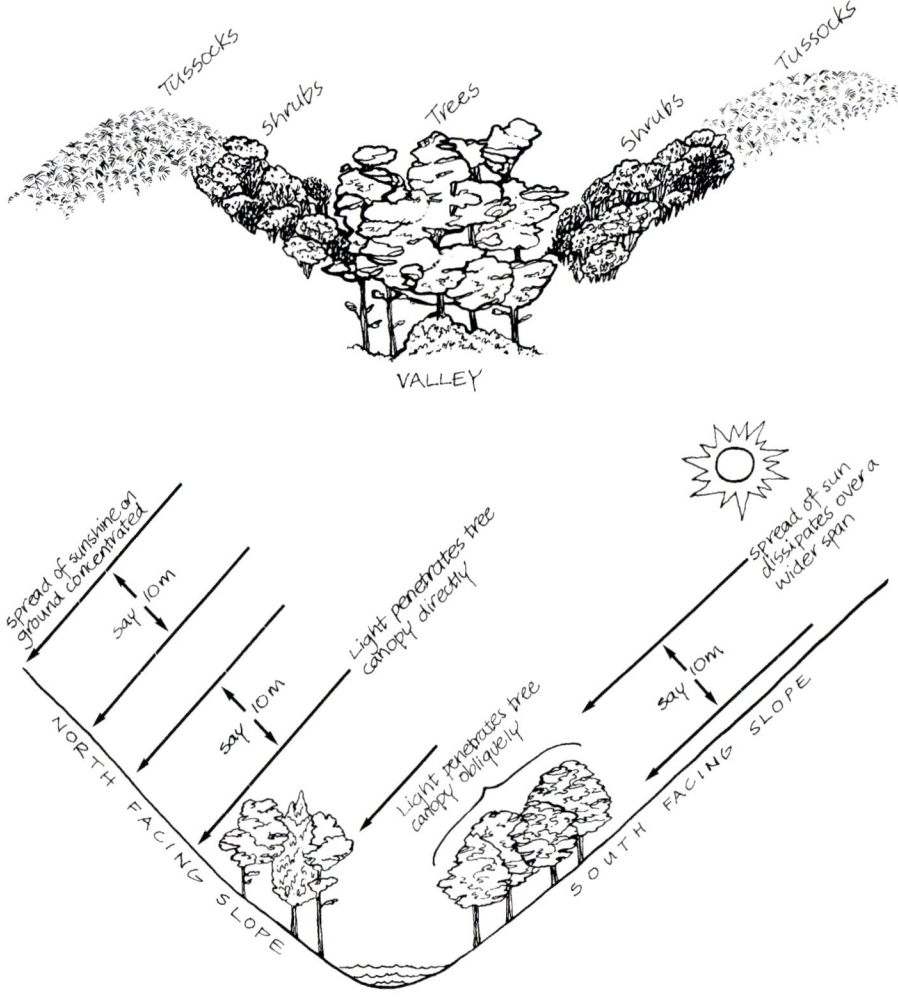

The diagram shows how the rays of the sun are dispersed on to uneven topography, with certain areas receiving more sunlight than other areas. Valleys are always wetter, with lusher growth. They can support more – and taller – vegetation than the drier hilltops can.

Orientation and altitude are two microclimatic factors that affect valleys prone to frost. The microclimate of your property will be affected by the way it is oriented to the sun. North-facing slopes are warmer than south-facing slopes, and east-facing slopes are usually more moist than west-facing slopes.

These examples show that many microclimatic factors interrelate, permitting some plants to do better in some areas than in others.

The seasonal variations in the position of the sun relative to the earth affect the heat that is retained or dissipated in a garden. For example, the low sun angles in winter can completely shade the garden, resulting in a cold and wet site that in contrast is sunny and dry in the summer. This point has particular relevance to the location of structures. If you place a sealed driveway on the sunny side of the garden you are wasting an area that receives maximum winter sun. A driveway should be placed in a shaded location that is cold and boggy in winter, and therefore less desirable for garden plants. The same considerations should be applied to structures that cast long shadows, causing frost pockets.

RECOGNISING THE NATURAL ECOLOGY

On open flat land, there is less microclimatic variation than on land with an uneven topography. Compare Wellington's suburbs: Seatoun on the coast is warmer in winter but susceptible to salt wind, while Karori and Upper Hutt, both inland, are colder and thus prone to frosts. A change in plant species behaviour is evident over a small distance. Deciduous trees are more colourful in the colder parts of the Hutt

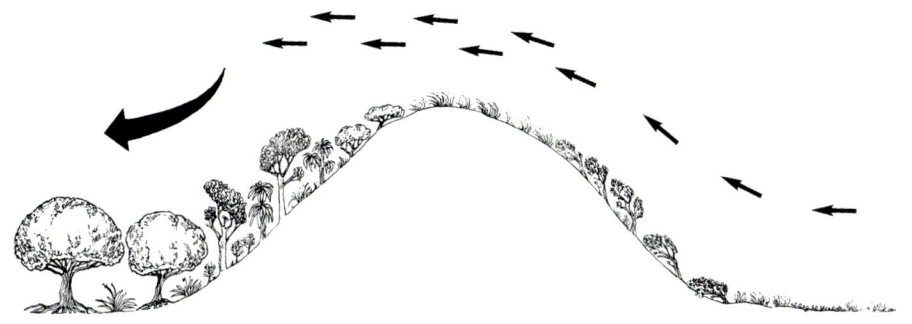

As the wind ascends a hill it builds in pressure. Plant growth at the top of the hill will appear harsher, with hardier plant species dominating where it is drier and more exposed. There is more shelter on the leeward side of the hill, and greater variety of plants, which grow taller and are often lusher because more moisture is available. The gardener must be able to recognise these variations in a landscape and also within a garden.

Valley, yet tend to be burned by the salt wind in Seatoun. Frost-susceptible plants, such as hibiscus, are not found in Karori or Upper Hutt, yet are found in Seatoun.

In Christchurch, coastal New Brighton can be compared with St Albans and then with the Cashmere Hills. Each locality has a totally different microclimate, and this is clearly seen in the localised dispersion of specific plant species that grow only in certain favourable areas. For example, the tall trees of inner Christchurch city are splendid, towering specimens in Hagley Park, but in coastal New Brighton the salt winds prune them significantly, and only deformed specimens can be seen along the beach frontage. In Victoria Park, on the Port Hills, only tree species like pine and cedar that can adapt to the summer droughts survive.

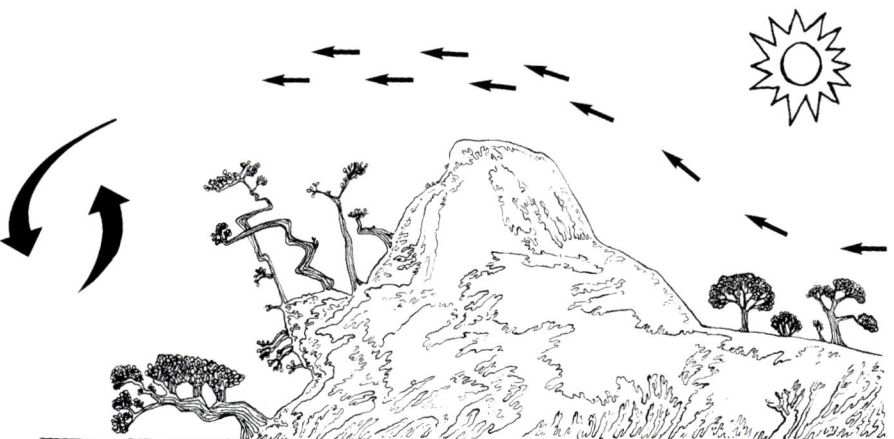

Those areas that face to the south and east, away from the sun, often have different vegetation from those areas that face north into the sun. This segregation of plant species is due to the evaporation of available moisture and excess transpiration from sun-baked areas. Particular site advantages can be easily recognised. Pockets of a garden may be warm and sunny while others are wet and shady, with different plant species dominant in the different areas.

The only places in which plants cannot exist are in total darkness or permanent freezing zones where liquid water or light is unobtainable. There is a plant for every other situation. Light and temperature are modified by latitude, altitude, orientation to the sun, proximity to large masses of water, and the change of seasons.

LATITUDE FROM TEMPERATE TO SUBTROPICAL

Zonation of species occurs with changes in latitude. New Zealand is situated between 34 and 47 degrees south. Zones of species occur with changes in latitude and can be seen by comparing vegetation, like mangrove swamps, in subtropical, largely frost-free northern areas such as Auckland at 37 degrees, with the vegetation of southern North Island areas, such as Wellington, at 41 degrees south, where frosts are regular. In temperate conditions subtropical species do not occur naturally. Compare the vegetation of subtropical Auckland with that of Wellington's more temperate conditions. Hibiscus, lantana, and bougainvillea all flourish well in

Auckland, yet are seldom seen further south than Taranaki and the Bay of Plenty. Ngaio and pohutukawa trees are rarely seen south of Kaikoura. Raglan, at 38 degrees south, is recognised as a latitude border where subtropical species merge with temperate plants. In Auckland, gardens grow softer plants like citrus, canna lilies, jacaranda, flame trees, and kikuyu grass.

On Wellington's wind swept hillsides frost-tender plants, such as the wild marguerite daisy and boneseed, thrive together with pohutukawa, puka, and ngaio trees, that are rarely seen in Kaikoura, down at 42 degrees. Further south, at 45 – 47 degrees, in the frosted regions of Otago, are the deciduous plants that have distinct seasons. Growth occurs later in these temperate zones, as the spring and summer seasons take longer to warm and are shorter. Arrowtown, in Central Otago, is more spectacular during May and June than the autumn displays in the North Island. Southern gardens are also special during these months when perennial plants flourish after surviving the cold frosty winter through dormancy.

FROST AND ALTITUDE

Frost is the factor that segregates temperate from subtropical plants. Once cell walls inside a plant fracture from expansion caused by freezing, all soft growth is damaged and the plant dies. Thus plants adapted to freezing temperatures usually have woody tissue and either drop their leaves in the winter or lie dormant beneath the soil at that time of year. Late frosts can destroy young tender plants that have been unable to protect themselves from freezing.

Many temperate plants, however, depend on freezing to trigger seasonal change. This process is called vernalisation and occurs when the temperature nears zero. Once daylight hours and temperatures increase, new buds on plants conditioned to flower in a frost zone begin to open in blossom and leaf. Many seeds also depend on freezing before they germinate. This process is called stratification. The seeds of apples, for example, germinate better after a cold period.

Altitude decreases temperatures. On the lower slopes of the Heathcote Valley in Christchurch, for example, there is a definite variation of vegetation in response to frost sensitivity. Plants such as pohutukawa, the sweet pea bush (*Polygala myrtifolia*) and several varieties of the Proteaceae family grow on warm sunny slopes. In ice-prone valleys and flat areas, twenty metres below, frost causes these plants to die. Other examples are the hibiscus and pohutukawa that grow in New Plymouth and Opotiki at a latitude equivalent to National Park. Growth of these species at National Park is restricted because of the cold temperatures so high above sea level. And as we have seen, pohutukawa is abundant in Wellington, but is non-existent in Upper Hutt, because of winter frost.

SOILS

Soils vary considerably over small distances and this is often discernible to the trained eye by the type of plant growth. Soils are found as clays, loams, and gravels; they can be stony, free-draining, or boggy. Coastal soils are usually free draining, sandy or gravelly, and always have a different type of plant growth from soils found in boggy inland areas. Coastal vegetation is hardy, smaller, and drought- and salt-tolerant, whereas inland vegetation is taller, lusher, and often supports totally different species. River basins have similar drainage properties to those of coastal soils.

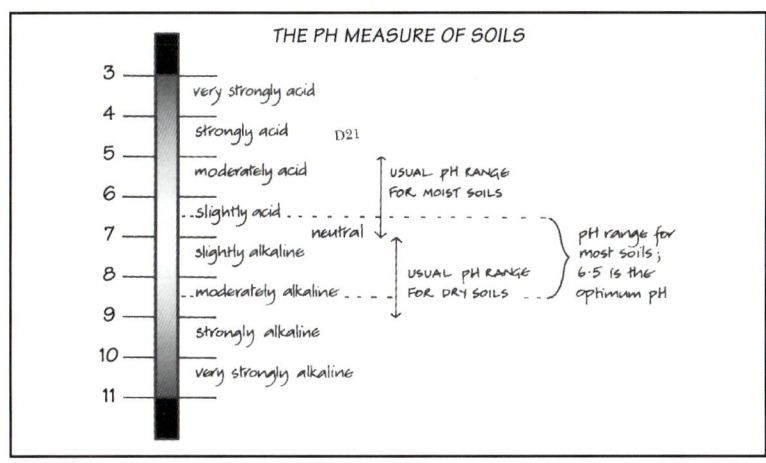

THE PH MEASURE OF SOILS

3 — very strongly acid
4 — strongly acid   D21
5 — moderately acid   USUAL PH RANGE FOR MOIST SOILS
6 — slightly acid
7 — neutral   pH range for most soils; 6·5 is the optimum pH
   slightly alkaline
8 — moderately alkaline   USUAL PH RANGE FOR DRY SOILS
9 — strongly alkaline
10 — very strongly alkaline
11 —

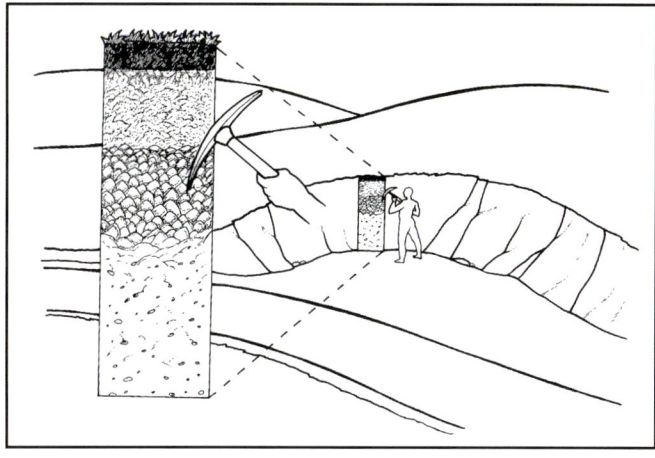

Good soils are the secret to successful gardening. They provide plants with the moisture and nutrients they require. Plant roots need room to wander within the soil particles and to have space to breathe. This is known as anaerobic respiration.

Drainage is an important factor in soil condition. Poorly drained soils are permanently waterlogged, so in situations where there is no free air or oxygen, anaerobic respiration occurs, resulting in acidic toxins developing within the soil. These toxins cause fermentation of vegetative matter, which is why waterlogged clay soils support feeble growth.

Another important factor in soil structure is the amount of water soaked up by the soil after the free water has drained through. This is called field capacity. Field capacity is dependent on the soil structure, the air gaps between soil particles, and the size of each fragment, together with organic content which provides plants with the essential trace elements. These elements and the moisture give the soil its fertility content, and plants depend on this for survival, especially in windy gardens. Sandy soils are fine, aerated mediums for plants to grow in, because they are well drained, but they are not good at retaining valuable moisture or nutrients and are, therefore, infertile. An arid windy garden can be turned into an oasis by improving the soil with compost or adding new topsoil.

(Left) Soil pH is the measure of alkalinity and acidity. The pH of most soils lies between 5.5 and 7.5.

(Right) Roadside cuttings often reveal the underlying layers of soil, or soil profile, of an area.

Native toetoe and flax have naturalised and are now dominant on volcanic soils in Tongariro National Park.

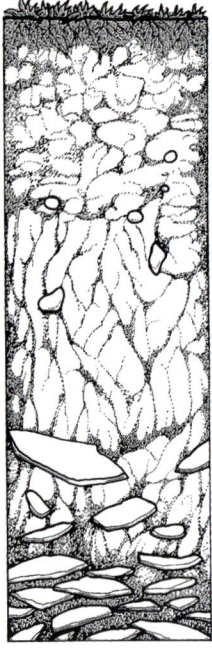

Sandy soils are finely aerated media for plants but, because they are derived from sandstone rock, do not retain moisture. This can be overcome by applying bulky organic manures and watering. Lime can counteract acidity and build fertility.

Nitrogen-fixing lupins have naturalised the river beds in Otago, where the gravel soils favour them in competition with other plant species. The lupin is a perennial, and its foliage dies back during winter frost, but in spring it re-emerges from strong roots.

pH BALANCE

Some soils are acid: others are alkaline. The pH level is measured on a scale where 7 is neutral, 14 is pure alkaline, and 0 is totally acid. Most soils range between pH. 5.5 and pH. 7.5.

Each species has its own range of tolerance and is best able to absorb its nutrients according to the acidity or alkalinity of the soil. Lawns do best in acid soils with a pH of 5, while vegetables do best in soils with a pH of 6.5. Among a range of plants, ericas prefer acid conditions with a pH of 4.5 to 5.5. Boronia, camellia, leucadendron, leucospermum, protea, telopea, blackberry, raspberry, strawberry, aubergine, and pepper plants prefer soils at pH. 5.0 to 6.0. Acacia, maple, grevillea, phlox, roses, citrus, stonefruit, beans, and tomatoes prefer pH. 5.5 6.5. Alyssum, clematis, dianthus, paeony, stock, stonefruit, currants, beetroot, carrots, and celery prefer pH. 6.5 to 7.5.

The rate of nutrient exchange within the soil from which plants obtain their food depends on the pH level, and the anion and cation exchange capacity (that is, the negative and positive ion exchanges of soil chemistry).

Boggy or clay soils are acid, with a pH reading of 5.5 or lower. Sandy free-draining soils generally have a pH of 6.5 to 7.5. The optimum pH is 6.5, a level at which most plants can exchange nutrients without the inhibition of acid or alkaline dominance. It is necessary to find out the pH balance of your soil before you apply fertilisers, especially acid fertilisers like sulphate of ammonia.

Soil testing should be done by a specialist, such as ESR or Landcare Research.

The pH level is dependent on the amount of leaching within the soil. The amount of water filtered through the soil particles affects the amount of nutrients that are washed away. Acid soils tend to bind and hold valuable nutrients, making them unavailable to plants. Some plants, such as oaks and pine trees, will acidify the soils. Boggy soils will also ferment and become acid, as toxin build-up from the lack of aeration will burn off the delicate root hairs of plants.

In waterlogged soils, certain bacteria which live without air attack the ammonia and produce nitrogen gas. This escapes into the air, thus resulting in a loss of fertility.

PLANTS AS INDICATORS OF SOIL FERTILITY

When considering weeds as indicators of soil fertility, it is important to remember that it is the prevalence of certain groups of weeds, rather than the presence of individual weeds that suggests what might be happening to the soil. An increase of weeds that flower in the summer and autumn may be a sign of neglect and

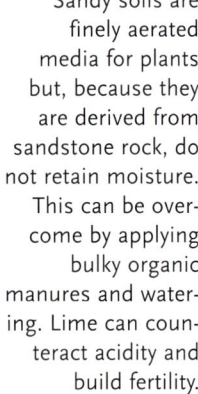

Limestone soils are alkaline but prone to dry out readily. Organic manures and watering build fertility.

declining fertility. Some weeds thrive in soils that are acid, others in soil that is alkaline: for example, an increase of dock and sorrel will suggest that the soil is becoming acid. Weeds that are successful will seek those nutrients present in the soil and take them out to recycle into organic content. If there is an inadequate supply of nitrogen, plants such as clovers and broom, which can fix nitrogen from the air, will appear.

Leaching is the natural process whereby water percolates through the soil, flushing out salts, nitrates, and nutrients with it. The persistent percolation of water through the soil reduces the nutrients available for plants, as minerals become diluted. The dilution of a particular mineral is indicated by a plant's appearance. For example, if the older leaves of the plant show yellowing (chlorosis), this may well suggest a nitrogen deficiency.

Growing plants will absorb nutrients into their own structure, putting into store what would otherwise have been lost through leaching. Deep-rooted plants explore the soil to a greater depth, bringing up minerals from lower layers and, equally important, opening up stiff heavy clays or rocky soils, making it easier for other plant roots to penetrate and find moisture. Winter-feeding plants are usually deep feeders and are a valuable wind shelter. The summer annuals are more important as a nitrogen store, and for the humus they provide when they die.

A weed is a plant growing in the wrong place because it is uninvited, and usually unwanted. But nature has a reason for these herbs that invade new territories: they can be useful in the early, establishing stages of a garden, providing shelter and protection for other plants, and also preventing soil erosion and water loss. Most new gardens are in a stage of healing. The original native vegetation has been removed and new growth is occurring. In windy locations, it is very important to retain such growth, even if the growth is weed.

Weeds growing between plants need not be a nuisance to a gardener. Provided they are controlled by introducing competitive plants, and are kept to a specific area, they offer a living mulch in dry weather, preventing erosion and loss of soil surface moisture, to the advantage of other plants. Weed growth can be especially useful in an exposed situation. For example, plantain, a herb often seen in arid coastal regions, is a valuable contributor to soil preservation and fertility along Cobham Drive, near Wellington Airport. When the herb was removed by former, unwitting gardeners severe soil erosion occurred.

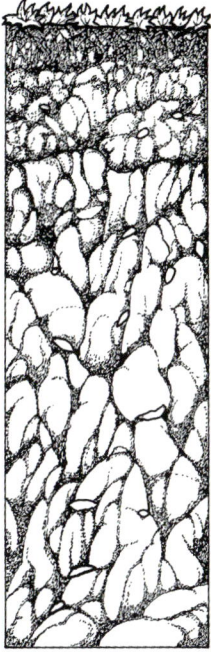

A typical profile of a poorly drained soil, showing the shallow layer of topsoil.

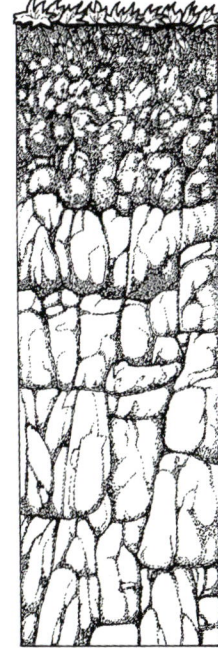

Clay soils have poor drainage but can support most growth if artificially drained.

Centranthus rubra, naturalised on rocky coastal cliffs, gives strong displays of white, red, and mauve flowers in mid spring.

PLANTS AS INDICATORS OF SOIL TYPES

The extensive existence of groups of species rather than of individual plants suggests what might be happening to the soil. Raupo, sedge grasses such as *Scirpus cyperacea,* and willows, for example, are plants that favour wet or boggy conditions and flourish in numbers only in these habitats. Plants with reduced foliage, or with strong, thick, or modified leaves like spikes, or with green stems indicate drier soils.

The effect of weather leaching nutrients from topsoil can also be gauged through plant indicators. Poor soils can be infested with noxious weeds such as broom and gorse seed. Patchy growth, with other species emerging through, can be the result of nutrient deficiencies. In areas of poor soils, legumes like clover have advantages and add considerably to soil fertility. They always look lush and green, even though other plants struggle. Pine trees also grow well in poor soil. If weeds such as groundsel, fat hen, chickweed, stinging nettle, and dandelion are flourishing, take note because they are adding nitrogen and usually indicate good soil fertility.

Because certain species thrive in soils that are either more acid or alkaline, the pH level in the soil can be assessed by identifying which species are flourishing. Wild buttercup *(Ranunculus repens)* is often found in wet pastures with a low pH level, whereas arid akaline soils with a high pH favour plants such as plantain, wild chamomile, and yarrow. Oak and pine trees tend to sour soils, and an increase of dock and sorrel suggests an increase in acidity. Azaleas and rhododendrons suit acid soils. (See **pH balance**, above.)

Vegetation analysis
EVALUATING EXISTING VEGETATION

Before you can begin to evaluate the plants on your site and the likely success of other plants you wish to purchase, you will need to have some background information on the habits of plants and the factors which directly affect their ability to grow successfully.

Wind-blown seed has naturalised on the south shore of Lake Hawea, Otago. Californian poppy, lupin, and alyssum have found a favourable habitat here.

The ability of any species to attain its optimum growth is dependent upon changing daylight hours, seasonal temperature changes, moisture, soil types, and adaptability to wind, salt wind, and frost.

The seasonal changes of the sun hours upon the earth affect the daylight hours through different months of the year. This in turn affects the temperature within the landscape. For example, spring is usually crisp to begin with, but as the sun hours increase the land gradually becomes warmer. As the season advances towards the longest day, 21 December, the temperature increases in response to the insolation of the sun's energy upon the land and sea.

The relationship between sun angle, availability of moisture, and growth in a garden over four seasons.

Time through the seasons

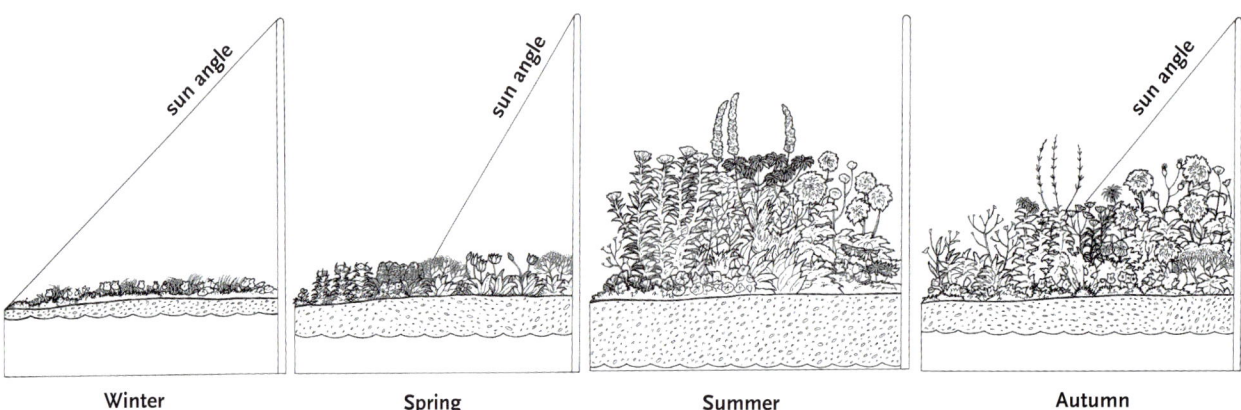

Winter   Spring   Summer   Autumn

You should now be ready to undertake your own evaluation of the plants growing on your site. This involves working through the following steps.
- Identify the types of plants.
- Consider the condition of the plants.
- Identify the habits and adaptability of existing plants to wind and salt winds.
- Note how the seasons affect your area in terms of frosts, salt, drought, and plant competition.
- Identify those plant species that will be compatible with the intended effect of your landscaping: for example, ornamental plants, seasonal plants, or shelter plants.
- Decide which stage of competitive plant succession has been reached on your site.

(See **Plant association/succession**, p.34.)

PLANT TYPES

In exposed dry or arid areas, or where extremes of persistent or salty winds occur, plants may have special modifications in their physical structure. These adaptations reduce the amount of moisture lost through transpiration and enable the species to thrive in the extremely harsh conditions. They can have one or several of the following leaf characteristics: curled leaves (for example, marram grass); thick, shiny, and waxy leaf skins (taupata); fleshy leaves (most of our succulent plants,

which may be grey in colour, like stonecrop); small leaves (cotoneaster); or fewer or sunken stomata cells (or pores) in their leaves, which may be hairy, furry, or leathery in texture.

CONDITION OF PLANTS

The condition of different plants in your garden – for example, their height, shape, quality and hardiness – is a clear indicator of the environmental extremes that occur in your area. Is the existing vegetation scarred, battered or exhausted as a result of other plant competition (weeds), water stress, salt burn, vandalism, starvation, pollution or exposure? How do these particular plants compare to plants in other local areas?

The shape and size of plants can tell you about the winds that blow in your area. Compare the shape of a tree in your garden with same species growing elsewhere.

The better the quality of plants you find growing naturally on the site, the gentler the microclimate. Remember that considerable microclimatic variation can occur within close distances.

PLANT HARDINESS

Some plant species have stronger salt and wind tolerances than others, and can flourish in harsh habitats where more delicate species suffer.

In harsh environments, hardy plant species that have adapted to exposed conditions (see **Plant types**, above) will dominate the weaker species. By discovering which plants flourish over the four seasons you will recognise those varieties best suited for each new habitat. For instance, flax may be swamped by other growth in favourable locations, whereas in a harsh environment within the same locality it will cover competing plant growth, because the softer plants cannot survive.

WIND AND SALT

Salt is a substance with which only specifically adapted plants can live. It is blown from the sea by wind and settles on the foliage of plants, where it crystallises and dries by absorbing moisture from within the plant's leaf – a reverse osmotic effect.

Quantities of salt which collect upon the soil surface create saline conditions, damaging to plant roots. Together with the drying effect of wind, salt is a menace to plants that are not adapted to it.

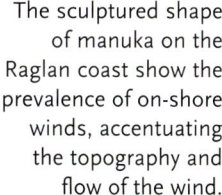

The sculptured shape of manuka on the Raglan coast show the prevalence of on-shore winds, accentuating the topography and flow of the wind.

Salt winds differentiate or devastate and maim plants. Plants that grow lee-ward of the prevailing salt wind survive, while those on the windward side can be blown over, dehydrated, eroded or stripped of their foliage. Disfigured, they lose their vigour and never reach their optimum growth.

PLANT SHAPE

The prevailing wind is reflected by the stunted shapes that plants grow into. Observe how trees in windy areas like Lake Ferry in the Wairarapa lean to one side and grow away from the origin of the most harsh wind, in this case the north-westerly, the prevailing wind.

Macrocarpa or pine trees will quickly out-grow their use for shelter and cause draughty undercurrents of increased wind pressure. They will also obstruct views. In this example, salt wind, drying soil, and needle litter all inhibit potential growth of desired garden plants.

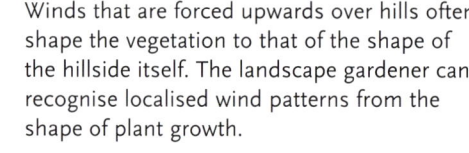

Winds that are forced upwards over hills often shape the vegetation to that of the shape of the hillside itself. The landscape gardener can recognise localised wind patterns from the shape of plant growth.

Wind-sculpted trees show the prevailing wind.

Species differences vary within close proximity when wind is increased as it is uplifted along most coastal areas and hilltops. The species frequently found thriving on hilltops are those that grow close to the ground; they are usually smaller than those growing downhill. Within 20 to 100 metres, vegetation characteristics can be

redefined. This is also evident along coastal areas, especially where hardy species, perhaps manuka or kanuka, taupata, karo, olearia, and coastal grasses that have adjusted to the loss of surface moisture and can endure the wind's onslaught as it blows over them, provide shelter for more tender plants behind them.

Wind can be cold, salt laden, gusty, warm, or move upwards or downwards, and affects plants in several ways. It will evaporate the surface moisture, burn the foliage, distort the shape of the plants, and 'prune' shrubs and trees.

If a tree is standing symmetrically – that is, shows even growth all round – you can assume there is no strong prevailing wind on that particular site. When trees lean to one side, as they do at Lake Ferry, the direction of the prevailing wind can clearly be seen.

But wind has more effect in some areas than in others. In sheltered areas where growth is lush because of adequate water, wind blowing from the occasional storm causes evaporation of surface moisture and increases plant transpiration that results in damage to soft growth. If such winds occur frequently over a season, new growth is pruned.

In Christchurch and Auckland, the presence of many tall trees suggests that the wind frequency and velocity there is far less than in Wellington. The winds of Wellington restrict the growth, height, shape, and also the species of trees found there.

It is always useful to observe those plants that shelter other plants from the wind, and to evaluate their contribution to the garden. For example, people believe that pine or macrocarpa trees provide shelter. But when they grow tall and straggly, they act as barriers, similar to large structures. The wind will bounce over them to be compressed on the other side, or roar underneath, with increased chilling velocity. The wrong type of shelter tree creates more havoc than good, as can be seen in many rural areas throughout New Zealand.

Pests and diseases

Pests and diseases also affect plant habits. In Auckland, for example, the humidity causes a greater prevalence of fungal diseases. These are less common further south because of lower temperatures and less humidity.

In areas of lush growth, aphids and other sucking insects will also attack young shoots and cause certain species to become deformed. A classic example is *Pinus radiata*. In its native habitat of California, it is much more slow growing than in New Zealand, because New Zealand has fewer insect pests and fungal diseases likely to attack this species.

Vegetation facts

Plant group habits

Plant species vary in type, and over time have evolved their form and habit into two groups. Monocotyledons, such as grasses, have a single seed leaf and parallel leaf veins. The important and unique feature of their adaptation is the way they grow from a crown at the base of the plant. This crown is surrounded by leaves that protect it from wind, sun, and frost. Dicotyledons, such as shrubs and trees, have seeds which, once germinated, produce two leaves. Plants in this second group have compound leaves that grow from branches.

All plants can be classed in three broad groups, according to their seasonal growth habits.

Annuals are plants that germinate, grow, flower, seed, and die within a 12-month period: for example, pansy, cornflower.

Biennials are plants that germinate and grow in the first year, then flower, set seed, and die in the second year: for example, tree mallow, beetroot.

Perennials are plants that flower annually, and continue to live year after year. Perennials can be further divided into the following sub-groups:

- Evergreen broadleaved trees and shrubs: for example, kowhai, hebe, daphne.

- Coniferous plants: for example, pine, macrocarpa, thuya.

- Deciduous trees and shrubs: for example, oak, birch, roses.

- Grasses: for example, toetoe, *Carex* species.

- Herbaceous softwood plants that sprout from a strong root system each spring, then flower, set seed, and are deciduous through the next winter, repeating this cycle each year: for example, rudbeckia, shasta daisy.

- Woody herbaceous perennials which flower each year, seed, and partially shed their leaves over winter, or during summer droughts: for example, valerian, marguerite daisy.

- Bulbs that usually appear above the ground to grow and flower for only six months, during their favoured season, then disappear until the following year: for example, daffodil, crocus, nerine, tulip.

Each group or sub-group has other typical seasonal habits: for example, all oak trees, which are perennial hardwoods, are deciduous in winter. Each group also varies in its matured growth height and growth rate. For example, bulbs are low growers, and herbaceous perennials and annuals seldom grow over two metres tall in a season, but this growth usually occurs at a faster rate than for most other plants. Plants like gunnera, rudbeckia, fennel, dahlias, and sunflowers can reach heights of up to two metres in six months.

For every situation within the landscape there is a plant of some type that has adaptations which are naturally suited to a specific climate. Lush-growing annual or perennial plants and evergreen trees thrive in the warm, moist conditions of subtropical climates. Biennial plants, such as giant bugloss (*Echium pininana*), have habits which give them the ability to tolerate salt winds and grow to a height of four metres in 18 months. Mosses and ferns do well where there is an abundance of water, soft light, and cool temperatures. Cacti and succulent plants, such as ice plant (*Disphyma australe*), *Carpobrotus edulis*, and century plant (*Agave americana*), are xerophytic. They are able to live in arid conditions as water is stored within their fleshy leaves. Grasses survive freezing temperatures and some drought, and cope with any abundance of wind. They will even grow again after fire. Agapanthus survive dry sun-drenched banks, as they store water in their roots and leaves. Other plants such as rhododendron, camellia and azalea, buttercup, dock, white pine

(*Podocarpus dacrydioides*), kowhai, and cabbage tree prosper in moist, acid soils. In soils of low fertility, leguminous plants like lupin, which prefer well-drained stony or sandy soils, usually flourish. Each plant has habits peculiar to its species and these habits are as numerous as the species themselves.

CHANGING DAYLIGHT HOURS

Changing seasons throughout the year affect the amount of daylight and the temperature – the two initiators of plants' life-cycle processes. The germination time for most seedlings is mid-autumn through to early winter and spring. Early summer is the most common time for flowering and seed formation, but each plant species has its optimum flowering time. For example, euryops flowers in the winter; arctotis in the spring; dahlias, crocuses, and nerines are flushing in the autumn. Photoperiodism is the term given to the direct response by a plant to the amount of daylight it experiences in a 24-hour period. This initiates hormones that trigger bud formation for flowering or growth.

Daylight is used in the process of photosynthesis to convert nutrients from the soil into organic matter. During the natural daylight hours, plants must produce sugars through photosynthesis. They can rest only in the dark hours. The length of the day, therefore, governs the amount of the sun's radiant energy transformed by plants through the seasons of the year. The active growth of all plants occurs in the spring and summer, as the number of daylight hours increases and temperatures become warmer. Hormonal controls trigger the budding time for fruit trees, spring blossoming, and also the fall of leaves in autumn as plants become dormant. Each species has habits that correspond to a particular predisposition to day length. For example, chrysanthemums flower in the autumn, whereas pohutukawa flower at Christmas, over the longest daylight periods.

Many of our ornamental house plants can be tricked into changing their habits. For example, chrysanthemums can be exposed to artificially induced shorter daylight periods over summer in order to initiate hormonal activity to form flowering buds. Through this artificial control of photosynthesis, they are able to flower out of season. The cut-flower industry depends on this factor to obtain higher prices for blooms outside the natural flowering seasons.

Although seasonal plant habits are triggered by variations of daylight, temperature further modifies their habitual activities. This applies to all plants, though each species' reaction to temperature is different. Consider the deciduous habits of trees throughout New Zealand. In their native environment of Europe, oak trees are naturally adapted to shed their leaves for cold snowy winters. In Auckland, the winter temperatures are comparatively moderate, but the oak still sheds its leaves each autumn, so that habit is dependent first on the number of daylight hours and secondly on the temperature.

Increasing daily sun hours, followed by the warmth of spring after a cold winter, and the availability of water signal an increased rate of spring growth. This is a characteristic habit of temperate plants.

PLANT ASSOCIATION/SUCCESSION

Evolving changes of species begin symbiotically. Primitive plants, such as lichens and mosses, break down bare rocks by clinging to them, and as they decay, they leave

behind fine silt. Gradually there is a build-up of organic soil from which grasses and small plants grow. Over years, taller-growing shrubs and trees emerge to dominate the species they replace. These in turn are overtaken by more dominating tree species which are more tolerant and better adapted to the changed conditions. However, only certain species finally dominate. Within the taller canopy of trees, only species that can regenerate or compete in shade emerge as the climax canopy: for example, beech in the Southern Alps; podocarps, rimu, and southern rata on the West Coast; or kahikatea (white pine) in wet Westland; and kauri in Northland. This evolutionary process shows how and why plants live with each other, in response to their environments. Plant succession occurs when, over a long time, one species competitively dominates another until a forest climaxes.

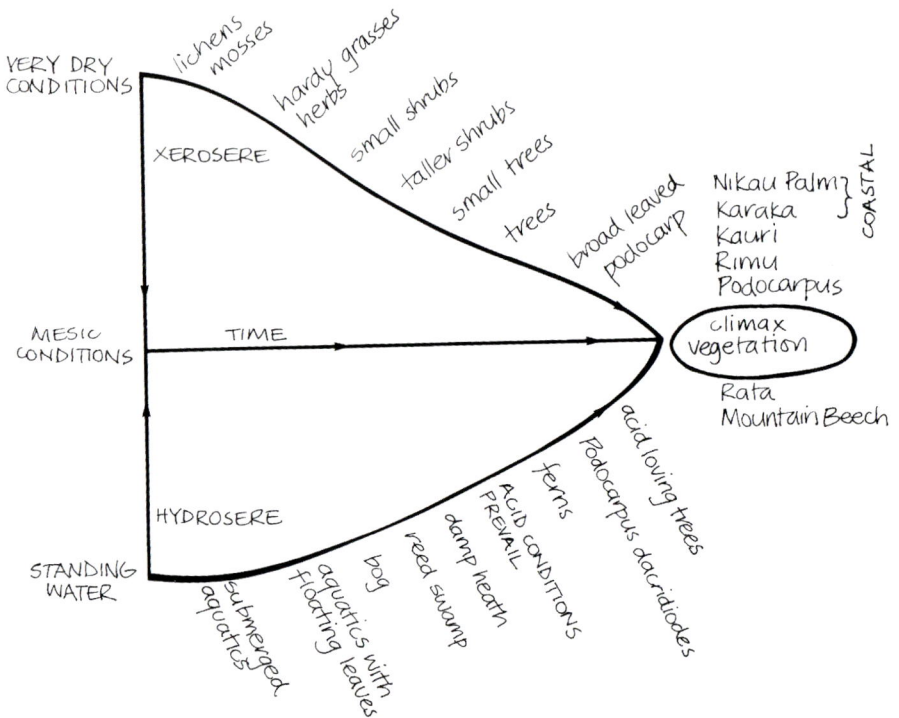

Plant succession, showing how the first colonising plants establish themselves, giving way to stronger dominating species as time passes.

If an area has been unattended for a lengthy period and is then cleared of vegetation, the natural cycle of competition, succession, and dominance is interrupted. Each small area of soil is subject to varied influences of wind exposure and insolation. This in turn affects the moisture available to plants and is affected again by the seasons changing. Seedlings have to endure these restrictions to be able to survive, and only plants that have adapted successfully to the conditions dominate each particular space. On cleared land, at the start of this cycle, hardy grasses and annual or herbaceous perennial plants, most of which are recognised as weeds, are the first to colonise exposed earth. With increased ground warmth, light, and available moisture in spring, these species grow aggressively, building up humus levels in soil as they die off and giving way to other perennial shrubs during the dry months of summer. Hardy shrubs compete with and succeed earlier established plants, and eventually they too become dominated by woody shrubs. Gorse, for example, grows in very dry conditions and succeeds through competition over

The natural cycle of plant succession can be observed in an area of undisturbed land. Over time, grasses give way to scrub such as gorse and broom, which in turn is succeeded by taller growth such as kanuka and larger trees.

pasture and other rank growth, but its seedlings need light to flourish, and later, when shaded, it has difficulty competing with other plants. Gorse is then succeeded by taller native growth. Through time, clones of indigenous trees that germinate in shade and in the shelter of existing scrub growth become more dominant. The neglected vegetation is eventually succeeded and the area is transformed to native forest. This is evident where native bush is becoming more prevalent by regenerating through natural competition and succession.

Minor plant succession also occurs on a small domestic scale. Freshly turned earth will quickly become covered in weeds, such as chickweed, grasses, dandelion, and fat hen. These plants are temporary, as garden shrubs soon dominate, using the available light for photosynthesis, and weeds retreat into submission. This is the secret of low-maintenance landscape gardening. By understanding plant succession you will be able to recognise an existing plant's compatibility with introduced new plants.

NATURAL PLANT COMPANIONSHIP

Plants in the wild with similar habits usually form associations of colonies in specific habitats where they are able to flourish. Clones of species growing closely together indicate favourable growing conditions for successful species.

The symbiotic lives of some plant communities even involve their demise and decay, providing food for other

Naturalised coastal vegetation has established in gravel soils on the Wairarapa coast. Here flax and muehlenbeckia, together with rocks, form a stunning landscape.

species' growth. Clover, broom, gorse, wild sweet pea, and lupin are some plants from the Leguminosae or pea family. Legumes all have nodules on their roots which are host to a relationship between algae and bacteria. The bacteria are able to fix nitrogen which the plant needs for growth. Coniferous plants, such as pine trees, have a fungus known as mycorchiza on their roots, and this supplies them with phosphorus, another important growth mineral. Species with tap roots bring minerals from deeper soil levels to the surface; and as nutrients are collected from different sources, stronger, more hardy plants shelter weaker ones, living as companions.

COMPETITION, BALANCE, AND DOMINANCE

Plants exist in a continual state of competition for space, nutrients, moisture, and light. The ability of a plant to grow to its optimum size at its optimum rate depends upon how well its tolerances are suited to the environmental conditions of a particular site, and its relative dominance over other competing plant species. This can be understood by observing the growth habits of plants that are isolated from others and contrasting them with the habits of groups that are intermingled with various other species.

In the wild, plants grow naturally in groups. In valleys or on ridges, they clone where favourable moisture, soil, and climatic conditions prevail. The stronger, dominant plants survive against the competition of other aggressive species. This response is closely related to the orientation of the plants to the sun and to the availability of water. Along the south-facing cliffs of Cook Strait, where there is dampness, flax dominates. On the north-facing cliffs, which receive more sun, there is a predominance of gorse.

Each small area of soil is subject to the varied influences of wind exposure and heat absorbed from the sun. These factors, as well as the changing seasons, affect the moisture available for plants to survive. This moisture is also affected by the changing seasons. Seedlings have to endure certain restrictions to be able to survive in a windy climate, and only those plants that have adapted successfully to the site will dominate each particular space.

Even when a species adapts to local climatic factors, other and more aggressive plant species will smother those that are weaker than themselves and eventually may take over. On cleared land, spring growth will die during the dry summer, and each season it will give way to hardier shrubs. Through time, this natural community of plants will exhibit a diversity of species, but one species will dominate because it has the optimum growth habits for the given conditions. If an area of vegetation has been unattended for a lengthy period, clearing that vegetation will interrupt and set back the natural cycles of competition, plant succession, and dominance.

This is an essential consideration when planning a garden in terms of maintenance. The more the garden approaches a natural balanced state, containing plants suited to the environment and existing with those that are equally competitive, the less maintenance will be required. Nature will work on itself.

When introducing new plants into your garden, ensure that the plants' natural habits are similar to those of the other plants around them, and that they are compatible with those of existing plants. Otherwise your efforts will be lost.

PLANTS THAT COMPETE WITH GORSE

In situations where gorse is dominant, plan a planting scheme where equal competition will occur naturally. For example, toetoe and most of New Zealand's native trees will grow happily with the gorse, and will finally succeed it by growing taller in a competitive search for light. (Strong salt-laden winds will prune gorse into dry kindling, making it a fire hazard, so the planting of hardy natives amongst it will also help reduce this danger.) Fast-growing plants like *Virgilia divaricata* will compete with gorse, provided the windy areas are free of both salt and frost. In salt-air environments, use trees like ngaio, which will quickly succeed gorse. Gorse needs full light to survive against competing plants and is vulnerable to excessive salt-laden winds. If you plant species that are successful in these habitats, you can create an ecology of your own choice which will naturalise harmoniously with the existing vegetation.

Boneseed (*Chrysanthemoides monilifera*) grows naturally with gorse on the Wellington hillsides because it is competitive and equally suited to the same habitat. These two species can be distinguished by the different colouration in the groups of cloned plants: boneseed flowers are a brighter yellow than the gorse. Darwin's barberry (*Berberis darwinii*) can also be seen competing successfully with gorse in this area.

Biennial plants like tree mallow are able to endure harsh, frost-free sites, tolerate salt winds, and grow to a height of two metres. Plants such as taupata and karo will grow similarly in such habitats but are slower, longer-term survivors. There are also deciduous plants, such as salix, poplar, and elm, and weeds like fennel, which lie dormant over winter and consequently evade the harsh, salty conditions that prevail along Wellington's south coast at that time.

All plants in the wild naturally balance themselves with other plants that they compete with. Those that cannot compete are not present and have retreated in the face of more successful plants.

CONCLUSION

To become familiar with a site's limitations you need to evaluate all plant growth within the site. The existing plants that are compatible with your purpose can then be used as an aid to establish new plants. For example, the marguerite daisy will grow a metre high in a season, recovering quickly from severe salt burn, and can be used in exposed sites to protect those slower-growing plants which, in time, will succeed it. This is a long-term process. Instead of eradicating all established growth, aim to work with the existing healing that has already taken place and plant compatibly amongst this growth so that favoured plants may in time dominate the wind garden. If you have a scorched-earth attitude and totally clear the land, other problems will arise, such as aggressive new seasonal growth, wind and water erosion, and perhaps a loss of shelter.

Weed growth contributes to the build-up of soil fertility, protection from the wind, shades from the sun, and can help to conserve the humidity around each plant. A plant growing on its own in an exposed area suffers a lot more than when it is grouped together with other plants, which give natural protection in much the same way as animals huddle together to keep warm.

This series of diagrams below illustrates stages in gorse control using two different environmentally sound techniques, with tree lucerne and pine, from stage 5-8.

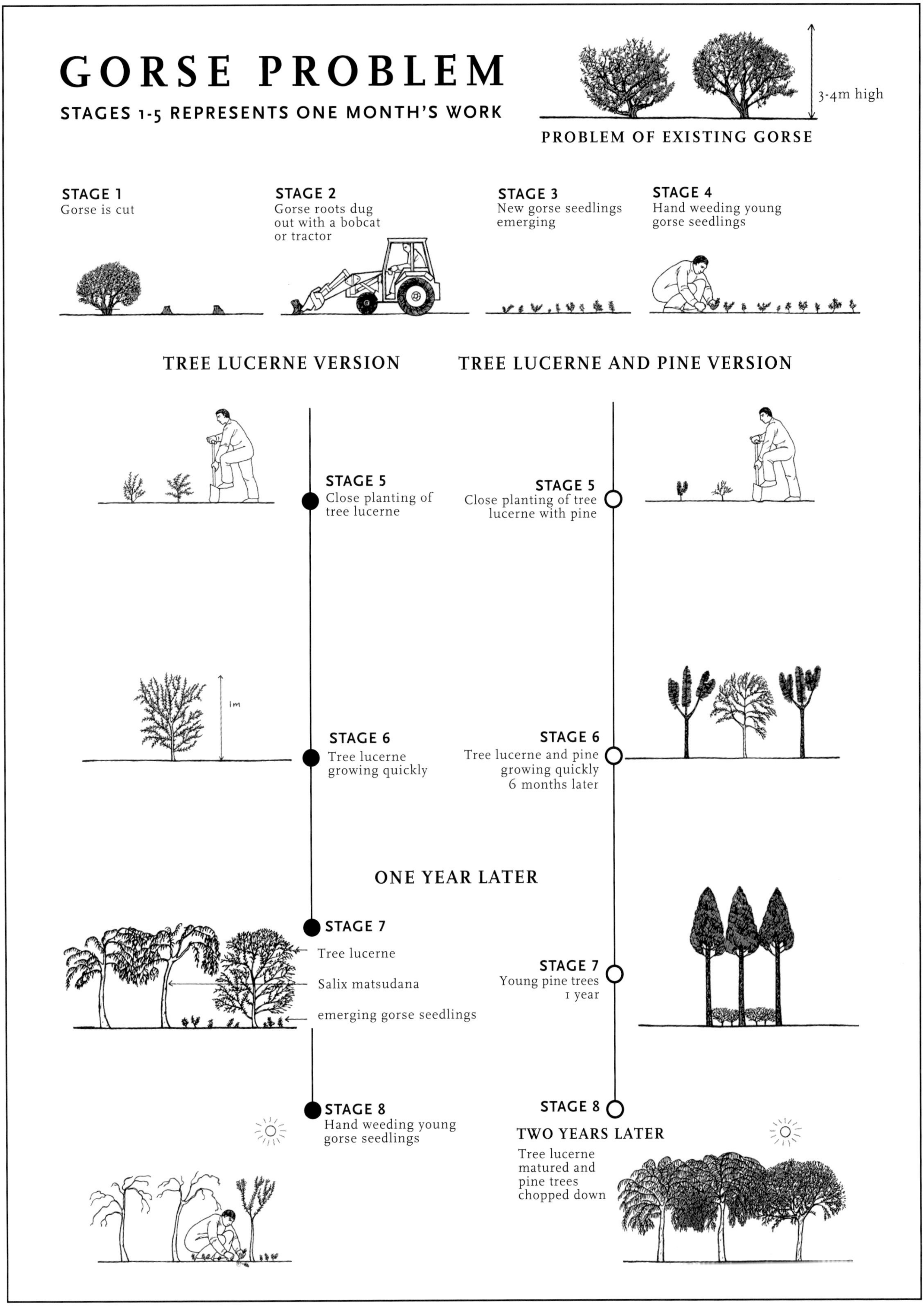

GORSE PROBLEM
STAGES 1-5 REPRESENTS ONE MONTH'S WORK

3-4m high

PROBLEM OF EXISTING GORSE

STAGE 1
Gorse is cut

STAGE 2
Gorse roots dug out with a bobcat or tractor

STAGE 3
New gorse seedlings emerging

STAGE 4
Hand weeding young gorse seedlings

TREE LUCERNE VERSION

STAGE 5
Close planting of tree lucerne

STAGE 6
Tree lucerne growing quickly

1m

TREE LUCERNE AND PINE VERSION

STAGE 5
Close planting of tree lucerne with pine

STAGE 6
Tree lucerne and pine growing quickly 6 months later

ONE YEAR LATER

STAGE 7
Tree lucerne
Salix matsudana
emerging gorse seedlings

STAGE 8
Hand weeding young gorse seedlings

STAGE 7
Young pine trees
1 year

STAGE 8

TWO YEARS LATER
Tree lucerne matured and pine trees chopped down

Competition between plants is dependent on several microclimatic factors such as the presence, absence, and exposure to salt wind, wind, drought, and freezing temperatures. Each new location is different: contrast coastal regions with windy, dry, and frosted inland regions. The compatibility of your chosen garden plants depends on the competition you create when you combine your new plants with those already thriving.

Always observe plants in environmental conditions that are as close as possible to those of your own site. This will ensure that variables of light and temperature, the salt content of wind, and the availability of moisture do not give an undue competitive advantage or disadvantage to the new arrivals in your garden.

Typical of Northland with its kauri, tree ferns, and mangroves, this habitat shows the influence of higher temperatures and more rainfall.

The severe alpine climate of the South Island produces a sparse and hardy vegetation.

The seasonal habits of plants are most obvious in frosted areas with deciduous species.

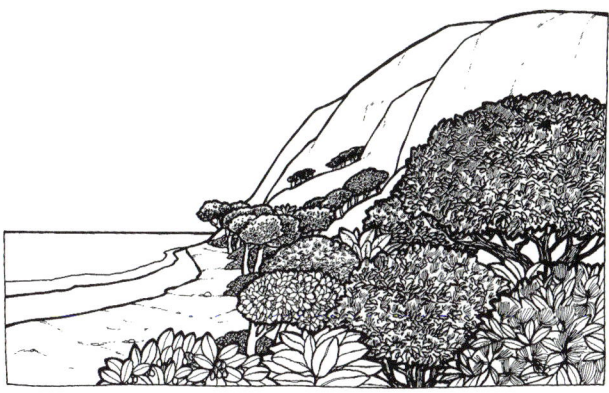

This west coast habitat in the Wellington area receives late afternoon sun, salt-laden but warm winds and usually no frost. Puka, pohutukawa, taupata, karaka, and ngaio flourish here.

The central North island area around Tongariro is a habitat of acid soils with snow tussock, toetoe, flax, and ericas.

In high-altitude habitats in the South Island, beech trees succeed where there is ample rainfall.

A typical New Zealand coastal habitat: marram grass, pingao, toetoe, gazanias, horned poppy, flax.

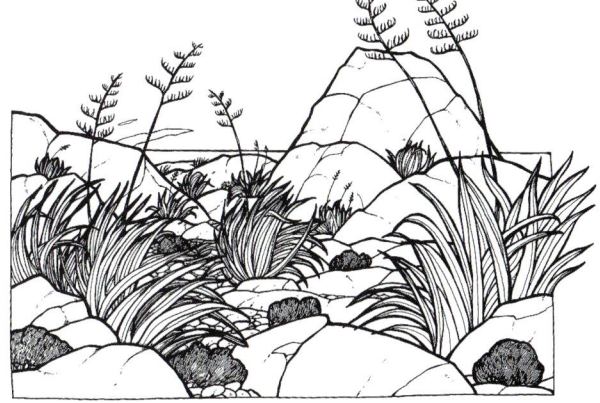

Although plants in coastal areas and river valleys have access to water, their differences are often pronounced because of the influence of other factors such as soil and temperature.

Although swampy areas are often considered problems, species such as gunnera, willows, raupo, flaxes, and toetoe flourish there, producing a distinctive landscape.

Conifers, larch, and mountain beech have developed an association in this Otago habitat because of similar adaptations and habits.

Section 2

Making the garden

Site planning

By now you will have an understanding of the principles of landscape design and the process of site and vegetation analysis. It is now time to apply this knowledge to your own place, and develop the garden which meets your needs.

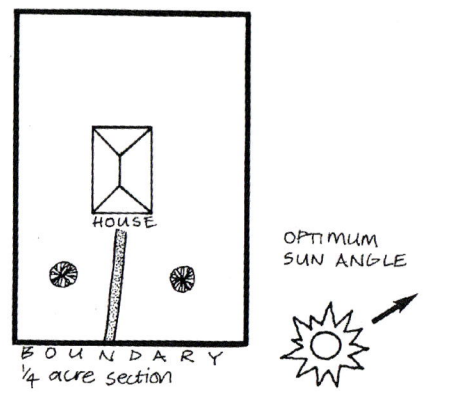

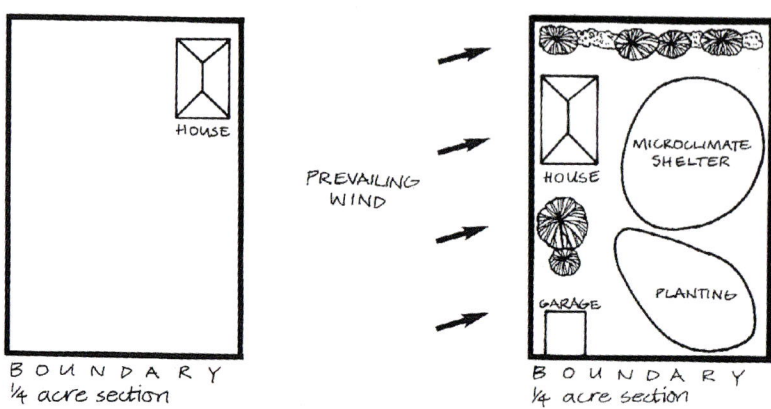

Positioning a house in the middle of a quarter-acre section often destroys the full potential of such a property.

Placing the house at the rear of the property will give the front of the site more sunshine than if it were shaded by the house.

Placing the house on the windward side would create sheltered areas and allow more positive spaces for outdoor activities.

Drawing a scaled site plan

This chapter begins by explaining how to construct a scaled site plan, then goes on to discuss ways of preparing your site for a garden which will extend its natural limits by using earthen mounds, cluster plantings, secondary mounds together with cluster planting, and fencing with Sarlon cloth.

A scaled site plan allows you to foresee the layout of your garden, its future size, the impact of shrubs and trees, and the effect of pathways through the site. Discussion, debate, and modification of the plan will enable you to develop practical and pleasurable solutions to your garden needs.

For an exposed garden, you must first plan the shelter belts, earthen mounds and cluster plantings within the boundaries, before designing those pleasurable microclimatic areas within.

When planning on a domestic scale it is often better to focus on a central area of the garden, nearest the living area of the house, rather than to expand too quickly on a larger scale. This way you obtain better intensified use of an area within

Display gardens, like the herb garden in the Wellington Botanic Gardens, shown here, need to have a plan.

the site – say, a courtyard – and avoid taking on too much work to begin with. Larger areas within the garden can be planted out in fruit trees or ornamentals, or be used as practical recreational spaces.

It is best to draw up your plan on an average scale of 1: 50 centimetres. That is, each centimetre on the plan is equivalent to 50 centimetres (i.e. 0.5 metre) of your actual garden. For example, a fence-line 5 metres long would measure 2.5 centimetres on your plan.

Start by drawing your boundaries using a scaled ruler. Then position the existing solid physical elements such as the house, garage, driveways, paths, large trees, and favourable shrubs. Position the house so that the other spaces can evolve.

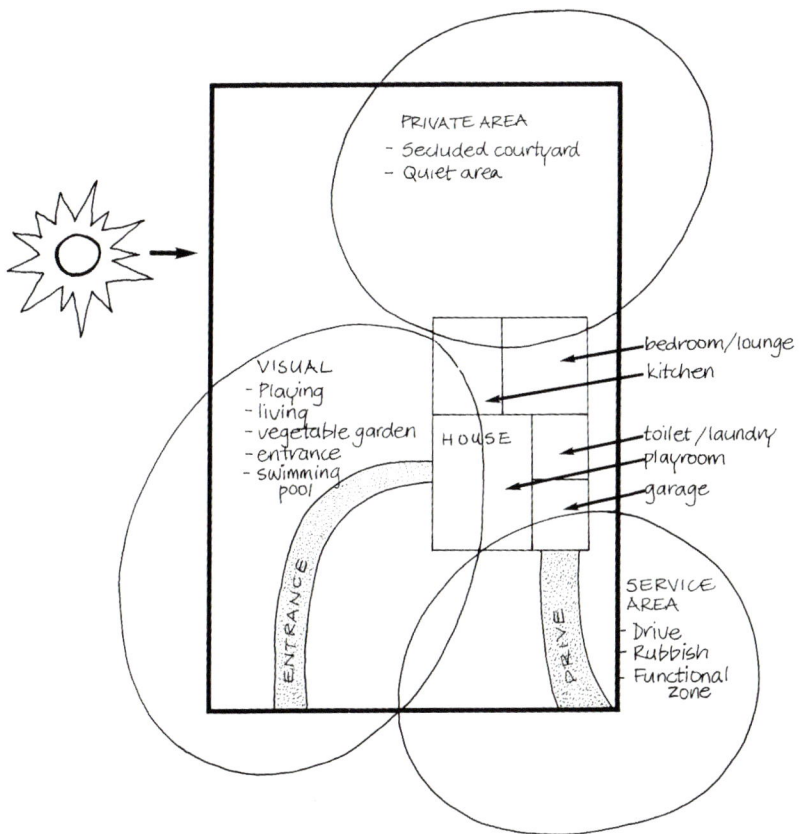

Locate north and south. Take note of winter and summer sun angles as well as the morning and evening sun. Focus on pleasant and distasteful vistas, and also take note of humps and hollows, wet and dry areas. You can then use this site plan as a base for your site analysis. Consider the functions you require of your site. Are you going to have to alter access and path routes? Do you want service areas for parking, rubbish collecting, or washing lines? Do they need to be relocated or given clearer definition? Have you decided on ways to improve social areas?

Having recognised the existing positive/negative features and determined the recognised changes to your layout, you should be able to consolidate the theme you wish to pursue and so begin to select appropriate plants, especially in the early phases where shelter planting is required. (Refer to the next section for more detail.)

After working with the relevant elements on your plan, you may find you need to draw several versions. Photocopies of the original base layout and notes will allow you to generate alternatives as you refine your ideas.

Spatial arrangement for windy sites

Once the building site is located, you then must prepare shelter in forms of mounds, and cluster plantings (see **Site preparation**, p.49–61). This will give you the benefit of establishing shelter in a natural way, saving time and money. In windy areas, establishing this protective growth takes a lot more time than it does in sites with more favourable climates, so you need to plant your shelter as soon as possible in order to enjoy its effects.

Within your site design there are now two established factors:
- dwelling space
- mounds or shelter planting.

These provide the frame or skeleton of the site.
Now look for the other major functional and recreational areas, merging them together, so that they flow into one another to your advantage.

These may include:
- Service area: washing line, rubbish bins, workshop and storage areas, car parking, car circulation, and garages.
- Entrances: these should be direct and flow easily.
- Garden character: the aspects that create the character of the site – the style that you, the owner, reflect naturally to others. It may be formal or informal, ostentatious, or more humble. The point is that the style you choose formulates the character of your site. (See **Themes**, p. 12.)
- Recreation areas.

With these requirements established, you can then design your garden using the design principles explained in Section 1 of this book. Bear in mind scale, character, style, maintenance requirements (wild garden or mown lawns?), and function.

The detailed ornamental gardens can be positioned once the building work has been completed. Over time these gardens will mature and intensify.

Ideally, the house should relate to and flow into garden spaces. The living area, for example, should connect to the outdoor recreational areas, like the courtyard, used for sitting, playing, or barbecues. Likewise, vehicles should be sited away from the family areas so that there is no disruption to sleep, and no unwelcome intrusion from smells, pollution, and noise. Access to car parking, however, should be direct. The laundry, too, should relate to the service area of your yard, used for hanging out the washing or storing rubbish.

- LEGEND -

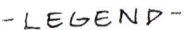
EXISTING TREES

PAVING

BRICK PATH

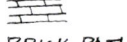
NEW PLANTING

GRASS

EXISTING BUSH

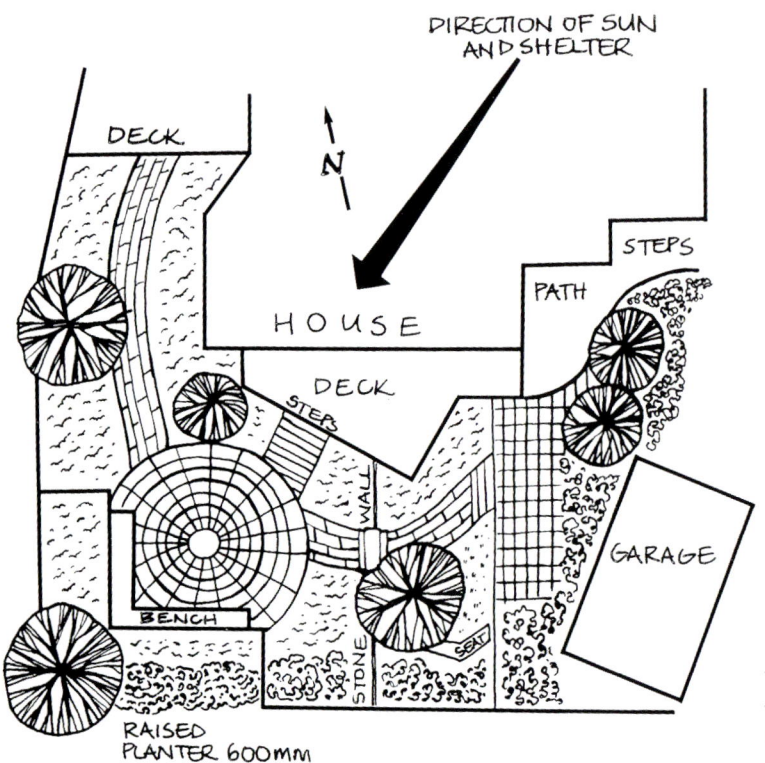

The house is positioned to block the wind and to allow a courtyard to be built in a sheltered area on the site.

You can now look into the detail of your house and garden design, and relate intended functions to their appropriate areas, as mentioned above. These details can be play spaces, courtyards, water activities such as swimming pools, ponds, or fountains; pathways or entrances. Once the spatial arrangement within the site has been finalised, you follow it up with planning the decoration using such aspects as colour, texture, and paving. Places of play or recreation can be bright and cheerful, using flowers, paint, and paving. Relate these aspects with the section on aesthetics in Section 1 of this book.

Entrances and pathways

Entrances and pathways should be located in areas where they are less likely to create draughts or wind funnels. For example, avoid locating your driveway entrance directly into the prevailing wind. (This is common on sites where function is the prime aspect.) In fact, it is like leaving the front door of your home open to the elements of weather. If it is impossible to change the location, then try to curve the entrance or pathway so that the access is bent and the draught deflected or bounced away. The simple relocation or rearrangement of your entrance can prevent those damaging wind gusts from entering the inner areas of your site.

A curved path now deflects 60 per cent of the wind.

The direct driveway was remade and curved, with gravel mounds put along the sides and then planted. This prevented the wind from gushing directly up the drive and forced the flow to bend away.

Planting with toetoe, *Brachyglottis greyi*, flax, agapanthus, and arctotis, now mature, 18 months later.

The mounds here are curved, bending the wind so that it loses strength, and providing privacy from the street. Quarry gravel (containing no soil or weed seeds) was used. Young flaxes and toetoe were planted into the gravel and watered regularly during the first season. The result is pleasing to the eye and effective in dealing with the wind.

Mounds can be built on these passageways to buffer draughts, and can be further planted with wind-hardy ornamentals.

Wind will follow the easiest route, blowing strongly down straight driveways. Bend the drive and cluster planting in areas where the wind pushes through to block the wind's path, thus reducing its velocity.

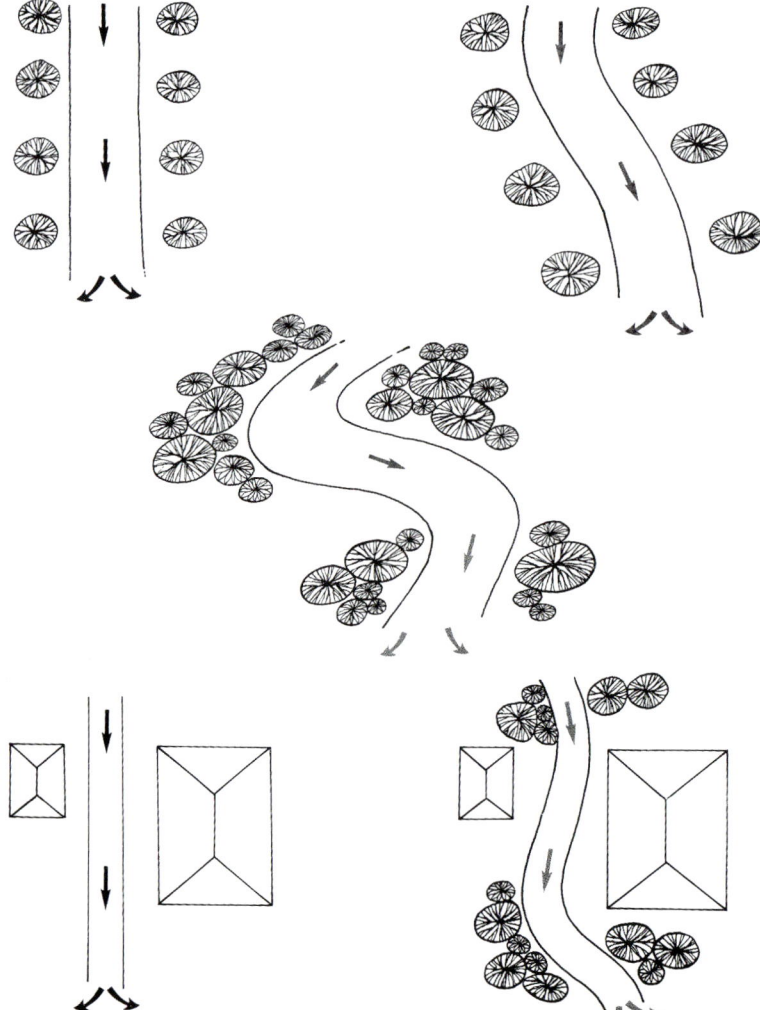

The entrance to your site marks a transition from the public to the private space. This sense of privacy is enhanced if the change is also marked by a change of direction, surface, level, sense of enclosure, and view. Create a sense of arrival with either a gate, pergola, arch, posts, or a bower of trees. Your garden can help improve the quality of your entrance by using shape, scent, colour, and texture, with movement flowing through the site.

Therefore begin the planning of your garden at the point of entrance to your site. Let the plants there 'signpost' the theme your garden reflects, as well as creating the sense of successful movement from public to private realm.

Your site may already have clearly defined passageways. Ensure these are natural passages which connect the various parts of your site. People will usually shortcut across two paths at right angles, so make sure your paths follow the natural lines between the places you wish to connect. Curving the line of paths also creates interest and invites further progress.

The width of the path indicates the frequency of use and the degree of public accessibility. Have a wider path for your main entrance and narrower paths for those areas you wish to be private. Intimate spaces in your garden, which are partially blocked by shrubs, may have a narrow curving path through the line of vision.

Surfaces can vary from the formal durable surfaces of concrete, asphalt, and rounded pebbles to the cracked paving and stepping stones of informal paths.

When constructing pathways for your garden consider the function of your path and let its width, surface, and layout enhance the movement between all parts of your site.

Coastal properties exposed to constant salt winds are ideal for flax plantings that provide some shelter along pathways.

(Below left) The straight, sloping entrance before landscaping.

(Below right) The path has been reshaped into a curved and stepped descent through the garden, making it more interesting to look at and more interesting to be in.

New plants, battered by the prevailing wind, are establishing themselves.

The plants are now settling and taking a strong hold.

Ponds impart a feeling of relaxation.

Water, streams, and ponds

The reflection of the sun on the water, with flowering water lilies, frogs jumping on to floating leaves, fish swimming underneath, and the placid buzzing of mating dragonflies, are parts of a simple fantasy that can be so easily created in a natural wind garden. Water is always a bonus in any garden, giving it variety, peace, and serenity.

Water can be used as a theme, beginning as a trickle and gradually building up into a pond, perhaps focusing on a fountain. Or it can be a waterfall over rocks, either within a human scale or with just a faint fall which allows you to hear the soft splashing of water.

It can be as simple as a pond created in a poorly drained area of the garden which would have otherwise been a bog. With a little excavation and a plastered lining of clay slurry or clay paste on the bottom and sides to inhibit seepage further, a simple pond is easily created. Or you can go to the cost of building a pond to your desired shape from cement and stone with an in-built water pump. All these methods enhance the garden's theme and create a focus for relaxation and contemplation.

Conclusion

The design and style of a garden should be envisaged in a drawn concept. Spaces should flow into one another and be connected so that they relate in unison with the structures on your land. Look at the intended garden's influence on space: where it could interfere with access or block out sun and desirable views. Notice damp, shady, and low areas that are susceptible to frosts over winter months; these pockets are ideal for driveways or car-parks and garages. Use space positively, reserving favourable sunny areas for outdoor living.

A garden plan should be weighed up in terms of the time needed to accomplish the total effect, and the costs of establishment and maintenance. Consider priorities and plan to build the garden in affordable stages. Schedule a time frame for completion and aim to be as practical as possible by beginning simply and leaving provision of detail until later. It is advisable to consult a landscape designer who has experience with the kind of garden you wish to create. Materials, as well as the supply of good-quality plants and the services of specialised trades people, all vary in value. Shop around for resources and compare the quality of products with their cost. Prepare a budget for the essential work, and finish other stages of planting, paths, seating, paving, ponds or fencing later, when more money is available. It's best to save the money first and then begin work, rather than having to stop half way, leaving an unfinished effect that can quickly deteriorate.

A newly planted garden takes time to evolve to its optimum through natural competition within the confines of nature. So it is important to estimate the time span needed to establish dominant growth, or the garden might revert into a wilderness. You may, for example, wish to establish trees first. But remember that regular maintenance will be required over the time it takes for them to mature, which can be many years. Sometimes landscaped sites can have a dull impact if the planting is too spaced out. When left, quicker-growing plants will become too tall and choke slower growth, resulting in the death of favoured varieties.

In other words, you must plan ahead of the seasons to introduce plants that will flourish and blend into the existing ecology within your estimated time span.

Site preparation

Creating microclimates using wind deflection

On an exposed site identify the most sheltered comfortable places and plan to create other microclimates by reducing wind pressure. Observe where the wind moves, swirling past barriers. Wind takes the most direct route but can be bent on to a new path by placing a series of obstacles in its way, so that it travels above rather than through the site. Constructing fences or building structures, such as garden sheds, in draughty spaces can provide some shelter, but buildings and houses sometimes act as funnels for wind, as it blows along each of their sides. Shaping the ground with humps and hollows, making mounds, using rock placement or establishing shelter and cluster plantings are ways wind is lifted upwards and over, deflecting turbulence. This is a long-term project. Planted mounds take time to establish but are highly beneficial, enjoyable, and attract wildlife.

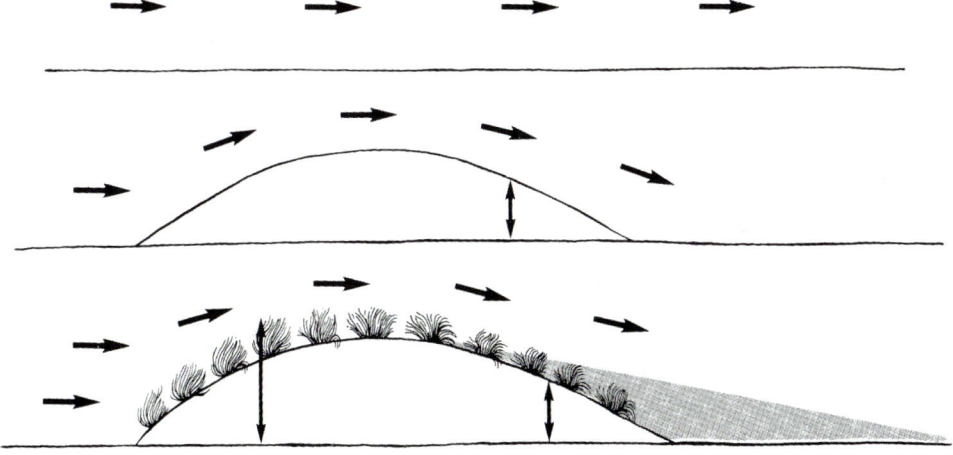

Mounds are effective in lifting the wind, creating effective shelter in the lee of the mound. Planting on the mounds adds height and helps to deflect the wind further and filter it, creating less turbulence.

The music block at Wellington College of Education, before planting (left) and five years later (right).

Wind will take the most direct route, blowing over a barrier, swirling as it moves. It is necessary to deflect the turbulence further by creating secondary mounds and other cluster plantings within the site to reduce the wind even more. This can be accomplished by placing secondary mounds and secondary cluster plantings in the wind's path.

MOUNDS AND SECONDARY MOUNDS

These are very effective for providing shelter on level or undulating landscapes, especially in those areas where there is an abundance of salt wind, as they are solid barriers from which wind is deflected, lifting it upwards and over. A series of these mounds placed strategically throughout the site will assist enormously with wind deflection. It is important to note that a height of only two metres is adequate for human comfort and will benefit most garden plants. The higher the mound, the greater the uplift of wind, causing a stronger rebounding effect on the other side of the object. Taller shelter belts or buildings increase wind pressure. A series of low, one- to two-metre mounds that bounce the wind upwards is far more effective. It is very important to take note of this fact!

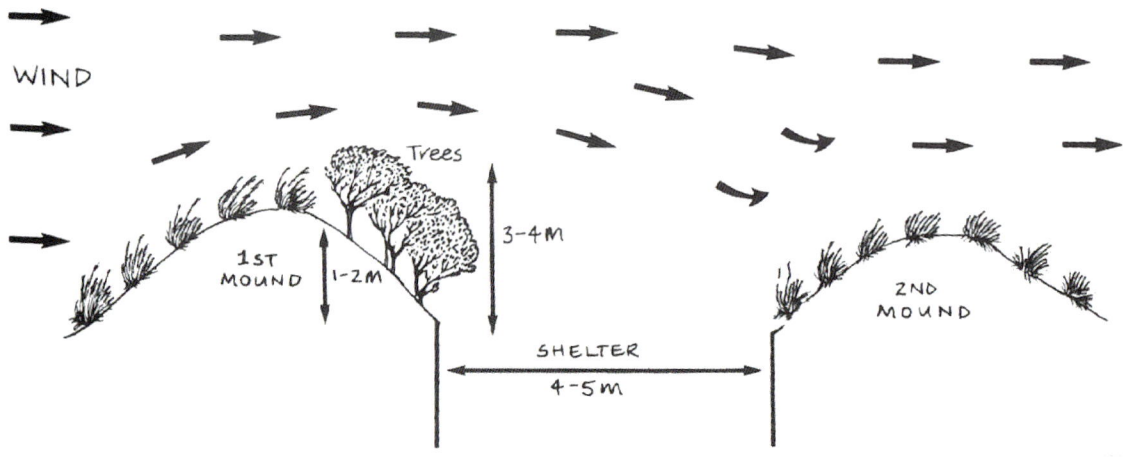

Mounds provide shelter extending to twice the distance of their height. A second mound helps to deflect the wind even further.

Mounds can be made using poor soil or even rotten rock. Placing easily grown plants such as toetoe on the mounds adds height at the top to deflect and filter the wind, decreasing its velocity, thus providing added shelter. Broom, tree lucerne, and other leguminous plants (usually taken for weeds) are also beneficial in providing shelter for future growth, and play an important role in re-building poor soils. A series of such planted mounds placed throughout the garden will assist enormously with wind deflection, as wind will tend to blow a few metres above the garden, rather than blowing through it.

Mounds deflect wind by lifting it. They provide privacy and can be permanent features on a street frontage, allowing shelter for off-street parking. This mound has not needed any maintenance in ten years, and is self-sustaining.

(Left) Formation of the mound and the first planting.
(Middle) Growth of the mound after the first year.
(Right) The matured mound with toetoe and karo.

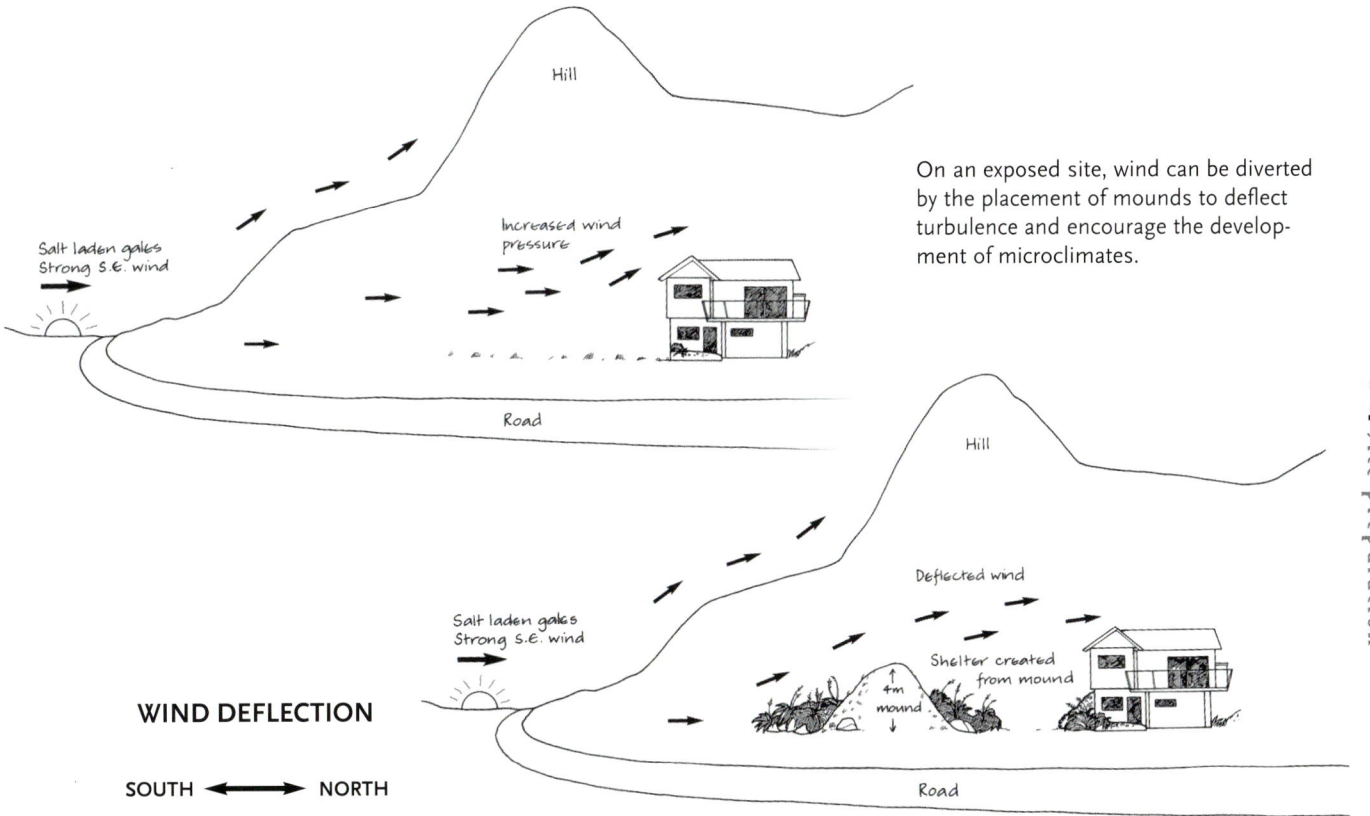

Hill

Salt laden gales
Strong S.E. wind

Increased wind pressure

Road

On an exposed site, wind can be diverted by the placement of mounds to deflect turbulence and encourage the development of microclimates.

Hill

Salt laden gales
Strong S.E. wind

Deflected wind

Shelter created from mound

+m mound

Road

WIND DEFLECTION

SOUTH ⟵⟶ NORTH

The mound shown in the sketch above: karo, flax, and olearia on a gravel mound, ten years later.

This house is situated on a hilltop with excellent views but is exposed to all winds. Small mounds were designed to allow cluster planting to mature, deflect the wind, and provide some shelter within. Those areas where views are to be retained are planted with low-growing plants.

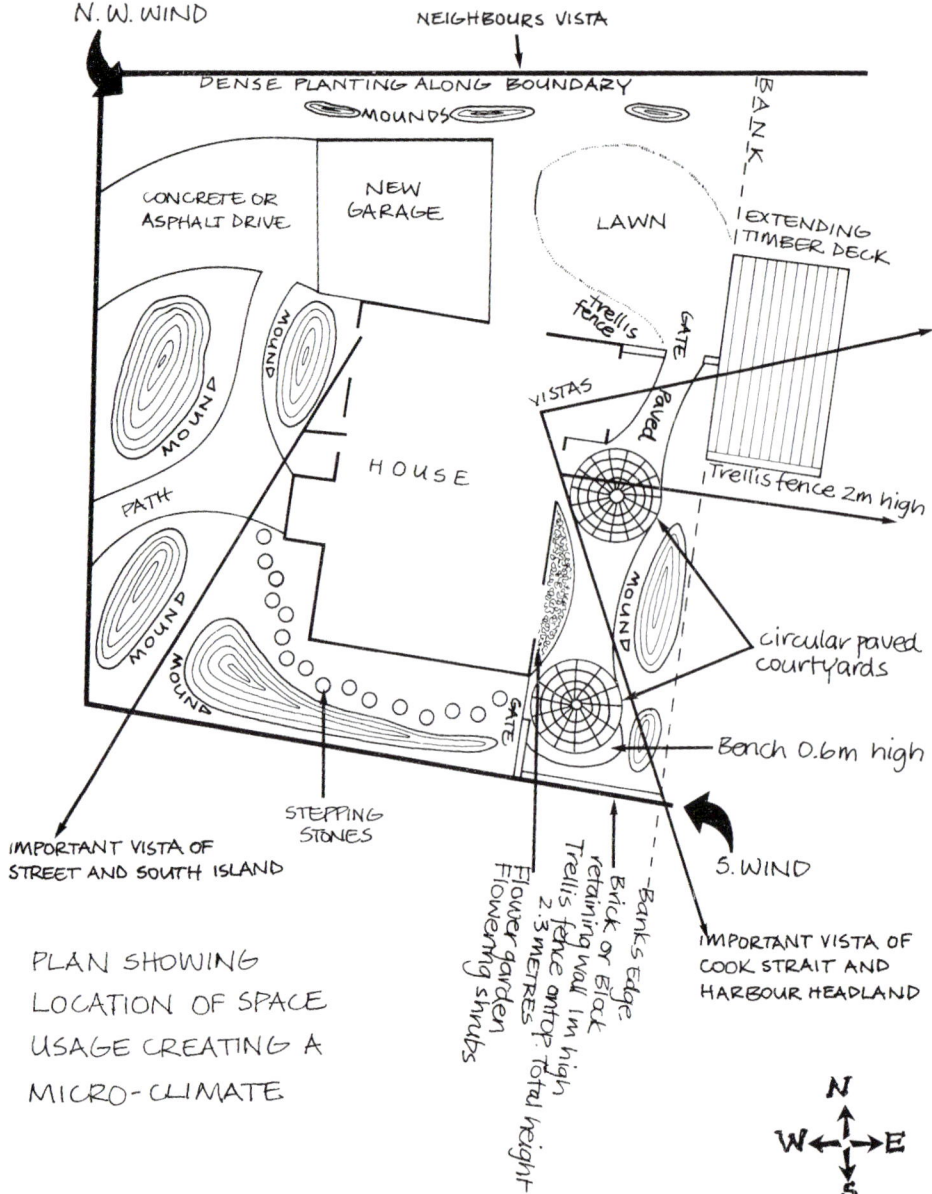

N.W. WIND

NEIGHBOURS VISTA

DENSE PLANTING ALONG BOUNDARY

MOUNDS

BANK

CONCRETE OR ASPHALT DRIVE

NEW GARAGE

LAWN

EXTENDING TIMBER DECK

MOUND

MOUND

Trellis fence

GATE

paved

VISTAS

Trellis fence 2m high

HOUSE

PATH

MOUND

MOUND

circular paved courtyards

MOUND

MOUND

Bench 0.6m high

STEPPING STONES

GATE

IMPORTANT VISTA OF STREET AND SOUTH ISLAND

PLAN SHOWING LOCATION OF SPACE USAGE CREATING A MICRO-CLIMATE

Flower garden Flowering shrubs

Banks Edge: Brick or Block retaining wall 1m high Trellis fence ontop 2.3 METRES: Total height

S. WIND

IMPORTANT VISTA OF COOK STRAIT AND HARBOUR HEADLAND

N
W ← → E
S

Mounds can be made up to 5m high to deflect strong prevailing winds, as in this farm property in the Wairarapa.

This mound hides a pump house. The weeds were grazed back by cattle and followed with the planting of *Cortaderia selloana* 'Variegata'. (Top) Planting begins. (Middle) Six months later. (Bottom) One year later.

The construction and growth of the mounds at Wind Gardens, Houghton Bay.

CLUSTER PLANTING

Cluster planting is a technique in which carefully selected tree and shrub species are grouped together so closely that they grow into each other, filling in all the gaps. This has a sheltering effect similar to that of mounds. Cluster planting should be planned carefully, and you should choose only suitable plants which will grow vigorously in competition with each other. Select a variety of integrated plant species such as toetoe, flax, or olearia that not only look attractive but also balance themselves with competition, thus forming that vital shelter. Some planting combinations can be a collection of shrubs, small conifers, and hardy foliage plants.

This site in Wellington is exposed to extreme north-west winds that descend over the Makara hills. To deflect the wind, a former straight path that gave access to the front door was changed into an S shape. The prevailing wind is lifted upwards over two mounds planted with tussock grasses, seen along the edges of the path. The taller-growing plants such as virgilia, toetoe, and ake ake were planted at the rear, with marguerite daisy bushes for quick cover. The slower-growing natives emerged and began to dominate three years later. This wind garden shows mound planting that is easy to maintain and is aesthetically pleasant for a frosted, wind-blasted site.

This series of pictures shows how the landscape planting has established itself over time, with minimal maintenance in an exposed, salt-wind environment where only the strong survive. It shows how a self-sustained garden can mature into the future. (Middle) Garden at one year old. (Bottom) Six years' growth.

(Top) Early planting completed.
(Middle) One year's growth.
(Bottom) Six years' growth.

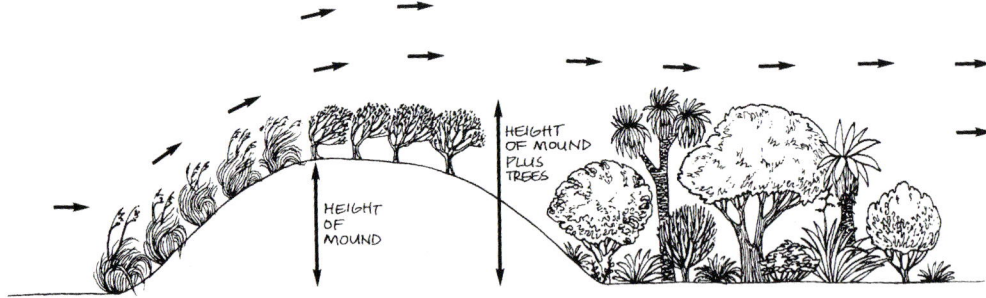

Mounds and plants need only be 2m high to provide comfort.

HEIGHT OF MOUND PLUS TREES

HEIGHT OF MOUND

In this rural garden in Greytown, Wairarapa, a mound has been formed to deflect wind, then planted densely with protea, grevillea, *Artemisia arborescens*, *Santolina chamaecyparis-sus*, *Argyranthemum frutescens*, *Arctotis stoechadifolia*, *Osteospermum fruticosum*, *Euryops pectinatus*, *Echium candicans*, hebes, ake ake, and a mixture of herbaceous perennials. This garden has been particularly successful in withstanding frosts and abundant wind. The mound, along with suitable planting, has made the best use of this exposed site, creating sheltered microclimates within for more delicate plants.

Mixed plantings are superior to single-species planting as some individual plant species will always do better than others because of microclimatic changes.

In the domestic garden, cluster plantings should also be a carefully planned mixture of varying species to attain the shelter height required. If you know the heights of mature plants, then you can plan cluster plantings in areas that face directly into the prevailing wind. Consider orientation and organise the planting so taller plants are in areas where height is essential for shelter. Place smaller species where lower levels of growth are desirable. You can then use this planting as a backdrop to other ornamental species, as long as it does not shade sun-loving plants in other garden spaces. Consider the growth of your plants over time; look for long-term results.

Cluster planting: a selection of trees and shrubs mixed together in compatible groupings designed to reach a desired height and block the force of wind.

Up-draught on exposed hillsides can be very difficult to shelter. Close planting of toetoe and *Olearia albida* helps provide some protection.

Cluster planting along Cobham Drive, where strong, closely-planted flax and toetoe have matured, providing shelter for over 25 years.

Cluster plantings can also take the form of mixed hedging, with trees and shrubs grouped together to fill in the gaps where wind could pass.

Clustered groups of plants scattered throughout the garden will help deflect wind by lifting gusts over the tops.

The library entrance at the Wellington College of Education before work began.

The site has been mounded and planted with grasses so that strong wind can be seen dancing through them, providing shelter and a pleasant outlook.

SHELTER BELTS

Pine, poplar and macrocarpa planted in straight lines of single species are the most common shelter belts found in rural areas. However, when they have grown tall and straggly, they act as barriers similar to large structures. Wind bounces over them to be compressed on the other side, or roars underneath with increased chilling velocity. Poplars grow anywhere from 20 metres to 60 metres high and are too tall for shelter belts. They cast long shadows and their roots sucker along the surface soil, taking up moisture and wasting valuable space, and with age they become susceptible to rust diseases. The wrong type of shelter tree does more harm than good.

Young eucalyptus and tree lucerne are an ideal combination for quick shelter on open, wind-blasted land.

It is wise to vary species so that planting then develops a thick strong canopy and supports the large variety of parasitic insects and bird life needed for biological control against plant-sucking insect pests in orchards and gardens. Each planting must be carefully chosen to suit local conditions with respect to frost, wind and salt tolerance. A mixture of beneficial plants has a longer and healthier life as a group. When some species age others take charge.

If longer sunshine hours in sheltered areas are desired, plant taller trees along south-side boundaries so that any shadow falls away behind. On the north-facing boundary of the garden, plant a shelter belt of mixed species that beautify and grow to between two and three metres high. Shelter belts should be a mixture of trees with grass-type plants such as toetoe, cabbage tree, and flaxes which enrich the soil and provide shelter, as long as they are crowded together. In time, hardwoods and conifers will succeed others that are quicker growing but not as long lived.

An old shelter belt can be transformed by either removing top-heavy trees such as pine and macrocarpa, or strengthening the existing vegetation by filling in wind-funnel gaps under the trees with earth mounds and then planting into them. However, shelter belts are less desirable than well-planned cluster plantings.

WIND PROTECTION AIDS

Wind protection aids can be artificially created. Remember that wind deflection from mounds and the filtering of wind through vegetation have far greater advantages than solid fencing. Sarlon cloth, a woven plastic cloth, is a good wind filter that can be battened on to fence posts, providing immediate protection, and can be purchased in various thicknesses. This type of fence placed through a mound acts effectively against strong winds.

(Left) Wind cloth secured to stakes provides instant protection and helps significantly in establishing new plants.

(Right) The site two years earlier.

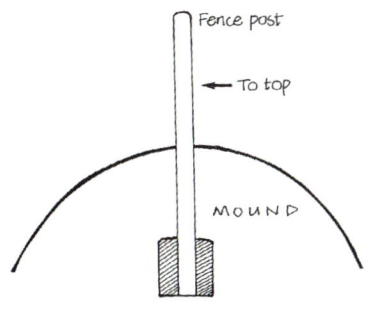

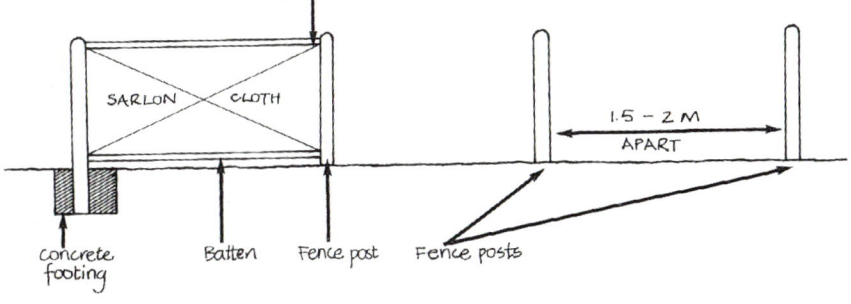

Mounds with Sarlon cloth attached to tall fence posts can be used in severe cases to take the full force of gales. Fence posts should be treated and cemented into a base.

Sarlon cloth between fence posts filters the wind effectively. Use it where salt-burn damages plant growth, or where instant shelter is required.

The wrapping of Sarlon cloth around a circular staked frame for each plant is simple and effective, but is not the most attractive sight.

An important consideration with individual cultivation is to make sure each plant is securely staked, so as to prevent the wind from rocking the newly forming roots. Without staking the young roots will be constantly torn, and the plant will die. Remember also to prune back the newly planted taller plants by as much as half their foliage.

Trellis screens provide immediate shelter and can be used imaginatively. They capture the warmth of the sun's rays in what would otherwise be a wind-chilled zone, especially in exposed, south-facing areas.

Trellis fencing built around a courtyard helps shelter the outdoor area from swirling winds. Photo at top left shows site before construction.

Trellis fencing will filter wind force, providing good shelter within.

A small vegetable garden between two properties. Here the wind would usually funnel through, so a glass sliding door was erected to block the path of the wind flow and allow sunlight to come through.

TERRACES

Terracing, built along contour lines, reduces erosion, spreads water evenly over the ground and increases your usable garden space. On sloping land, construct a series of terraces by building low walls that lean back into the slope of the hill, and back-filling with free-draining soil. By planting shrubs and bushes such as pohutukawa, virgilea, ngaio, toetoe, and flax along the edge of the terrace you will deflect wind and provide shelter on the flat space behind.

Terracing reduces erosion by slowing down surface water run-off.

Planting the edges will provide shelter on the terrace by deflecting the force of wind.

Working with the natural ecology

Different climate zones

When gardening and landscaping, try to recreate the beauty found in nature. Each new place is host to local flora and provides opportunities for certain types of gardens. Harsh environments suit only hardy plant species whereas favourable climates suit a greater variety of plant species. Inland zones are subject to wind and frosts but are free of salt and its drying effects. On lakeside properties, gardens closest to the water's edge are a few degrees warmer than field locations.

Cold, frosty mountain environments, such as that at Glenorchy, are ideal habitats for the red snow tussock, *Chionochloa rubra*.

Lakeless, land-locked areas do not receive warmth re-radiated from the sea during cold nights as coastal areas do, and consequently experience very cold frosts. Marked seasonal variation makes deciduous species a good choice here.

Northern areas, where minor freezing occurs, are nearly always warm, enabling a great range of plants to flourish, including jacaranda and coral trees, canna lilies, frangipani, hibiscus, and lantana. However, diseases and pests can be a problem in the humid climate of the north.

Seasonal change is not as distinct in northern areas as it is in more temperate regions. Quick growth generally occurs all year round, and competition between plants is far more intense. Cottage gardens need continuous maintenance as weed growth is rampant and species contest strongly for dominance. Gorse, manuka, bracken, kikuyu, and pampas grass are also aggressive invaders here.

The choice of plants to grow becomes more restricted in colder gardens with greater seasonal variations. The coming of spring and the strong colour of autumn leaves are seasonal highlights. In winter, snow and ice make the landscape barren-looking, although slow-growing conifers become more colourful as temperatures begin to drop. But in summer, temperatures at midday usually soar. Herbaceous perennial plants such as echinacea, rudbeckia, aster, helianthus, helichrysum, statice, and gypsophila all love hot summers and thrive here, as do wild species like thyme and lupin.

Coastal zones are generally dry, windy, and exposed to salt, but are free of frost. If very close to the sea, expect microclimatic contrasts. Most often the need here is to create shelter from wind. For trees try pohutukawa, ngaio, and Norfolk pine. For shrubs, try taupata, karo, cottonwood, tamarisk, and manuka. These evergreen

(Left) Beachfront landscaping. The garden before landscaping begins.

(Right) The garden during construction.

The built garden. The work was completed in one day.

shrubs and trees are slow growing but are long-term survivors. For ground cover, plant marram grass or pingao mixed with gazania and lupin. Xerophytes, such as succulents, and nitrogen-fixing plants that thrive in poor soils are also well suited here. Plants introduced into a coastal environment must be of a similar type to these, chosen because they can prosper in this harsh dramatic climate.

A beachfront planting of *arctotis* in Collingwood, Golden Bay.

Arctotis in gravel soils at Island Bay, Wellington.

Street planting of *arctotis*.

Different colours can be mixed in street plantings.

This street garden at Devonport, Auckland, features spring bulbs and *Arctotis stoechadifolia* planted in a bank under cherry trees.

Orientation and sun angles

The lie of the land and its orientation in relation to the sun must also be clarified, as this determines which plants are able to grow.

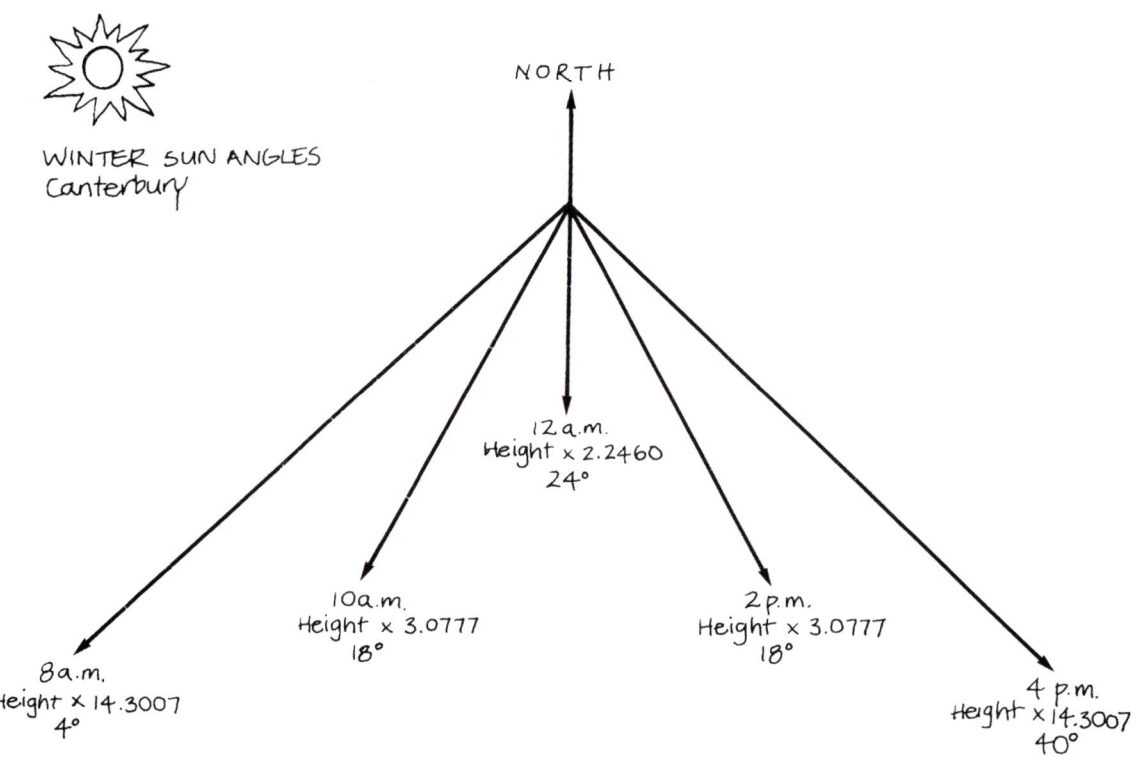

Winter and summer sun angles and the distance of shadows cast.

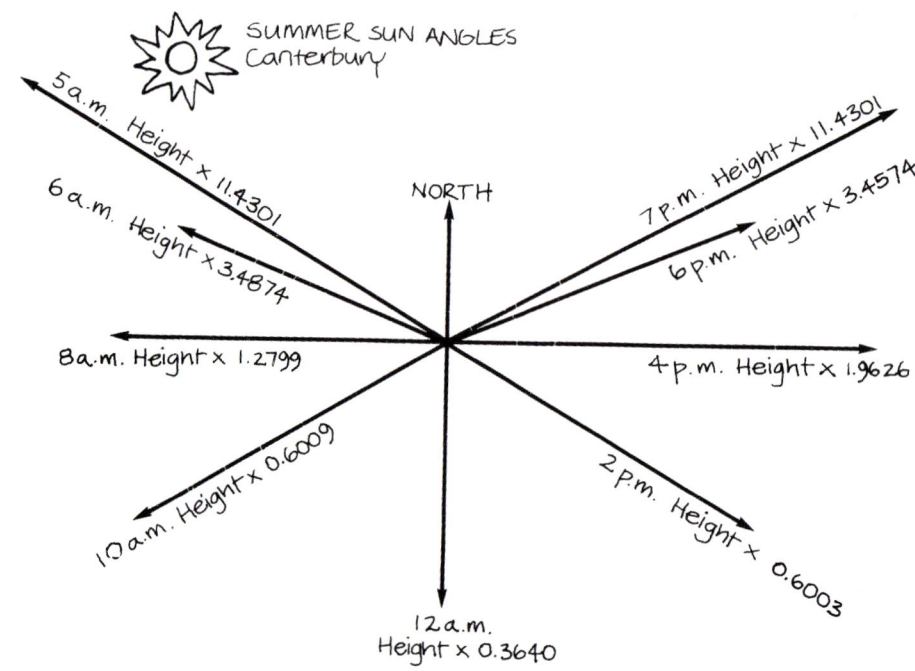

Observe and define seasonal sun-angle changes, contrasting the availability of sunlight and shade from summer to winter. Notice winter shadows that create cold and damp pockets within the garden: they will disappear as sun angles become more direct overhead with the coming summer. Hills, shelter belts, and structures within the landscape cast shadows that have profound relevance in gardens, reflected in the distribution of local species and variations in their growth quality.

When shaded for a long time, plants that favour full sun are succeeded by species that prosper with much less sunlight. When selecting plants you will need to know which are suited to full sunshine or shade and are therefore appropriate to particular areas. By removing objects that shade, such as large trees or sheds, the sun is able to penetrate and warm new pockets within the garden so plants can grow. Species that thrive in the shade, however, cannot prevail in sunny habitats. Knowledge about these interrelationships is important in planning and planting.

Soil preparation

As plants have evolved to survive in certain habitats, it is important to recognise soil type so you can choose the correct species for your area. Soils that are waterlogged, drought stricken, dry or nutrient deficient all affect plant quality and growth rates.

Is the soil clay or sand, loam or peat? You can assess the soil structure and its water-holding capacity by taking a wet sample and rubbing it into a putty between the hands. The soil structure is displayed by the way it adheres together and breaks apart. If the soil is poorly drained, the sample becomes a fine paste with a clay consistency. If the sample breaks up into small particles, the soil has a good texture for drainage. To create an ideal soil medium, mix together equal quantities of peat, loam, and sand.

Loam: It is best not to work this soil physically, as the structure deteriorates through continual digging. A good loam, such as volcanic ash, falls apart easily. Compost always aids loam, as it adds to soil structure and fertility.

Peat: This soil is derived from the decay of organic matter and is usually found in poorly drained areas. Liming peat soils helps to neutralise their acidity. Lime comes from crushed limestone which is found naturally as a sedimentary rock rich in calcium, so by adding lime or dolomite to an acid soil, hydrogen ions in acid molecules are displaced by ions of calcium, magnesium, and potassium.

Sand: This can be improved by adding compost and organic mulch, both of which make sandy soil better able to retain moisture. This helps to establish some perennial plants that thrive in dry conditions.

Clay: This kind of soil needs to be broken up so that air and water can percolate through it. This is easily done by digging in coarse sand and organic matter. Organic matter is very important in modifying the effects of clay, transforming it into a loam soil type; improving drainage also gradually aerates clay. Once air gets into the soil, acidity decreases naturally by simply leaching away. A good dressing of lime or dolomite can be added to improve the acidity of a clay soil further.

Topsoil: Poor soil, bare of plants, can be the result of the erosion of some pure rock, such as limestone, or of pollution, as in an oil spillage. If the original topsoil is completely removed from the site, only rocky soils remain. This often occurs in new housing areas. New, clean topsoil is usually required if you want to establish a garden in an area such as this.

As a general rule, plant species prefer fertile soils with good drainage and an adequate water supply. Therefore, it is generally safe to introduce a loamy topsoil with sufficient organic material that is free of weeds. In exposed areas, dehydration from wind and sun soon depletes available soil moisture, so good loamy topsoil is a necessary requirement for plants to survive and succeed here. Note, however, that not all ornamental plants favour such a growing medium, which can also encourage aggressive weed growth and strong competition. Garden plants should be placed in soils they are naturally adapted to and thrive in: for example, many herbs and herbaceous perennial plants prefer average or arid soils, and coastal plants love free-draining mediums like sand or gravels, not clay loams.

Exposed beach areas have sandy, free-draining soil in which coastal plants flourish. These seaside species are able to dominate in dry gravel or sand, because grasses and other similar plants prefer a loamy soil that holds more moisture, enabling them to compete. If such a soil is placed in a coastal habitat, an uncontrollable weed problem can be expected.

Mulching

Freshly dug soil is also vulnerable to quick weed invasion. So, after bedding plants into the ground, continued regular digging has no real advantage and tends to dry out soil unnecessarily. As most nutrients are found in topsoil, reduce evaporation of surface moisture by mulching and keeping the ground covered in growth. Some plants that are thought of as weeds, such as plantain, yarrow, and lupin, prevent soil erosion and conserve surface moisture.

Urban planting in Stokes Valley, near Wellington.

(Top left) Before and during construction.
(Top right) Planting complete.

(Left) Mulching
(Right) Planted and mulched.

Water problems

Drainage is an important factor in soil condition. Water filtering through soil particles washes away both toxins and nutrients, and affects the pH level. Waterlogged areas are improved either by proper drainage or by digging in gritty sand and gravel so that air is able to permeate the soil, allowing water to percolate and leach toxins from these stagnant conditions. Boggy soil is usually acidic and can use a good dressing of lime as well.

Sometimes the existing soil needs replacing with new topsoil once drainage has been improved. Alternatively, you may decide to use boggy ground as a suitable place for building a pond. Excavate a shallow hole, then line it with fine clay to hold water. This creates an attractive place for fish, frogs, water plants, insects, and birds.

In very difficult dry locations, install an irrigation system, and be aware that in New Zealand the main holiday period occurs when the days are longest and the sun is at its hottest. Make some provision for watering if you are away from home: ask a neighbour or use a time-delay irrigation device.

Dry soils are always improved with the application of organic mulch or compost which helps retain moisture. Select xerophytic species for all year-round dry areas.

Using nature to create low-maintenance gardens

SYNCHRONISE PLANT SUCCESSION

Plant competition is aggressive. There is no mercy amongst plants. Species that cannot compete retreat in the face of those which are more successful. When adjusting plants to new habitats, or transplanting desirable species from one garden to another, the you must consider their ability to compete successfully.

If decorative species are situated in habitats with soil to which they are adapted, they gain ground and succeed through natural competition. However, disagreeable seasonal changes in daylight hours and temperature; adverse amounts of frost, moisture, wind and salt; and inappropriate soils all inhibit the success of species that have not been put into their favoured habitats.

The technique of putting species with the same habits, likes and dislikes together applies to many plant groups. Selected shrubs, planted in collections, compete with each other at a similar rate of growth. For the perennial border, choose species with similar growth habits to the established plants and introduce them into the garden during winter hibernation so that the new arrivals can compete once dormancy is broken at the beginning of spring.

When planning a planting programme for a given area, become familiar with the natural plant competition in that place and harmoniously combine species that have equally aggressive habits. Low-maintenance gardening is achieved when plant species with similar habits are combined together and balance naturally. Poor garden planning results in bare patches or spent growth that leaves room for weeds to infest. These areas have to be cleared to allow other preferred plants to survive, and this maintenance can become a chore.

However, the garden is forever growing and gaining height. Changes in competition between chosen species occur all the time and can be recognised as stages of plant succession. Planning succession or choosing the plants to dominate in the garden is essential to creating the desired effect and for maintenance.

When choosing a tree to plant, take into account the shading effect and competition for water it creates for other desirable growth. After a few years, dominating growth will need to be checked by pruning so that desirable species are not smothered. Aggressive weeds such as old man's beard or convolvulus can suffocate trees during summer, even though (because they are dormant during winter) the effects on tree health are not obvious at first. Other weeds, such as buttercup or yarrow, aggressively dominate in different seasons, making it difficult for plants to become established. If taller growth is removed, slower-growing, more delicate plants will flourish. If left to itself, the garden will go wild – which is fine, provided plants are growing in companionship, living together as one mass that dominates other unwanted growth.

In the herbaceous perennial garden grow taller species at the rear and smaller ones nearer the path so that over a few years the planting naturalises and has a dominant edge on smaller weeds or herbs. The same principle applies to planting trees. Taller trees suppress smaller tree species by shading them. Camellias, azaleas, and hydrangeas are some species that prefer shade: here they naturalise and symbiotically flourish as companions.

When introducing new plants, determine the stages of succession developing within the existing vegetation. Planting combinations need time to mature, so you may need to observe these plant dynamics over an extended period in order to assess how aggressive and competitive species are. A cottage garden or a shrub planting, for example, can take several years to climax; some trees mature over decades. The life span of chosen species must be considered and each plant collection organised so that groupings succeed each other over a calculated period.

Last season's flowered annuals are spread over the bare soil.

Helichrysum, aster, and calendula seeds are thrown over bare soil.

(Left and right)
Germination begins.

(Left) Emerging weeds
are mulched over the top,
along with bark.

(Right) Plants take hold
and dominate weeds, and
flush into the winter.

(Left) Next spring the
geums are in full bloom.

(Right) Summer flushes.

(Below) Asters dominate
over the Easter period.

PLANTING FOR INSTANT AND LONG-TERM EFFECTS

Some plants grow quickly and some slowly, so when planning your garden, allow for changes in rates of growth to occur over time. To create a grouping of harmonious plants, plan for the immediate and long-term effect together. If the spaces between newly planted trees are filled with smaller, short-lived plants, the landscaped work looks pleasant and is decorative from the beginning. The extra cost to accomplish an immediate as well as a long-term effect need not be great.

Annual plants, such as pansies, cineraria, primula, petunia, begonia, and helichrysum, are useful fillers in a newly landscaped garden. They make a quick splash of colour and then die, providing a store of humus important for successive layers of establishing plants. Perennial plants begin to flush in spring, gain height over summer and die back in winter, allowing other slower-growing species gradually to emerge. Short-lived shrubs, like fast-growing daisy bushes, make quick use of available space and smother likely competition. Slower-growing trees and shrubs need care in their early establishing phase, but after a short while begin to take over available light. Toetoe planted in a windy coastal situation provides quick shelter, while other plants, like five finger (*Pseudopanax lessonii*), grow at a slower pace. However, within only three years the established pseudopanax will succeed to form a pleasant hedge and provide needed shelter, even if the toetoe are removed.

By choosing plant species which are short lived and fast growing, together with those of slower but durable growth, a harmony of favourable plants that can compete against undesirable plants eventually emerges into a flourishing dominant group. This is a key to success in low-maintenance gardening.

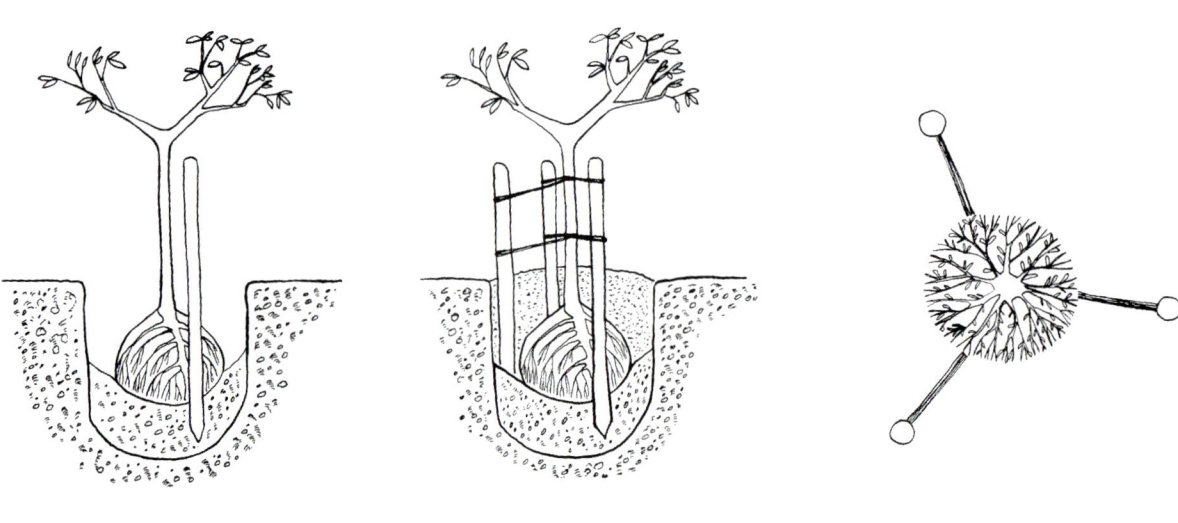

Stake trees well in exposed situations. Rubber ties help support the trunk and prevent the roots from being wrenched loose.

(Left and below) Re-vegetation along road reserve, with one-year-old plants establishing themselves.

(Left and below) The planting has matured and stayed strong for over ten years, with minimal maintenance, by choosing the correct plants initially. Who needs a fence?

PLANT COLLECTION AND PURCHASING FOR WINDY AREAS

Having studied the site for its limitations, climatic advantages and disadvantages, and having formed your spaces from a design, you can now look to healing the landscape with careful plant selection, blending new plants into the natural ecology, so that they can compete and survive naturally and still give the beauty sought.

Boundary planting with toetoe and flax in the early establishing phase.

Choose plants of equal vigour, maturation, height and durability. Look at the range of suitable plant species and list them. (See **Section 4** for examples.)

The selected plant species must be able to acclimatise and dominate the aggressive weeds and eventually succeed them, otherwise, they will die or have to be continually pampered. Agapanthus, for example, will smother onion weed. Toetoe and most New Zealand native trees will compete with gorse. Cornflowers, dahlias, and strawflowers, semi-matured, will compete readily with new weed seedlings, as they mature quickly, utilising available light.

Gather various species which you have identified and enjoyed within your neighbourhood. If these plants are accessible, then collect the seeds and take cuttings from them for propagation. Seek beyond humanised plant habitats. A hike through a local wilderness area is essential to obtain an awareness of the variety of species in your area. These plants will have acclimatised to any equivalent microclimate and stand the best chance of survival.

For individual plants to be viable, they must be healthy and acclimatised at the time of selection. Hardened-off plants (young, soft plants that have re-adjusted to tougher conditions) are able immediately to survive harsh winds that will eventually sculpture the site. They must be tough specimens. Too often people make the mistake of purchasing trees and shrubs when they are in full flower, fresh from the nurseries. This is a common error, as the nursery trade is aimed towards selling on visual impact, seducing customers with bright displays of flowering plants and lush vegetation. Be careful and selective, as the plants straight from the nurseries are usually too soft to be able to withstand windy conditions. Look for plants that have been hardened off, pruned back to last season's growth, and preferably are pot-bound (that is, the plant roots are ready to burst their container). Plants grown locally are likely to be hardier than those that have been imported from warmer climates.

Preparing the site for planting.

Plants matured, three years later.

(Right) Pine trees block the view and cast long shadows in winter, but provide only short-term shelter.
(Below) The pine trees have been removed, restoring the view, and the mound reshaped and planted with mostly native grasses and shrubs. In a few years it will provide long-term shelter for the garden.

PLANTING TECHNIQUES

When planting for shelter, consider the following points.

Select strong plants which have acclimatised to your particular site. If you introduce plants that have been grown in a protected environment, they are susceptible to severe damage once planted in an exposed location, because they are unable to adjust to the new local climatic conditions. It is easy to lose new plants which have been propagated in milder climates. Plants grown in Auckland, for instance, and then planted in Wellington, suffer badly for the first year or may never recover from the initial shock.

Hardened-off plants may be unattractive to look at, as they may be dormant or pruned back, but as long as they show abundant healthy bud formation they are ideal. It is the future you are planning for, and it is those buds and hardy stems from which the new foliage will grow.

These plants should be pruned back to at least half their size, enabling them to acclimatise naturally. This is a golden rule of gardening. When transplanting, prune back the lush foliage, to save water loss and reduce the initial shock.

It is better to select the correct type of plant rather than one that just looks pretty! Fresh stock purchased from nurseries is often delicate and is unsuitable for direct planting into windy environments.

As a rule, plants that are pot-bound or have been in their containers for an extra season are usually tougher than fresh stock. They will have built up enough resistance to withstand the shock of adapting to a new and harsher environment.

The rootball needs time to secure its new roots in the soil. Gardeners often call this a period of sulking, and it can last up to two years. All roots must be firmly in contact with the new soil. Any air gaps left around the rootball will dry out the plant.

Where good soil is absent, it is necessary to introduce new topsoil in order to achieve success.

Staking is necessary for plants that tend to sway in the wind. Planting close together is also a valuable consideration in an exposed location. Spaces between plants in exposed situations create draughts.

Autumn, winter, and early spring are best for planting, as the day length is shorter and the nights longer. A greater availability of water occurs, even if it is only the night's dew. Summer planting will succeed only if plants are constantly watered, usually during the hottest time of the day, when the plants endure their greatest stress. Water must soak into the soil thoroughly.

Young trees should be staked and lightly pruned back to shape so that there is enough root to support the new growth.

Try to organise the planting so that plants will grow harmoniously together rather than smothering each other. The taller-growing plants should be planted at the rear, with smaller plants in front; or alternatively, the more aggressive species at the rear, with the less aggressive plants near the front where they can be easily tended. Plants grouped in threes or fives have a stronger visual impact than individual plants standing on their own.

(Left) Plants are arranged for their correct growing positions.

(Right) Plants are then planted directly into the turf.

(Below) Thick mulching with pine bark will suffocate the turf grasses and reduce weed growth.

Plan to create shelter against wind by planting hardy, wind-tolerant plant species, thus creating a future microclimate where other vulnerable plants will succeed because they have the protection to do so.

Companion planting will encourage a longer procession of flowering through the seasons. Begin by preparing the soil in the late autumn, and plant primulas, pansies, stock, and wallflowers for the spring garden, to be followed up with spring planting of dahlias, helichrysum, and sunflowers, and summer plantings of salvia and aster, creating a prolonged display of flowering plants.

PLANTING IN INLAND AREAS

Areas exposed to wind and subject to winter frosts have a unique beauty, as they lend themselves to strong seasonal variation. Each season expresses itself through changes in plant appearance, in flowering, foliage colour and dormancy. The correct selection of plants is important. Hardwood trees, conifers, and herbaceous perennials are safe choices for planting and are naturally slower to grow in frosted areas. However, their eventual growth and shelter can be more effective than in coastal regions, because of lack of salt-laden wind, which always has a pruning effect on plants. Earthen mounds are useful in areas where constant prevailing winds occur. In colder regions during winter months, there is far less wind than in summer, and cluster planting is a simpler procedure to introduce.

Inland areas like Martinborough, in the Wairarapa, can be very dry, frosty and windy. Here, macrocarpa trees were removed to allow natural light to come back so that the ground could be planted and mulched.

After two years, mainly native planting is taking strong hold, giving a pleasant, sheltered landscape.

When selecting plants for windy situations in frosted areas, certain considerations should be looked into:

- **Rainfall and water source:** Areas such as Central Otago or Martinborough are hot, dry and frosted in winter, so select plants that can cope with those conditions.

- **Soil type:** Stony greywacke soils suit plants that can feed themselves from nitrifying bacteria or mycorrhiza from coniferous plants. A combination of these useful plants will build up organic matter vital for other plants in the starved soils. The fertility of soils is the governing factor in the rate of growth for wind gardens.

- **Compatibility:** Plants here must live harmoniously together, attaining their optimum in vigorous growth and evolving naturally into their own mutually protective wilderness.

During summer, inland areas usually have warmer midday temperatures. This fact provides a choice for deciduous plants. Conifers and herbaceous perennials thrive here and are the envy of a coastal gardener. Echinacea, rudbeckia, aster, helianthus, helichrysum, statice, and gypsophila all love hot summers.

Shelter planting can be a mixture of *Cedrus deodara, Pittosporum tenuifolium* and *P. eugenioides, Cortaderia toi toi, Olearia alba, Laurus nobilis,* Douglas fir, cabbage tree, ceanothus, lupin, flax and photinia, and pussy willow (*Salix spp.*) for wet situations.

ORCHESTRATE SEASONAL TIMING

If flowering plants in the garden are planted with others of similar habit, there is no continuation of flowering through the year but rather an invasion of weeds. Such gardens are regarded as 'at their best' during summer. However, within the restraints of each season, gardens can always look great. The key to continued seasonal flowering is timing. Plan for seasonal succession and maximum effect, using plant habits to ensure a continued birth, flowering and decay of various species. In this way, maintenance becomes a pleasure – a simple task of removing spent foliage.

When temperatures increase with advancing daylight hours in early spring, before the main growth period begins, bulbs emerge, often in harmony with long grass. The marguerite daisy grows steadily through winter in frost-free

(Above left) Macrocarpa trees in Martinborough have been felled to let the daylight in. The stumps are left to rot and new young native trees and shrubs are planted directly into the soil.

(Above right) The same site two years later. The tree lucerne in the background and wind cloth along the fence line have helped shelter the new planting. The new growth and foliage colour provide a pleasant contrast. Compare this photo with the ones on page 59, looking at the same site from the other side of the fence.

Colourful perennial gardens are hard work to maintain but are well worth the results. In this Otaki garden, poppies also make a strong show.

areas, and flowers in spring with cornflowers that bloom until the longest day. Perennial and annual plants like primula, watsonia, wallflowers, polyanthus, iris, and forget-me-nots all flower in spring. When such species die, summer bloomers like bishopsweed, shasta daisy, godetia, and hollyhock take over. In turn these species die back, after seeds are set, allowing other plants, such as aster, dahlia, coreopsis, rudbeckia, and salvia, that grew in early summer, to take charge in autumn and flower until long after the first winter chills are felt. Stock, polyanthus, primula, pansy, and helleborus usually flower through winter, though this is a time of relative rest.

Regular planned plantings of a variety of species encourage long flowering periods through the seasons. Annual plants – for example, primula, calendula, Californian poppy, cineraria, pansy and stock – should be sown in trays in early autumn and sheltered from freezing, two seasons before they are planted in the garden with spring bulbs and hardy shrubs. In winter and early spring most perennial plants that can easily be increased from root division should be placed into their preferred positions with bulbs and late spring-flowering annual species, such as cineraria, calendula and cornflowers. In spring, follow this up by planting helichrysum, sunflowers and other summer-flowering annuals. Salvia and aster, planted in early summer, will emerge in the autumn garden. This type of organised planting offers a wonderful range of flowers.

Think of plant themes with colour, such as white or blue gardens, with texture and foliage effects or with strong scents. Look at collecting groups of species suitable for the site and style of garden that can be picked for cut flowers.

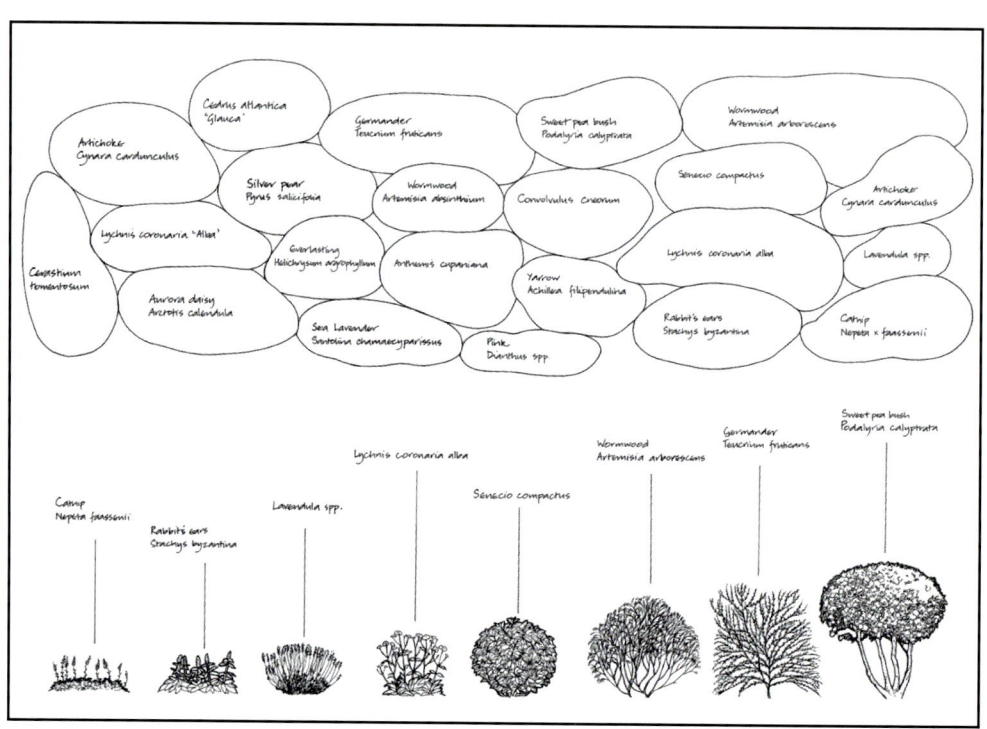

Planting ideas for a grey garden.

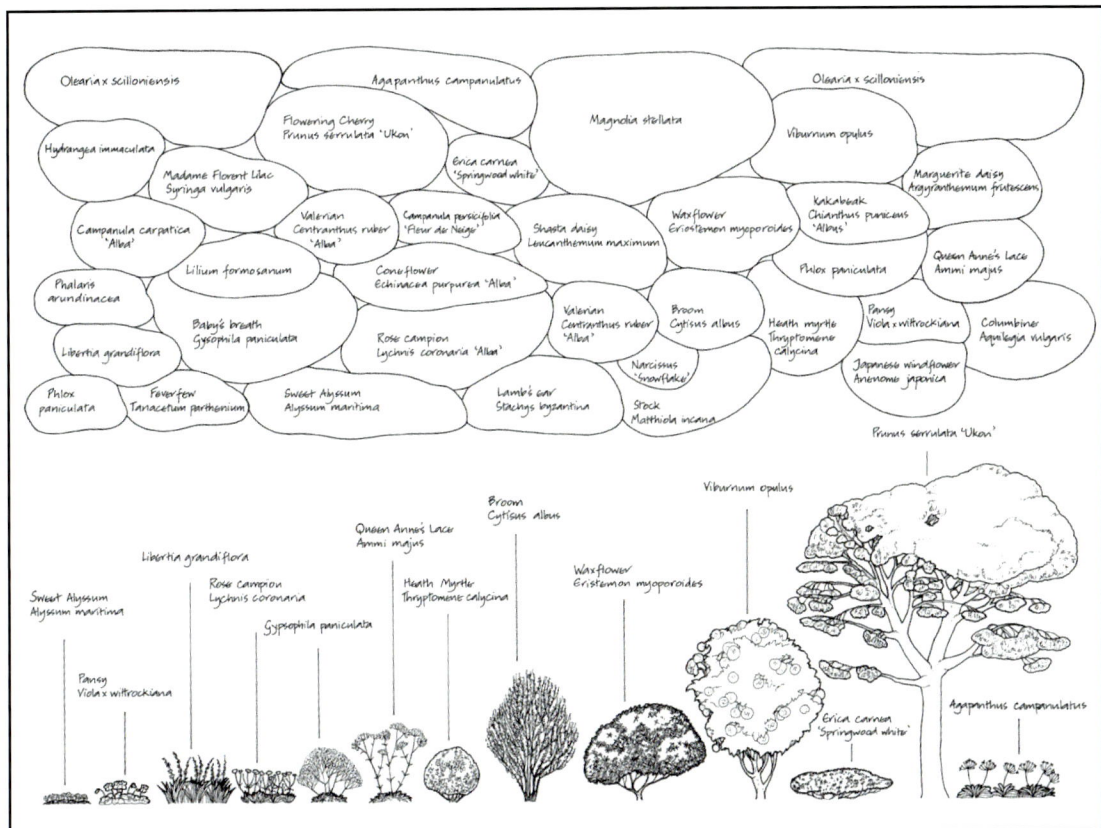

Planting ideas for a white garden.

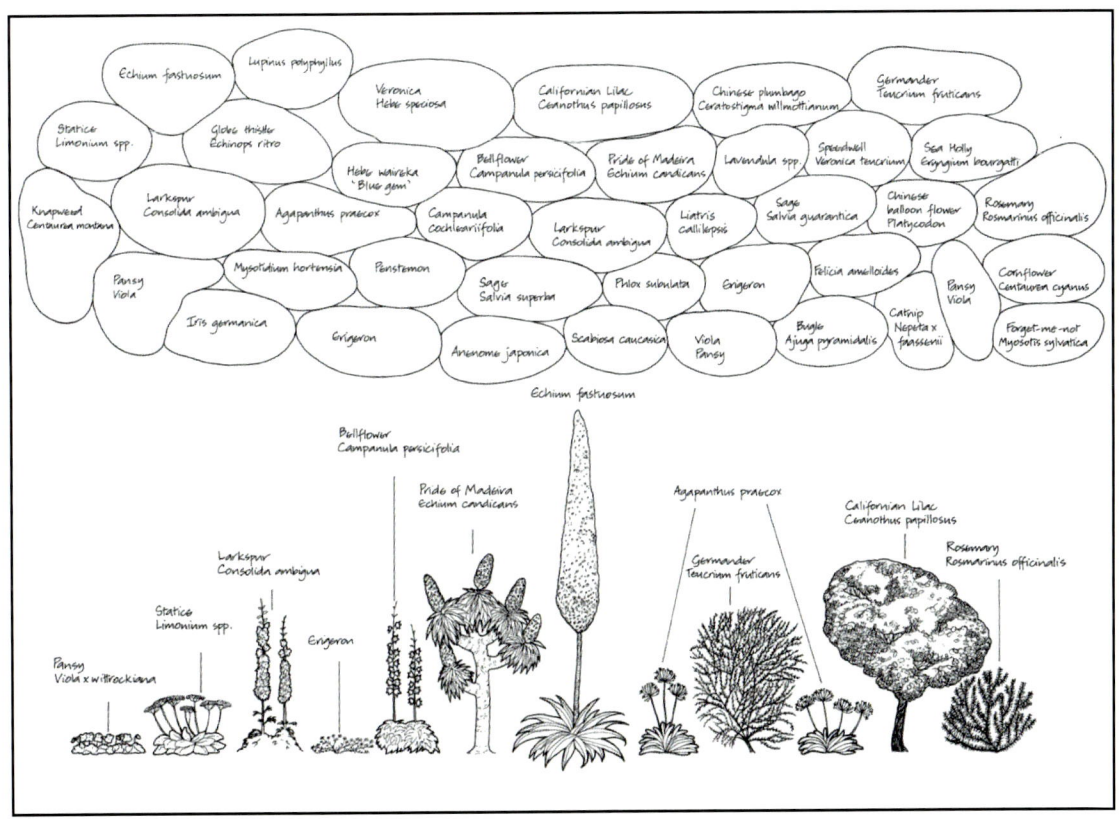

Planting ideas for a blue garden.

Use established vegetation

A vulnerable time in flower gardens is when herbaceous plants become spent and have seeded, leaving space for a new flush of weed germination. However, certain weeds growing between plants in the garden need not be a nuisance. In most cases it is better to have the soil surface covered in preferred low weeds or herbs that are companions to the desired garden plants. Examine the existing weeds and determine what they are, their value and their habits. If compatible, and provided they are controlled within a specific area, they can be an advantage. Use weeds and herbs to shelter new plant species from wind and sun. This weed growth contributes to the build-up of soil fertility and, used as a living mulch in dry weather, helps to maintain the humidity around each decorative plant by preventing loss of soil surface moisture. For example, plantain is a herb often seen in arid coastal regions and is a valuable contributor to soil preservation. Seasonal weeds like oxalis cover the soil surface quickly and suppress other unwanted weeds, inhibiting their germination. Oxalis has a decorative flower and temporarily smothers low ground when it flushes in spring. It is absent through summer and autumn. If oxalis is a problem, the wrong plants are growing in association with it. Its presence can either be accepted as a groundcover, or plants should be cultivated which easily compete with and suppress it. In warmer areas, groundcovers like forget-me-not and calendula grow with oxalis with ease. In colder areas, ivy or periwinkle, bergenia or hosta grow in shaded areas under trees. Other weeds such as nettle and chickweed are also useful groundcovers, enriching the soil. These weeds are seasonal and soon retreat as summer approaches. Over-planting weeds with taller-growing plants that establish themselves is a natural way of weed control.

In rural areas, winter planting of trees and shrubs directly into existing pasture works well, provided the new plants are at least 500 millimetres above ground

Sand-dune restoration along Brighton Beach, Christchurch. The area is fenced off to prevent people from trampling over establishing plants such as marram grass. Lupin, arctotis, and *Senecio angustifolius* can all be seen growing well.

level, so that they have at least enough height to compete with the rush of new spring grass growth. The long grass is useful to prevent rabbits from chewing newly planted trees and also to limit moisture loss from bare ground. Often, in pasture plantings, mulching can be difficult, expensive, or inaccessible. Some people find the appearance of long grass untidy, but over time (two years plus), the new plantings will take hold and develop a naturalness of their own.

If grass growth is too choking, then the simple tramping down of grass with your feet will allow your young plants to breathe. Remember that grasses peak over the late spring to early summer months, so this is really the crucial time to check on your young plants, whereas during the other months grasses recede whilst your trees are still growing.

(Left) Boundary planting into turf.

(Right) Planting takes hold 18 months later.

Watsonia will compete strongly with wild grasses in clay banks around Auckland.

Similarly, planting advanced grades of natives into gorse or manuka areas will eventually give rise to native bush. Your additional planting will enhance the natural process sooner.

A landscape planting of chosen dominant vegetation that harmoniously suppresses noxious plants is achieved by working with the ecology and the factors of plant distribution, competition, balance, succession and species habits.

Trees and shrubs are often planted with large gaps of several metres between them. Here, in a short space of time, weeds and grasses begin to flourish. This type of planting requires regular maintenance. As a general rule, in all gardens, plants should shelter each other, covering the ground closely. Fill in the gaps between perennial species with quick-growing, short-lived annuals. When all available space in the garden is planted out, there will be little room for unwanted species.

Planting new fragile species next to taller existing shrubs helps them to establish, provided they are in positions that receive the required sun and water. Established growth shelters young tender plants and protects smaller species from wind and dehydration by shading them from the glaring sun. It also insulates them, as older plants absorb the evening dew that can become frost.

In the cottage garden arrange plants so that taller, quick-growing perennial species are at the rear and smaller flowering plants near the front, otherwise the smaller plants become lost. The golden rule for a herbaceous border is that an east-to-west orientation is preferable, so that the garden can have all-day sun. Gardens positioned to face north to south cast shadows and do not do as well, requiring more maintenance.

Looking after the garden

People have always tried to conquer nature. They do so today in domestic gardens boasting straight rows of symmetrical planting and manicured lawns controlled by lawnmowers, which disturb the peace of suburban weekends. In such gardens, clearing spring growth and infestations of weeds can become an obsession or chore rather than a pleasure. Tedious hours spent in the reluctant maintenance of an unnatural and poorly planned garden give little satisfaction.

Style and scale dictate how much maintenance is needed. Tamed gardens always require the most upkeep. Theme gardens, too, require careful upkeep and planning. The cottage garden initially involves similar effort, but the job becomes easier as the seasons progress. The secret is to let the garden naturalise. The best garden is one that flows with nature and is easy to maintain because plants that grow well in your area have been selected.

However, although the natural garden that is allowed to go wild requires less upkeep, it needs pruning into shape when shading and crowding become too great. Warmth and abundant spring rainfall after dormancy during winter promote rampant seasonal growth, as evidenced by an invasion of weeds. This lush growth always needs to be checked to allow favoured plants to survive.

Aim to achieve an arrangement of plants chosen for their effectiveness within the desired garden style, and for their compatibility with the existing vegetation and climatic conditions. If there is an extensive weed problem, and your garden needs a great deal of maintenance, then several factors of compatibility have been overlooked. A balance of introduced and existing plants must be found so they can live harmoniously and evolve into a dominant plant cover.

Understand how the healing processes really work. This important aspect is too often overlooked. Landscapes tend to be artificially dominated without consideration of the valuable natural healing processes already taking place.

Often the natural environment has been disrupted by land clearance with fires and bulldozers. The first plants on a cleared site leave behind nutrients and soil for other plants to re-utilise in the form of weed growth. This is the first stage of plant regeneration. By blundering on and removing such growth or reshaping the landscape, many years of valuable healing which has already occurred can be undone. The natural building of soil fertility from the decay of organic matter is interrupted. Again we must recognise and work with natural forces.

Organic methods

Organic ways of maintenance are best for growing plants, as they ensure that natural balances are retained. Chemicals that pollute the food chain cause imbalances in the environment and threaten human health. Humans and other animals living on organic foods and herbal mixtures are healthier, as they are not exposed to toxic synthetic chemicals. Although organic methods can be more labour intensive to begin with, the results are well worth the effort.

Organic gardening methods realistically promote a symbiosis between people and nature. In the wild, various plant species are found in colonies, grouped in different areas as the topography of the land allows microclimatic changes to occur. Strong healthy plants compete successfully and flourish as the weak and dominated plants recede and are replaced – a natural balance that recycles itself. In the long term, these ecological principles dictate what happens, so it is much easier to work with nature than against it.

Integrated mixed plantings are advisable on any horticultural site or in any garden. Diversifying crops and garden species that mature at different times allows natural rotation to occur. You should plan on harvesting quantities that are easily produced.

It is best not to risk damage to the earth by over-cultivating, which results in disease build-up and starves the soil. Cultivate carefully-selected companion plants which encourage health, rotate crops, and leave fallow areas to recover. It is very satisfying to grow species that are integrated together in harmonious association without chemicals. Striving against the balance of natural order increases problems.

The herb garden at Dunedin Polytechnic.

An organic vegetable garden in Pakiri, Northland. Marigolds are planted as companions with vegetables to deter insect pests. Borage is allowed to spread as a groundcover. Mulching and composting are intensive, and the garden feeds five people all year round.

Composting is the key to health and quality in a garden. Even a small property can find a corner for a compost heap or bin; larger properties should have several. Commercial gardening firms, city councils, and large organic gardens often produce compost for sale in bulk.

COMPOSTING

Compost is a collection of organic plant material that has decomposed to a humus which is rich in nutrients. In the wild, the top layer of soil on the forest floor is the most fertile, being built up from leaf litter, and surface roots seek sustenance from it. This is nature's way of recycling organic matter back to plants. In late autumn fallen leaves decompose and are absorbed back into the soil through winter, readying the earth with new nutrients for the flush of spring growth.

Compost or humus is always a bonus to any soil structure. It aerates the soil, helping to retain moisture and preventing nutrients from leaching. The granulation of clay, for example, does not progress adequately without the presence of a certain amount of humus.

When soil is dug or turned, new weed seeds surface and soon germinate in the bare open space. Rather than continuously turning the ground, destroying the soil structure and causing it to become puggy, it is better to add compost on top of the soil and grow plants into it. Compost on the garden enables plants to become stronger and have better resistance to disease, as organic matter provides nutrients and trace elements that are gradually released. So, although it takes time and effort to make, compost is the key to the health and quality of any garden.

Using horse manure, sheep droppings, and cow dung in compost can sometimes be a problem. Seeds that have been eaten by these animals remain whole, and when manure is added with compost to the soil, unwanted weeds may be introduced to the garden, infesting it with species like stinging nettle, clover, ryegrass, and dock.

Sandy soils benefit greatly from compost and can in time turn into good soils. Even gritty rock soils which dry off in the summer can be improved by the addition of compost.

When a site is cleared of its vegetation, it is important to leave as much humus as possible so that it can recycle back into the soil. Some tired soils may be left

Raised beds for growing vegetables organically are labour intensive but have excellent results over weedy, poor soil.

Tree lucerne provides quick shelter and enriches the stony soil.

in pasture for a year or two, so that the growth can produce increased humus levels; grass, clover, and even lupin are used for this purpose.

MULCHING

Mulching involves the scattering of organic matter such as bark chips and rotted sawdust on the soil surface. It is beneficial, as it helps to retain the surface soil moisture and reduce evaporation, and reduces the oncoming weed competition, provided that the wind does not blow the mulch away. Over a period of time it can also provide organic matter for the soil. Mulches are not so essential if plants are deeply rooted, but are host to beneficial insects and ground bugs that naturally aid the recycling of organic waste into humus, which has nutrient value in any garden.

Mulching straight after planting is advisable as the bare soil invites competitive growth from new weed seedlings. For example, freshly planted flowering annuals take approximately two months for their foliage to touch and shade the surrounding bare soil. Mulching the bare ground around these bedded plants helps to suppress new weed germination by preventing young, unwanted seedlings from reaching light. If organic matter is unavailable, use pebbles or small stone chips as a groundcover, though the reflection of the sun on the inorganic surface creates a dry environment for growing.

NITROGEN

Soils are formed from the weathering of rocks, but very few rocks contain nitrogen in any form. Most plants obtain their nitrogen from the decay of pre-existing plants or animals. This process of decay is the result of bacterial action. The sugars and starch of the dead plant or animal are broken down into water and carbon dioxide, which escapes into the atmosphere and helps to maintain the supplies necessary for photosynthesis.

Bacteria also attack the complex nitrogenous compounds (proteins) of the dead plant, and change them to ammonia gas, which is absorbed by the soil particles if the change takes place in the ground. Otherwise the ammonia escapes to the air, to be washed down by rain. This is the process of putrefaction. In all fertile soils, further bacterial action takes place, changing the ammonia first to nitrites and then to nitrates. This change does not occur if the soil is very acid, since the bacteria that bring it about cannot tolerate a very acid medium. One reason for adding lime to the soil is to make this action take place. Ammonia is retained by the soil as nitrates are readily washed away; they are not held by the soil.

It is important to remember that when you apply an organic mulch such as fresh sawdust to a garden, it will rob the plants of free nitrogen within the soil, resulting in slower growth. (The yellowing of older plant foliage is usually an indication that the plant is starved of nitrogen.) The rotting-down process can sometimes take 12 months, and only after that does the nitrogen become available for plants to utilise.

Clay soils need to be broken up so that air and water can percolate into them, and this is easily done by digging in coarse sand with a good dressing of lime. Once the air gets into the soil particles, the acidity will decrease naturally, from leaching alone.

Pests and diseases are always present in the wild but are countered by the natural mix of integrated species and predators that increase and decrease in numbers as food sources are available. Healthy plants, if attacked by pests, usually recover and become optimum specimens of their particular species. Strong plants withstand attack and survive competition as the seasons change.

Pests should not be completely eliminated from the environment. Bugs and mites are a part of the natural ecology, and draw other predatory insect and bird life into the garden for food. Bugs, stick insects, earwigs, butterflies, dragonflies, cicadas, and mites attract praying mantises, spiders, ladybirds, hedgehogs, and birds of all sorts.

Trying to rid your garden completely of pests is always going to be a losing battle. The garden and its plants and flowers are the natural homes of these creatures and it is best to maintain a natural balance with them. Besides, the garden would lose much of its beauty and harmony without them. Living with and becoming part of the balance of creation is a joy that only a garden offers and provides.

An imbalance in the natural order results in an unwanted abundance of pests or disease. Snails, for example, are pests that multiply very quickly. Face the problem early by handpicking them when they first appear. This will prevent new waves of snail populations from establishing themselves. A wandering hedgehog will make a meal out of those mavericks that persist.

Predictably, most insect pests like aphids begin to emerge with soft growth and warming temperatures in spring. To be successfully countered, their predators must be already established in the garden or field. It is essential that beneficial insects survive winter, and they can do this if there is a variety of plants about for them to live on and shelter among. Many plants harbour beneficial and predatory insects and birds that keep pests in balance through natural means. Leave the organic litter of autumn on the ground to decay naturally over the winter months. Beetles, for example, live in bark mulch, and ladybirds or hover-flies survive the winter in curled leaves.

Healthy plants usually survive insect attacks, so long as the plants themselves are not stressed by drought or shading from overcrowded competition. Some species such as the kowhai are even adapted to insect attack: strong kowhai trees usually recover from attack by the kowhai moth which defoliates the tree over summer.

Strongly-scented plants such as artemisia will deter opossums. Most scented herbs such as thyme, calendula, basil, and mint in the vegetable garden will help deter aphids.

Species of the Apiaceae family such as parsnip, wild chervil, fennel, angelica, dill, and wild carrot can be grown with a crop or in the orchard to attract predatory insects such as hover-flies, ladybirds and parasitic wasps. These insects are clumsy fliers, so large Apiaceae flowers are good landing platforms. The pollen and nectar of these flowers also provide a food source in early spring when beneficial predatory insects can build up their numbers while their prey are not about. In summer, aphid and mite populations quickly explode but predatory insect numbers are much slower to increase. The earlier they get protein from pollen, the sooner they are able to breed, increasing predatory populations enough to check pests whose populations peak near the longest day.

Mixed plantings of carefully selected species are also successful against pests and diseases. Some insects can be discouraged by integrating a variety of crops with mixtures of other beneficial plants that act as deterrents. For example, inter-plant vegetables or fruit trees with strongly scented herbs such as artemisia, rosemary, pyrethrum, and lavender. Aim for compatibility which strengthens plant health and the ability to recover from natural disorders. With mixed cropping, parasitic insects have a wider habitat. In infested areas, it is best to address the problem by diversifying and growing other crops.

Pests or diseases will flourish in areas where one particular crop is grown in bulk. Large vineyards in California have succumbed to grub infestations which have destroyed millions of dollars' worth of work and investment. The rabbit problem in rural South Island areas has been caused by prolonged grazing of stock on pasture, which is the ideal environment for rabbits to flourish. On pasture they can see their predators clearly throughout 360 degrees. A change from conventional farming of stock to raising trees or growing long grass would help reduce rabbit numbers. Forests create an environment which this pest dislikes, because of the lack of open dry grass and clear vision.

Growing the same crop repeatedly on the same land also leads to disease build-up. Diseases or pests are kept at bay or eliminated by the absence of the host source on which they feed. By planting a diverse range of crops and rotating them (multi-cropping), infection is starved out and a balanced environment encouraged.

Diseases occur more commonly when humidity and temperature are high. The sickness of cabbage trees in northern New Zealand is believed to be caused by a virus associated with warmer temperatures. Further south, from the lower half of the North Island and throughout the South Island, where the climate is cooler, specimens of *Cordyline australis* appear to be free of this disease. Roses, too, suffer more from disease in humid northern areas like Auckland than in drier areas like Hawke's Bay or Canterbury. Soft moist tissue promotes fungal disease. In humid conditions, species like dahlias are prone to problems with mildew. Try to keep plants as dry as possible by watering the ground and not the foliage or flowers.

If you know the life cycle of pests and diseases, you can plan and prepare for vulnerable periods. Some crops can be planted and harvested early, before seasonal pests and diseases naturally occur. For example, during summer, humidity causes fungal diseases like blackspot on some plants such as celery. Winter-grown celery is less susceptible to blackspot because the temperature is cooler.

Hygiene is important in gardening, because lack of control of diseased plants encourages fungi to spread. The removal of infected growth helps to reduce the spread of disease. When old decaying tissue is left on plants during wet conditions, rot problems can be assured. Rough wounds left after pruning cause branches to rot inside trees. (See **Pruning**, p. 92.)

Pests and diseases affect plant health. Karo (*Pittosporum crassifolium*) is frequently attacked by scale, which is an insect that attacks new shoots and distorts growth, deforming leaves and sucking the plant's sugars. Although the tree survives this, it would grow twice as fast if the scale insect was absent. Manuka is attacked by multiple generations of sucking scale insects, which leave a residue of honeydew that the fungus 'sooty mould' feeds upon, resulting in the manuka's blackened stems. In addition, sucking insects like aphids can transmit viruses from plant to plant and deform species such as cabbage trees and flax. Symptoms of bud attack are not revealed until months later when the shredded and torn soft new growth unfolds.

Pests and diseases also affect competition between plants. Plants exposed to drought or planted in unsuitably shaded locations, or which are overcrowded or dominated by stronger species, tend to be weakened. Stressed, weak plants are prone to disease and pest attack because they do not have the strength to resist. As the weak plants die, they are competitively replaced by specimens that survive attacks. So it is important to choose plant species carefully. Select strong varieties that are naturally suited to the surrounding conditions, and position them so that they grow to their optimum and need minimal care.

Mixed plantings and multi-cropping, correct plant selection, the timing of planting and harvesting crops, hygiene, good soil health, and the absence of chemicals all help naturally to reduce any exaggerated numbers of pests and diseases. Natural climatic seasonal changes and predatory activity can then keep problems in balance.

SPRAYING

Spraying with toxic inorganic chemicals such as insecticides or herbicides creates disorder in the natural ecological balance and affects continued competition between insects and plants. Spraying insect pests or weeds with chemicals is a quick-fix method that becomes expensive and exposes the garden to new problems as weeds and pests continue to build up resistance to ensure their survival.

You can either live with the fact that these pests exist or use sprays to clear them. Spraying is usually a temporary fix and its residue – often found on celery, for example – can be harmful to health.

Years of experience suggest that the results of using herbicides have not been satisfactory. Spraying is an instant and convenient solution, but long-term results are another matter. In areas of uncontrollable weed infestation, the use of herbicides can do more harm than good. Take, for example, a problem of three-metre high gorse spread over an area 300 metres long by 20 metres wide. It is far more effective to use natural eradication methods. One method is to cut the gorse by chainsaw and use a digger or bobcat to extract roots from the ground. As many generations of gorse seeds remain in the cleared area, once the bare ground is exposed to sun and moisture it immediately needs to be planted. Tree lucerne, toetoe, lemonwood, and tortured willow grow quickly and shade new gorse seedlings as they begin to sprout. One year later, the partial shade from the almost three-metre high trees, together with long grass, inhibits most of the gorse regrowth. In contrast, unnecessary spraying with a herbicide under the new trees devastates all growth, creating open sunny spaces that are ideal for more flushes of gorse and where new weed seeds can germinate. As spray drift also affects the health of other desirable plants close by, it is best not to spray at all. When the ground is wet and soft, you can use a leather gardening glove to pull out young gorse by hand. Then let the grass grow long, to inhibit further regeneration of gorse seeds, which depend on light for survival.

All plants strive to continue their species and each new generation evolves stronger genetic capabilities. Some weeds develop resistance to sprays and, with no competition from other plants, take over an area. A new spray then needs to be developed – at considerable cost in effort, time, money, and damage – to solve this new problem. Spraying boiling water over weeds has the same effect as herbicides, which usually suppress soft weed growth for about 90 days only. In the future, the environmentally sound method of spraying steam over weeds will be increasingly favoured.

Insecticides devastate all insect life and upset natural cycles. From the human standpoint, the damage done by insecticides is not seen immediately, but the balance of pests with beneficial insects like bees, ladybirds, and praying mantises is destroyed. Although pest numbers may be reduced for a short period, some always survive. It is impossible to eliminate any pest problem totally, as surviving insects develop a resistance to the chemicals used. These individuals then pass their immunity on to future generations. This eventually creates an unbalanced environment among insects. Extra costs are involved as recurring problems need to be dealt with again in the future. Moreover, both the gardener and local wildlife are exposed to toxic chemical sprays that leave residues in the soil. The use of organic sprays like garlic helps to deter pests without any harmful side-effects.

Creating a symbiosis among wildlife and chosen plants is the key to avoiding the use of sprays, and to low maintenance. Do not upset the natural order, but work with plant and insect life to create harmony within the environment. Plant a mixture of strongly scented species that act as deterrents to insect pests. Use compost to encourage healthy species that are strong and competitive.

ROTATION OF CULTIVATED LAND

Rotation gives soil a rest so that fertility can recover. As land lies fallow, the nutrients within it are released and utilised to heal the soil's natural balance.

Fallow land can be left in pasture for a few years so that grasses and clovers increase in density before being ploughed or dug back into the soil, building up the organic content and improving the soil structure. This can also be achieved by sowing lupin seed and digging or ploughing the young seedlings back into the soil.

One method of successfully managing the domestic vegetable garden is to have a series of raised plots to grow crops that are rotated at different times. Plots that are resting are re-composted, while others are harvested. Old tissue decomposes and other fresh crops begin anew. This is a sure way of growing healthy vegetables.

Weeding

To ensure survival, plant species have various effective and sometimes sophisticated techniques of seed dispersal and germination. Some seeds attach themselves to the coats of animals that carry them to new areas. Some, that are eaten by birds, need to be exposed to acidic stomach conditions before they can germinate. Others germinate only after stratification through freezing. Some have a short fertility period and lose their vigour if not immediately embedded in the ground, while many others can lie dormant for years. Weed seeds are always arriving in the garden, and bare ground is quickly covered with new weed growth from reserves of seed in the soil. When conditions are favourable, germination begins and so does the competitive struggle to survive.

Some juvenile weeds, chosen because of their particular habits, should be allowed to cover low ground. These weeds grow with and shelter other young plants. Rather than constantly clearing them away, or mistakenly pulling out the wrong plant, wait until weeds are semi-mature, then pluck them out. Generally weeds are easy to pull out of the ground at flowering, when the plant's energy is used to complete seed formation. Whole roots, even of strong taprooted species that surface among tall grass, like fennel, dock, wild sea radish, and ragwort, pull out easily at the time they flower. Stubborn roots need to be grubbed out and left to dry in the baking sun. One good day of selective weeding every six to eight weeks is enough to maintain order among plants in the garden.

Where grass becomes a nuisance, it can be mowed or hand-pulled and the ground thickly mulched with its remains. Sometimes it is better to place a considerable quantity of clean topsoil on top of existing weeds like grass so they are smothered and then rot down. Planting directly into this topsoil, and covering any bare earth with thick mulch such as bark helps to inhibit future weed growth and conserve soil moisture.

Find out if unwanted weeds have annual or perennial habits and then decide how best to deal with them. A little effort plucking off flower heads, just before weeds are ready to disperse their unwanted seeds, reduces plant numbers and saves much monotonous future weeding. If onion weed, for example, is neglected and allowed to flower, its seed quickly spreads and a large-scale invasion takes place when germination begins. However, unlike the annual Californian thistle whose prolific airborne seeds float far and wide, the seeds of fennel do not spread through wind dispersion. This herbaceous perennial species forms tight colonies as its seeds drop close to the parent plant. The removal of flower heads prevents the increase of future generations, but its roots also need to be removed before the colony reduces in size. A 'weed eater' or line trimmer is a useful tool for controlling growth. Seedless weeds can be left on the ground to decompose and return nutrients to the soil.

Harmful creepers or vines like clematis grow several metres during summer months, choke other desirable plants, and kill them within one season. They are difficult to control and should be pulled out or chopped back as soon as they are found. Dipping bindweed re-growth into a container of Roundup disperses the chemical to the roots and kills what remains of it in the ground. Convolvulus can flower in both summer and autumn. Always be on guard for these noxious weeds and do not let them set seed. Take swift action and make sure flowers are plucked from the plant.

All removed seed heads should be destroyed. They can be burnt or put in the rubbish bin. They must not be added to compost.

Watering

Summer droughts dehydrate plants, so watering is needed when conditions become dry. Identify water sources such as springs, surface or underground streams, and ponds that can be used to reduce the effects of long dry periods. Good soil with plenty of compost or humus in it conserves soil moisture, and mulching reduces surface evaporation. Established plants seek moisture in deeper layers of the soil, which gives them an advantage over plants dependent on watering.

To minimise maintenance, it is important to select plants carefully and position them in gardens correctly. Plants that suffer from water stress have a lower resistance to pests or diseases, are prone to insect attack and die readily. They should be removed to accommodate stronger plants that favour more arid conditions.

Watering systems can be helpful in dry gardens during summer, but they can easily over-water the ground and leach nutrients from the soil. Over-watering also causes new weeds to sprout. Mechanical systems that have not been installed properly tend to water areas unevenly, leaving some plants to dehydrate while others rot. If watering is neglected just once on a hot sunny day, plants with underdeveloped small roots will easily die. This often happens when there is no one to look after the garden during a holiday away from home or when the irrigation system is forgotten or faulty.

Watering by hand is a good way to stay in tune with the garden. A hand-held hose not only conserves water but gives the right amount of moisture, and ensures that individual care is given to each plant. It is essential to spend time in the garden to relax, observe, and feel its needs.

Fertilisers and pH balance

These are a practical concern. It is essential to know the soil pH before applying fertilisers as they can acidify or upset its balance. Accurate soil testing should be done by specialists like Landcare Research, and fertilisers must be applied in the recommended quantities. When used excessively and applied too intensively, they burn and kill plants.

To grow a specific crop, a detailed analysis of soil pH and nutrients is needed. With a little homework, the nutrients lacking in soils can be supplemented. For example, if soil is too low in phosphorus for a particular crop to grow successfully, animal urine, potassium chloride, or potassium sulphate can be used. Vegetables do best in neutral soils with a 6.5 pH. If soil is acidic, lime is needed to balance the pH.

It is important to know whether the fertiliser is organic or inorganic. How the fertiliser affects the health and quality of the crop should be considered. Will it unbalance the pH or leave toxins to be absorbed into food? Synthesised fertilisers such as NPK contain all the principal nutrients that plants need. By law, packets must be labelled with all the ingredients. A good general garden fertiliser to use is Nitrophoska Blue Special (N:P:K:S 12:5:14:6): 30% ammonium nitrate, 15% dicalcium phosphate, 10% diammonium phosphate, 34% potassium sulphate, dolomite, and small amounts of borax, molybdenum, manganese, iron, zinc and copper.

Animal manures are good, but solid dung material contains only 1% nitrogen, 0.3% phosphorous and 0.5% potassium. When used undiluted, the high concentration of solid manure can burn and kill some plant species. Mammals get rid of water-soluble materials in their urine, so this is a more valuable fertiliser than solid manure, and is best collected soaked into sawdust or hay from the floors of stables and cowsheds. These water-soluble nutrients are readily washed away by rain. But if this urine-soaked sawdust has rotted to a neutral organic material, it can be used as matured compost which gradually releases its very valuable content. Poultry manure is three times stronger and better than solid animal manure because birds excrete liquids and solids together. However, undiluted poultry manure can also burn tender plants because of its high concentration of ammonia.

Sulphate of ammonia is the secret to establishing lawns successfully. On a poor, patchy lawn, mosses or flat weeds such as dandelion grow more quickly than grass. Sulphate of ammonia lowers soil pH to between 5 and 5.5,which is ideal for growing grass. It contains 21% nitrogen and 24% sulphur, plus oxygen and hydrogen. To apply, mix three parts sulphate of ammonia with one part super phosphate, and water into the lawn so the grass is not burnt or damaged.

Valuable nutrients are taken away from lawns when clippings are removed after constantly cutting. Mow the lawn on a sunny day, and leave the cut grass where it drops. It will dry out quickly and its nutrients will be recycled back into the soil.

Pruning

Provided that water is abundant and the climate is warm, plants will grow all year around. Over a period of time some grow to great heights and need to be checked, as they block out essential sunlight from smaller plants that live suppressed in their shadows. All deciduous plants produce growth each year and lanky extensions sometimes need to be removed to make sure more delicate plants have enough light to flourish. Shade also inhibits the growth of cottage gardens, as they depend on open sunlight. Pruning in all these situations becomes an essential maintenance task.

Be careful when pruning: some species re-grow easily, but others do not recover well. Usually, soft-wooded plants recover more easily than hardwoods. It is best to prune away older material during winter, leaving young wood to grow. Make sure that cuts are clean and done on an angle so that moisture will flow off the branch and the wound will dry quickly. Clean cuts dry quickly and heal better. Painting cut branches helps healing too.

Flowers are a special beauty to enjoy, but they are also the reproductive part of the plant that sets seed to continue the species. Removing dead flowers by hand helps to prolong the flowering period of perennial plants. Once the parent plant has flowered, the formation of seed is demanding on its sugar resources. If spent flower heads are removed before the seeds are formed, some plants try harder to produce more seed and flower again. By pruning away dead flower heads on species such as delphiniums, roses, and dahlias, the energy reserved for seed formation in the parent plant is used to continue flowering. This practice not only prolongs flowering but doubles or triples the number of blooms produced. This is an old and well-known practice among good gardeners. Monet, the great nineteenth-century impressionist painter, had a wonderful garden that inspired much of his work. To ensure prolonged flowering in his garden, he employed gardeners to prune away dead flowers before they seeded.

Annual plants, however, should be allowed to seed naturally for propagation the following year.

Pruning back spent plants after they have finished flowering allows other species to emerge and dominate the garden display in their season. Ornamental plants that grow quickly in spring, for example, become spent over the longest daylight period near Christmas. After flowering, these species need to be cut back to allow other plants with autumn-flowering habits to flourish. Often the beauty of plants is seen only in a brief flush, like a snapshot, when the garden is at its seasonal best.

Transplanting

When plants are transplanted, they need careful attention while they re-adjust, and should be watered during dry periods. If transplanting is done on hot sunny days during summer, the shock can exhaust and kill the plant. Winter is a good time for transplanting trees and shrubs as they are less stressed by lack of water and so have a better chance of survival. Deciduous trees and bulbs are easily transplanted while dormant. Cool day temperatures, long nights, and an abundance of moisture all benefit plants in a new location.

To support themselves, plants usually have the same proportion of roots as they have branches. Once a plant has been lifted, the damage to delicate root hairs means it is difficult for the plant to feed itself. While the roots re-adjust after transplanting, the foliage is overworked to sustain the plant. Therefore, when the plant is bedded into its new location, it is wise to prune back lush foliage so that moisture is contained and not lost through leaf transpiration. This important technique prevents dehydration. Cutting back foliage enables the plant to balance growth above the ground with the need to give its roots time to establish new growth below the ground. Most commercially produced plants are grown in containers so their roots are not disturbed when planted out.

Never transplant any species in full flower as it is in a weakened state, with all its resources concentrated on producing seed.

Examples of wind gardens

Houghton Bay, Wellington

The objective here was to create a pleasant garden in a domestic situation. This particular site is my own garden, situated 100 metres from the sea at Houghton Bay, on Cook Strait. It is located in a part of Wellington that was once the rubbish tip, and is therefore a man-made site without natural soil. The original land was levelled as each tip face was filled.

The site lies in a narrow valley exposed to strong north-westerly winds and salt-laden southerlies – an almost impossible location, and one typical of Wellington. The original vegetation that grew here was sparse. There were a few taupata and karo, both small native trees found in the coastal regions of New Zealand. The rest of the site had an infestation of fennel, a dormant perennial capable of growing to two metres during summer.

On analysis of the site, certain facts became clear.

- Wind would have a damaging effect on new plants. Both the north-westerly and southerly winds would break and twist the plants. Salt from the sea breeze would settle on the leaves and cause the burning of younger foliage, completely destroying plants that had no protection. Only by cluster planting could I provide protection from the wind and create shelter within which the more vulnerable plants could survive.

- The southerly winds are predominant during the autumn and winter months, whereas the spring and summer months have a preponderance of strong north-westerly winds. The seasonal nature of the wind patterns is reflected by the fact that deciduous trees and shrubs of certain species do survive here, because they are dormant over the winter months when most of the damaging winds occur. (For example, poplar trees can be found in this area, although their foliage burns off after the first strong southerly gale in the autumn. This is a clear example of how seasonal variations in climate can allow deciduous plants to live in a salt-laden environment.)

- The winters cast long shadows in the valley, creating damp cold areas. In the summer months these areas become sun-drenched, dry, and warm. In other words, there is great microclimatic variation within a small area.

- The weed growth during the spring and summer months is very aggressive, and can easily suffocate desirable plants.

- The Cook Strait coastline has an interesting and varied collection of naturalised plant escapees, and these provide colourful displays over the spring months.

These facts governed the design of the garden. I had to work within the limits of nature, and this meant that I had first to deal with the wind.

Certain parts of the site receive more sun than others, and there is a considerable contrast between the shaded, cold, and boggy areas and those that are warm and sunny. This is an advantage, as it allows for variation in design.

The location of the house was most important with regard to the winter sun angles and wind deflection. It was placed at the very rear of the site, tucked up against the hill, where it is private and sheltered, and receives the very first morning sun. The garden was planned so that to gain access to the house you would take a delightful walk through the garden.

Landscape planting

Mounds planted with toetoe were built along the front and side boundaries, creating shelter from the winds that had previously howled through the site. Secondary mounds together with cluster plantings were placed throughout the site, further deflecting the wind within the garden. The following species were chosen, and it took one season for these cluster plantings to provide adequate shelter.

Trees:
Karo (*Pittosporum crassifolium*)
Taupata (*Coprosma repens*)
Pohutukawa (*Metrosideros excelsa*)
Cabbage tree (*Cordyline australis*)
Five finger (*Pseudopanax lessonii*)
Ngaio (*Myoporum laetum*)

Shrubs and grasses:
Toetoe (*Cortaderia toi toi*)
Flaxes (*Phormium tenax, P. cookianum*); and varieties such as Maori Chief, Rubra, Rainbow Maiden, Tricolour, Yellow Wave
Euryops arbrotanifolius
Marguerite daisy (*Argyranthemum frutescens*) of which there are several different colours
Tree daisy (*Olearia albida*)
Tree mallow (*Lavatera arborea*)
Pride of Madeira (*Echium candicans*)
Agapanthus (*Agapanthus praecox*)

Groundcovers:
Cape weed (*Arctotheca calendula*)
Dimorphotheca (*Osteospermum fruticosum*)
Gazania (*Gazania linearis*)

These hardy coastal plants were planted en masse in every vacant, planned space, and very quickly formed an ornamental barrier for the winds to bounce off.

The site was still not complete, as the location of the driveway and garage had to be determined, and it was important to get maximum potential from these service areas, without affecting the concept of the site layout. The site had to be observed over a full year's seasonal range to pick out those areas most vulnerable to salt burn and shade. I decided to place the driveway along the shaded side of the garden, and the garage in the spot which suffered most from the southerly gusts. This location made good sense: because it was difficult to grow plants here, shelter was provided by the new garage.

Now I could focus on the finer details of the garden. Secluded seating areas were formed, and many ornamental, colourful, and scented plants were added to surprise and please.

Winter is an ideal time to plan the garden for the seasons to come. Winter planting consisted of textured foliage plants such as flax hybrids, conifers, ericas, camellias, sweet pea bush, gazanias, primulas, and the pampas grass *Cortaderia selloana* 'Variegata', which is less vigorous and more colourful than the parent pampas grass.

Spring planting consisted of more delicate annual plants like pansies, primulas, cinerarias, petunias, calendulas, and cornflowers, as well as roses and bulbs, creating a flush of spring flowers, which then gave way to summer plants such as dahlias, rudbeckias, roses, asters, and cosmos. Once the marguerite daisies had passed their best, I pruned them back hard, to allow the summer plants more room to grow; I do this each year, immediately after Christmas. The summer plants are allowed to bloom for as long as they are able, and this phase can last until the end of May.

Late autumn is the time to lift the dahlias from the soil. It is an ideal time to reshape the garden, improve the soil with compost, spread blood and bone fertiliser, and turn the soil where needed. It is also the time to eradicate aggressive weeds, such as couch. Most of these weeds are dormant through the winter, when the salty winds around the Cook Strait foreshore are predominant.

Weeding is an important task in the early spring, to eliminate the potential spring flush of unwanted growth. This is a pleasant task on a sunny day, and simply involves identifying unwanted growth at a very early stage and removing it before weeds are allowed to develop and absorb valuable space. If desirable plants are able to dominate the ground in the early spring, they will have a head start, enabling them to compete with the invasion of new unwanted growth.

As the spring days warm the site, all these plants begin to express their individual beauty, providing a unique display. Only 200 metres from the high-tide line, delicate plants can grow in places previously blasted by salty winds, provided that their shelter has been engineered correctly. The garden always has a good range of flowering plants and texture throughout the year, even during southerly gales. The more delicate plants are grouped amongst hardier plants which provide vital protection by creating microclimates in which they and other plants can flourish. Working with nature is the secret, and this requires a knowledge of each plant's tolerances. This is one good reason for visiting other gardens and observing how similar plants behave under different environmental conditions.

The author's garden, showing how different flowering periods are arranged so that the garden is in flower most of the year. When one species is spent, another is budding to flower.

(Left) The shortest and coolest days of winter are from June to August, when most plants lie dormant.

(Right) From September through to October daylight hours begin to increase. Although temperatures are still cool, forget-me-nots, calendula, and honesty begin to flower.

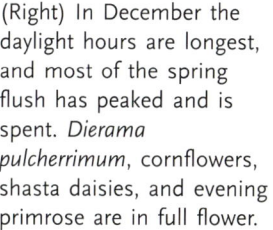

(Left) November into December roses begin to flower, and gazania, watsonia, lychnis, and geum are flushing.

(Right) In December the daylight hours are longest, and most of the spring flush has peaked and is spent. *Dierama pulcherrimum*, cornflowers, shasta daisies, and evening primrose are in full flower.

(Left) In January we see dahlias, bog sage, and rudbeckia in flower.

(Right) From February to March the climate is at its warmest and driest, and watering the garden is essential. Evening primrose and dahlia continue to flower, with Port St John creeper and asters beginning to flourish.

April to May is the cooling-off period when the asters and bog sage have an almighty last flush, glowing with reflecting colours in the soft light.

Planting in sandy soils, like those at Lyall Bay, Wellington, requires careful plant selection and positioning. Pohutukawa and karo trees are planted along the boundary, and *Artemisia arborescens*, *Santolina chamaecyparissus*, *Argyranthemum frutescens*, *Arctotis stoechadifolia*, *Euryops pectinatus*, *Echium candicans*, and hebes spread down towards the middle. Watering is very important.

Wind Gardens

(Above) The planting three years later. See how the trees along the fence are beginning to gain height.

In the exposed sandy soil of a beach frontage, plants are clustered in the middle to gain some height, and smaller plants are placed nearer the path.

Construction of a seaside garden.

(Left) Construction of the garden using clean topsoil. (Right) One year's growth.

Three years' growth.

(Left) *Echium candicans, Argyranthemum frutescens, Osteospermum fruticosum,* and *Arctotis stoechadifolia* were planted into poor turf and left to survive for themselves. The correct positioning and use of plant material can give satisfying results. (Right) Beach street planting at Seatoun, Wellington.

The site before work was started.

The courtyard site was dug out to create an outdoor, paved space that would connect with the dining area of the house and make a safe place for young children to play. The rubble was re-used to form a mound, then planted. What was once an unsafe, high lawn was made more hospitable by creating three levels, so that the step edges could also be used as seats with clean surfaces for children's safe play. The trellis fencing and gate gave more wind protection and security.

The site before work was started – a dull outdoor space above a garage.

The space re-created into a courtyard.

The site before work was started.

The paved site.

Courtyard paving can be made interesting with textured patterns that harmonise with the environment.

Artistic use of hand-painted pebbles.

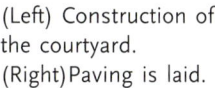

The construction of Zebo's bar, Southern Cross Tavern, Wellington.

(Left) Construction of the courtyard.
(Right) Paving is laid.

The courtyard three years later.

This courtyard has lasted more than 20 years and was constructed over a lawn. The space was arranged so that a new conservatory would flow on to both a wooden deck and a paved courtyard with shade and sun. In this way, four micro-environments could be made to suit whatever weather prevailed.

This site was a damp backyard that received little sun in winter. The planter was raised with a seat built in, bringing the garden to waist height, making maintenance easy. A deciduous magnolia is the feature tree, providing summer shade but allowing winter sun to penetrate the cottage planting. Paving with ceramic tiles eliminated dampness.

Wind Gardens

(Left) Before tree planting took place. (Right) At Hoon Hay, Christchurch, young trees are planted during winter, and staked.

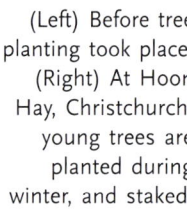

Four years on, the trees are taking hold.

Planting
into turf.

Plants maturing
18 months later.

Cleared blackberry
in a bush area
where natives have
been planted.
This will need
constant
monitoring, with
the blackberry
roots dug out and
left to bake dry in
the sun.

Plant selection & lists of species

Plant lists for different locations

Over the centuries, gardens have become representative of a vast global resource. Increasingly, with easy and cheap travel, people have collected foreign varieties of plant species and introduced them by seed and cuttings to new environments amongst indigenous plants. These new species are further hybridised into new forms called 'cultivars'. Often different flowering varieties have been bred for better-quality blooms, new colours or new dwarf forms. Cultivars or sport varieties may have genetic advantages that have been bred into the plant to aid its survival. 'Designer' plants are being raised to withstand disease and differing climates.

The domestic garden is often a confusion of plants behaving uncontrollably. Incompatible collections of plants require continuous costly maintenance. If neglected over a long period of time, a few dominant trees may grow too big and smother weaker species that pass away prematurely. So the correct selection of new plants, combined with horticultural techniques, plays a very important role in the success of a planting and its future maintenance. When selecting plants for a particular site, be it open farmland or a small courtyard, remember that plant habits remain the same regardless: stronger species grow to their optimum and suppress other plants.

Certain species that flourish in a particular habitat may be restricted or even absent in other similar sites only a few kilometres distant. Even though a plant can tolerate a certain temperature range, there are other microclimatic variables that influence competition between species – coastal sites are usually exposed to salt-laden wind; inland sites can be exposed to wind and frost; many areas are free of both frost and wind. Water and soil conditions and warmer or cooler air pockets further affect sites.

Before beginning to evaluate the plants on site and the likely success of those to be introduced, consider the location and other factors which directly affect their ability to grow successfully.

Soil type and fertility: Some plants need a rich fertile soil while others respond better to average or poor soils.

Rainfall and water source: Is there going to be water stress on plants seasonally or permanently? Try to choose plants that are naturally adapted to the climate so that watering occurs effortlessly with rainfall.

Exposure to wind: Is existing vegetation battered or scarred from salt burn or the effects of drying or cold inland winds?

Heat and light requirements: Many plants love full sun, others need shade.

Seasonal variations: Find out how the seasons affect your area – is it prone to frosts, drought, rainfall, and plant competition?

How to use the lists

First of all, determine a site's mature state in terms of shelter planting, and then select plants which are adapted to the relevant habitat. Plan for the years ahead. As all species mature at different stages there are always changes occurring within gardens as they evolve over time. In choosing plants suitable for the site, consider their association in terms of habit, seasonal change, growth rates, and dormancy and spread so that, over time, the selected species can naturalise in harmony.

In evaluating plant life on site as well as that to be introduced, work through these steps:

- Identify plant groups and habits.

- Check their adaptability to wind or salt wind. Note which plants shelter others from the wind, and evaluate their contribution to the garden.

- Consider their condition. How do individual plants compare to the same species on other local sites?

- Identify species that are compatible with the intended landscaping or garden, and with other plants on site and to be introduced.

The plant lists following indicate species with similar tolerances, providing a selection of plants for gardens and landscape work in a given situation. One of the main inhibitors of plant distribution is temperature, so the plant lists are divided into three temperature zones: areas where temperatures drop to -15°C; areas with temperatures down to -3°C; and entirely frost-free areas.

Within the three main temperature zones, variable microclimatic divisions are listed as A, B, C, etc. They are habitats ranging from coastal to inland areas, categorised by levels of wind and salt exposure: most severe wind (***); moderately strong wind (**); and light wind (*). The lists have been ordered in this way to help you choose plants that suit a specific environment, beginning with areas suffering the most severe salt and salt-free wind and ending with completely sheltered coastal or inland situations. Lists of trees, shrubs, herbs, grasses, groundcovers, creepers, climbers, ferns, perennials, bulbs, and annuals are included as appropriate within each habitat.

Each list describes a present-time garden situation. As you create a microclimate that decreases the influence of wind, whether salt-laden or not, and modifies extreme temperatures, you will have the opportunity to select from more of the planting lists than at first. Inland areas, not being affected by salt-carrying winds, offer the gardener wider planting options than coastal areas.

To demonstrate how to use the lists, here is an example. The site is exposed to salt wind and free of frost. For quick shelter, refer to List 3A and choose fast-growing plants that can be used for wind protection. Once the planting is established, plants from List 3B – those that need some shelter – could also be included. List 3C plants, which need even more shelter, can be used at a later stage. Once windless microclimates have been successfully created with shelter from established plants, softer

species (listed at the end of each category) can be used for the finer details of the garden. Frost- and wind-hardy plants from Lists 1A and 2A could also be used in this frost-free zone but may not be as competitive or reach their optimum as quickly as plants found naturally in a warmer climate.

At the other extreme, on a site where frosts occur, choosing plants from List 3 would obviously be a mistake unless they were positioned in a warm microclimate that suited that particular species.

Note that section 1 (temperatures drop to -15°C) has 11 microclimates (no section 1H or 1M); section 2 (temperatures drop to -3°C) has 10 (no list 2G, 2J, or 2M); and section 3 (frost-free) has 10 (no list 3G, 3H, or 3K). The lists have been lettered to show equivalent levels of wind and salt within each frost zone for easy reference between microclimates. For example, although the plants listed in List 1I are appropriate for a particular area, the creation of a warm microclimate which only ever gets very light frosts means that plants from List 2I could be suitable. Where there is no frost at all, plants from List 3I could be positioned close to sunny walls for extra winter heat. Summer-flowering annuals can be planted in any area, even frosted districts, provided they are set out after the last spring frost, and complete their flowering cycle before the first autumn frost occurs.

To survive, plants must be able to adapt to a location and climate as well as competing successfully with other species within their habitat. It is always best to make observations of plants in places which are as similar as possible to your own site. This will ensure that variables of light, temperature, the salt content of the wind, and the availability of moisture do not give an undue competitive advantage or disadvantage to the new arrivals in your garden. Plants grown in the north, for example, or purchased from nurseries there, are often too soft to re-acclimatise further south. Some nurseries apply a diluted solution of salt water to their plants to harden them slightly, and this seems to work successfully with some species. Other plants are just not able to compete or adapt to foreign habitats. Plant survival is dependent on the correct species being chosen for a particular area.

Temperature drops to -15°C
Inland wind: severe (***)
Coastal and salt wind: severe (***)

TREES

Cupressus macrocarpa 'Aurea' (conifer)
Common name: Monterey cypress. A competitive fast-growing evergreen tree that reaches 12m, only half as high as the macrocarpa. A far more compact and rounded tree, it is hardier against salt winds and is often used in rural and coastal areas along farm shelter belts as, when clipped, it can make an excellent large hedge. It needs bright sunshine, and can withstand dry and poor soil. Older trees tend to be spindly, causing draughts. It has fragrant leaves that are variegated yellow and green.

Propagation – late autumn to late winter: take cuttings from young plants or stratify seed.

Tamarix chinensis, T. japonica, T. plumosa
Common name: tamarisk. A competitive deciduous coastal shrub that grows to 5m in well-drained soil and sun. It makes a good hedge, surviving abundant salt wind or drought, and is also very useful for cluster plantings. In summer it has soft fine foliage, and from February to March showy pink-red flower clusters.

Propagation – late spring and autumn take semi-ripe cuttings; in winter take hardwood cuttings.

SHRUBS

Phormium cookianum (monocotyledon), P. colensoi
Maori names: korari-tuauru or wharariki. Common name: mountain flax. A small, competitive, New Zealand native evergreen from which a number of cultivars have been produced. Mountain flax is slow growing in moist soil and sun or semi-shade and reaches 1-2m. Nearly all cultivar flaxes can become untidy when used as ornamentals on windy sites as strong winds whip the leaf-ends, turning them into fibre. Birds love to drink the nectar from the flowers of all phormium species. This flax has pale green leaves which are more clumped than other flaxes and are also too feeble for weaving; from November to December spikes of pale yellow-green flowers appear followed by hanging seed-pods.

Propagation – in autumn by seed or division.

GRASSES

Briza maxima
Common names: pearl grass or quaking grass. Grows in open sunlight and well-drained soil to 60cm. Silver-white flowers that appear from December to January can be dried for floral decoration. This perennial rhizomatous grass self-seeds readily.

Propagation – in spring with seed; in spring and autumn by division.

Cortaderia fulvida (monocotyledon)
Maori and common name: toetoe. An evergreen, competitive, perennial grass that is moderately fast growing in poor well-drained soil and sun, reaching an optimum height of 2.5m. Toetoe is sometimes confused with the South American species, *Cortaderia selloana* 'Variegata' yellow pampas grass, which has a similar habit and appearance but differs in that it withstands only a light frost (see Plant List 2A). Toetoe thrives in well-drained, poor soil and sun; it is very useful in cluster plantings, because it buffers the wind, and on top of mounds accentuates the wind uplift. In spring 3m high silver-white flower fronds appear and attract nesting birds.

Propagation – autumn by seed; spring by division: selected forms by division only.

Poa astonii (monocotyledon)
Common name: coastal poa. Densely tufted blue-green grass, 75cm tall, forming clumps to 40cm in circumference. A native that grows on rocky coastal cliffs and beaches; will tolerate some drought. Decorative plant for seaside gravel gardens.

Propagation – by division.

Poa cita (monocotyledon)
Maori name: wii. Common name: silver tussock. A decorative golden-yellow green tussock with a fine-textured silvery appearance. Forms a densely tufted tussock 90cm in circumference and 40cm tall. Grows in poor, dry soils. Likes exposed windy situations. A hardy plant that will grow where many other plants would not survive.

Propagation – by seed or division after flowering.

PERENNIALS

Achillea millefolium (herbaceous)
Common name: yarrow. Competitive and withstands the harshest wind and salt-wind conditions. In well-drained soil and sun it grows to a height of 60cm and is particularly beneficial in building up soil and reducing wind erosion. Yarrow is sometimes used as a medicinal herb. From December to February it has decorative white, cerise, pale pink and deep red flowers that can be dried for floral decoration.

Propagation – late winter, early spring or autumn by division; early summer take softwood cuttings.

Sedum spectabile
Common name: shrubby stonecrop. A perennial herb easily smothered by tall grasses. Ideal for crib walls or rock faces, it is a xerophyte that is fast growing to 35cm in sun and sandy well-drained soil. Yellow and pink flowers appear from February to April.

Propagation – from spring to mid-summer take softwood cuttings of non-flowering shoots or by division; autumn or spring with seed.

ANNUALS

Lobularia maritima, Alyssum maritimum
Common name: alyssum. Is competitive, spreading and fast growing to 15cm high in well-drained soil and sun. Useful for decoration in rock gardens and paving cracks and at dry locations for soil conservation from wind erosion: naturalises along coastal areas. The tiny clusters of white or mauve flowers have a pleasant fragrance and appear at any time of year.

Propagation – in spring with seed.

Matthiola incana
Common name: stock. Grows as an annual in sun and well-drained soil to 60cm. This plant thrives in the path of wind or salt wind and can be found growing wild on beaches or near the coast. From August to May scented white, pink or purple flowers appear that may be either doubles or singles and are decorative in a vase.

Propagation – in spring with seed.

Malcolmia maritima
Common name: Virginia stock. A herbaceous perennial found growing in the wild in the most unusual places, such as on Wellington's Houghton Bay beach, amongst sand dunes and on cliff faces, clay banks, and in arid places where other plants are unable to compete. Flowers are colourful purples and whites, and are strongly scented in the spring, making an excellent cut flower. In its ability to survive harsh windy and coastal conditions it is similar in habit to the sea poppy. Has its place in any wind garden and should be encouraged to naturalise itself. Does not tend to take over and is easily controlled.

Propagation – in autumn by seed.

Temperature drops to -15°C

Inland wind: severe (***)
Coastal and salt wind: moderate (**)

TREES

Cordyline australis

Maori name: tii. Common name: cabbage tree. Competitive, New Zealand native evergreen that grows in sun and most soils that retain water to 9m. Wind hard, it is always welcome in shelterbelts. Frosts do not affect it, although it is more often seen in warmer areas where, unfortunately in recent years, it suffers from virus attack. So far there is no cure for the yellowing of leaves which eventually results in the death of the tree. As the growth is always from a central stem, upon maturity it begins to branch out into a tree with a long fleshy trunk; the older leaves die and as the tree ages, it can appear untidy. Once established, virus free, the tree is almost impossible to eradicate, as many side shoots appear, even after it has been chopped. Early settlers made chimneys from the trunks which, when the fireplaces were abandoned, grew back into cabbage trees. Broken trunks have been known to wash up on the shores and re-grow. Cabbage trees also grow freely from seed. Maori used the centres of the apex (the bud) as a food source. It is attractive for its tropical look and is grown as a specimen or for shelter. From October to November panicles of fragrant tiny, creamy-white flowers appear, followed during April and May by bluish-white berries containing black seeds.

Propagation – summer take stem cuttings; spring with suckers or seed.

Cupressus macrocarpa (conifer)

Common name: macrocarpa. A competitive, fast-growing, fragrant, evergreen shelter tree that reaches, in sun and poor well-drained soil, an optimum height of 20m. It is often used for hedging in rural areas along farm shelter belts. While able to provide shelter inland, in coastal areas it cannot cope with the strongest winds and the foliage tends to burn. Older foliage of an aged macrocarpa has a tendency to die, eventually becoming inadequate as a wind break by letting the wind funnel underneath. Macrocarpa can prevent other plants from growing around it by secreting a hormone in its needle litter which inhibits other seedlings. The thick canopy shades and keeps the ground around it dry, further retarding other potential growth. Although macrocarpa tolerates droughts, other tree varieties do a better job as wind deflectors and do not become so straggly.

Propagation – late autumn to late winter: take cuttings from young plants or stratify seed.

Populus alba

Common names: abele or white poplar. Large, competitive, deciduous tree used for shelter. In sun and moist but well-drained soil it is fast growing to 20m high; in autumn its green leaves become colourful bronze and golden-yellow before they drop.

Propagation – in winter take hardwood cuttings.

SHRUBS

Ceanothus papillosus 'Roweanus'

Common name: Californian lilac. A competitive, handsome evergreen able to grow in areas subject to strong winds. Grows in sun and most well-drained soil to 3m, providing partial shelter. Severe salt limits this shrub, but overall it is very useful for cluster plantings, banks, walls and as a garden specimen. It tends to become top heavy, so pruning is necessary to keep it bushy. The shrub is slow to establish itself in the early stages but, once secured in position, will dominate well, competing with other growth. Grows in frosted areas, provided it receives abundant sunshine and the ground is not boggy. From October to November the shrub is covered with tiny clusters of purplish-blue flowers which attract bees.

Propagation – in spring take soft-tip cuttings.

GRASSES

Cortaderia richardii (monocotyledon)

Maori and common name: toetoe. Fast-growing native grass. Can grow up to 3m when flowering between December and January. Flower plumes are slightly stiffer than those of *C. fulvida*. Very versatile, will grow virtually anywhere and will endure salt and frost.

Propagation – in summer, by seed.

GROUNDCOVERS

Cerastium tomentosum

Common name: snow-in-summer. Grows as a ground cover in sun and dry or well-drained soil. This perennial needs a gentle hand to establish it against competition from grasses. From November to January white flowers appear.

Propagation – in spring by division.

PERENNIALS

Cheiranthus cheiri

Common name: wallflower. Semi-evergreen competitive perennial or biennial that grows up to 1m. In open sun and dry or poor soils such as rock or sand, it is compatible with other growth and can even be found on beach sand dunes. The plant attracts bees and produces sweetly scented red, orange-red, mauve, yellow, pink or purple flowers from August to December.

Propagation – spring by seed and softwood cuttings; summer take greenwood cuttings.

ANNUALS

Calendula officinalis

Common name: marigold. Grows to 60cm as a competitive small bedding plant. In sun and well-drained soil it is able to naturalise along garden paths and in rock gardens. This is a very hardy plant that grows in open windy locations very well, but will burn with excess salt. Bright orange and yellow daisy-like flowers, that are sometimes used medicinally, appear profusely throughout the year. The petals are used in healing ointments and can be added to punch or drinks.

Propagation – spring or autumn by seed sown outdoors: self-seeds readily.

Temperature drops to -15°C

Inland wind: moderate (**)
Coastal and salt wind: moderate (**)

SHRUBS

Lavandula angustifolia, L. officinalis, L. spica

Common name: English lavender. Evergreen shrub that grows in sun and well-drained soil to a height of 90cm. This plant can make an attractive hedge, and the fragrant white or deep-purple flower spikes that appear from January to April can be dried for floral decoration.

Propagation – in summer take semi-ripe cuttings.

Lavandula stoechas

Common name: lavender. An evergreen that is slow growing to 50cm in sun and well-drained soil. It makes an ideal edging and can flourish at the coast but prefers to be sheltered amongst other plants. The fragrant dark purple flowers that appear from December to March can be dried for floral decoration.

Propagation – in summer take semi-ripe cuttings.

CULINARY HERBS

Tropaeolum majus

Common name: nasturtium. Aromatic, competitive and spreading evergreen or deciduous perennial plant. It is fast growing in moist soil and sun or semi-shade to 30cm. In colder regions it is grown as an annual. An attractive creeping plant, more noticeable when it flowers, it often smothers slower low growth on damp sites. Needs abundant water; dry summers retard its advance; it responds by going to seed or remaining small. In areas exposed to salt and wind, nasturtium survives protected by other growth. From October to May red-orange or yellow-orange flowers appear. The leaves and flowers have a spicy cress-like taste and can be used in salads.

Propagation – in spring with seed, tubers or basal stem cuttings.

PERENNIALS
Centranthus ruber (herbaceous)
Common name: spur valerian. Some consider this to be a weed, as it is a perennial with a strong will to live in the cracks of rocks or paving. It is an attractive herb, flowering mainly in the spring, although it will prolong into summer. The clusters of flowers are red, mauve, and white and in the wild they decorate hillsides and road edges with changing colour. Does not have the aggressive habit of a weed and will live compatibly with other plants without dominating them, but is able to survive impossible soils where other plants fail. Valerian is partly deciduous, relying on its roots as a food reserve, and grows well in temperate climates, surviving frost. It is an adventitious plant, an exotic plant that has naturalised in New Zealand, and is able to endure salty gale-force winds and recover well.

Propagation – in autumn or spring, by seed.

Echinops ritro
Common name: globe thistle. Hardy to wind, preferring dry sites. In sun and fertile well-drained soil it grows to 1.2m. Globe thistle is a good ornamental addition to the wind garden. From December to February tall stems of blue flower balls appear. The flowers are long lasting when picked and can be dried for floral decoration.

Propagation – spring with seed; in autumn by root cuttings or division; winter by division.

Eryngium maritimum (herbaceous)
Common name: sea holly. Grows in fertile, well-drained soil and sun to 30cm. The original coastal plant that its common name is derived from can tolerate salt air well, unlike its other relatives. From December to April blue or violet-blue flowers appear; these can be used fresh or dried for floral decoration.

Propagation – in spring by division; winter by root cuttings; species with ripe seed: selected forms by division only.

Helianthus tuberosus
Common name: Jerusalem artichoke. A competitive plant that prefers sun and well-drained soil where it is fast growing from 2-3m. The plant is hardy and able to thrive near the sea. It is an ornamental with bold foliage and bronzy, dull orange or yellow flowers which appear in April.

Propagation – in autumn or early spring by division.

Temperature drops to -15°C
Inland wind: severe (***)
Coastal and salt wind: light (*)

TREES
Pinus radiata (conifer), P. insignis
Common names: Monterrey pine or pine tree. A competitive, very fast-growing evergreen used for shelter. In New Zealand it grows three to four times faster than in California where it originates, because of the absence of pests and diseases, and the abundant rainfall and temperate climate. Pines are completely tolerant of winds, only burning off under severe salt wind, when they become leggy. However, they tend to become sparsely covered as they age, making them inadequate for shelter as wind funnels are created underneath them. When planted in clusters, young pines provide almost instant shelter for slower-growing plants to become established. This works well on open sunny sites with dry poor soils, drought and constant wind: here they grow to an optimum of 30m. Pines should be removed in 3-5 years and sold as Christmas trees, otherwise they will dominate the site.

Propagation – late autumn to late winter: take cuttings from young plants or stratify seed.

Salix matsudana 'Tortuosa'
Common name: tortured willow. A large, competitive and deciduous tree that is fast growing in sun and most soils to 15m. Quite different from the ordinary willow seen along river banks or wet areas, this willow is a hybrid produced specifically for shelter in rural areas, especially along boundaries of horticultural plots. Non-aggressive in habit, it does not sucker with rhizomes like its relative the poplar. Stands up to gale-force winds which deform its overall shape, causing more foliage to be produced on the sheltered side. In salt-free locations, it grows into a thick tree, providing excellent shelter to the site without cracking the pavement or sending its roots into drains and clay pipes. It is often combined with sarlon cloth to protect kiwifruit orchards. Young trees should be pruned back to half their size when planted, to allow trunk and roots to strengthen. Staking is essential to prevent the roots from tearing.

Propagation – summer by semi-ripe cuttings; in winter by hardwood cuttings planted deep in soil.

SHRUBS
Cotoneaster horizontalis
Common name: wall spray. Deciduous plant with dark-green leaves that grows in sun and well-drained soil to 50cm and has a horizontal spreading habit; ideal for banks. From November to December pink and white flowers appear succeeded by orange-red berries in autumn.

Propagation – in autumn with seed; in summer by softwood cuttings: selected forms by cuttings only

Cotoneaster lacteus
Common name: rock spray. An evergreen that is sometimes used for hedges, it grows in sun and well-drained soil to 4m. The shrub is useful in cluster plantings as it survives strong winds. From November to December pink and white flowers appear succeeded by orange-red berries in autumn.

Propagation – autumn with seed; summer by semi-ripe cuttings: selected forms by cuttings only.

Cytisus X praecox
Common name: Warminster broom. Deciduous plant that is fast growing in dry or stony soil and open sunlight to 1.45m. It is good as a nursery plant for sheltering and raising other trees. From September to November golden-yellow flowers appear that are attractive cut for a vase.

Propagation – in autumn with seed; in summer by semi-ripe cuttings: late summer for semi-ripe cuttings of selected forms.

Hebe odora
Common name: mountain hebe. An evergreen that is slow growing in moist but well-drained stony soil and sun to 1.5m. A good filler plant to use in shrub borders. From October to March white or pale pink flowers with blue tips appear.

Propagation – in summer take semi-ripe cuttings.

Viburnum japonicum
Common name: viburnum. A handsome, evergreen, ornamental shrub or small tree that is slow growing in well-drained soil with adequate summer moisture; will grow in shade or sun. Tolerates wind, and when grown amongst the shelter of other trees can cope with salt air. It needs assistance to establish in its early years and reaches 2-3m in height. From November to January it is covered with fragrant white flowers, succeeded by red berries in autumn and winter. Creates a good backdrop for other textured and coloured plants which contrast with its dark-green, glossy leaves. The bush retains its shape well and is seldom attacked by pests.

Propagation – in autumn with seed; in summer by semi-ripe cuttings.

CLIMBERS OR TRAILERS
Rosa wichuraiana
Common name: rambler rose. Competitive, deciduous shrub that is fast growing in sun and fertile, well-drained soil, but can take a few years to establish. They do well in wild situations, scrambling over other plants and fences, and providing summer colour from October to April, with fragrant flowers in white, red, orange, yellow, pink or lavender continuously in bloom. Very decorative in a vase.

Propagation – autumn or early winter by cuttings; summer by budding.

Clematis montana

Common name: clematis. Evergreen, fast-growing climber to 10m where sun is received for part of the day. Flowers for only a short period of 2-4 weeks, from October to November; the white or pink flowers can be cut and decoratively used in a vase.

Propagation – in autumn with seed; in early summer by softwood and semi-ripe cuttings or layering: selected forms only by softwood and semi-ripe cuttings or layering.

PERENNIALS

Helianthemum nummularium

Common name: sun rose. An evergreen shrub grown as a perennial in sandy or rocky well-drained soil and sun to 30cm. Good for overhanging walls and banks and can take a considerable amount of drought; however, it is short-lived. In mid-spring white, scarlet-red, copper-brown, orange, yellow or pink flowers appear.

Propagation – in autumn or late summer take semi-ripe cuttings.

Leucanthemum maximum, Chrysanthemum X superbum, C. maximum

Common name: shasta daisy. A competitive and spreading herbaceou perennial. In sun and well-drained soil from November to May it produces white flowers up to 1m tall, although the plant stays low to the ground; best suited to the cottage garden. The flowers can be dried for floral decoration.

Propagation – in spring take cuttings from actively growing plants or divide basal growth.

Temperature drops to -15°C

Inland wind: moderate (**)
Coastal and salt wind: light (*)

TREES

Acer negundo

Common name: box elder maple. A specimen tree that is fast growing in sun or semi-shade and fertile, well-drained soil to 17m. It has a decorative deciduous habit; in autumn the usually bright green leaves turn yellow before they fall. From September to November insignificant greenish-yellow flowers appear.

Propagation – autumn with ripe seed; late winter to early spring by grafting; summer by budding: cultivars by grafting and budding only.

Casuarina cunninghamiana

Common name: river sheoak. A large, competitive, evergreen tree that can grow in sun or shade. In poor sandy soil and windy areas without excess salt, it is fast growing from 10-15m. It can withstand drought, poor drainage and brackish or salty water. Is useful for shelter-belt plantings, providing good shelter for large sites. However, as it grows from a central stem and is not compact, it should be mixed with other trees. Its fine, needle-like foliage acts as a good wind filter. The red-brown flowers that appear from February to May are insignificant.

Propagation – in spring with seed.

X Cupressocyparis leylandii (conifer)

Common name: Leyland cypress. An evergreen tree used for hedging. Suitable for farm shelter, it is fast growing in sun and most soils, gaining from 70cm-1m a year; reaches 20-30m in 30 years. This tree has dark-green or grey-green leaves and stands up to strong winds. It needs plenty of room but is a better shelter tree than macrocarpa, as it retains its older foliage and stays more compact.

Propagation – late autumn to late winter: take cuttings from young plants or stratify seed.

Fraxinus excelsior

Common name: European ash. A deciduous specimen tree that needs a large open space where it grows in sun and fertile, moist but well-drained soil

from 25-30m. Very decorative in autumn when the usually dark-green leaves colour yellow and gold. In September and October numerous dark-purple flowers in dense clusters appear.

Propagation – autumn by seed; summer by budding of selected forms only.

Platanus orientalis

Common name: plane tree. A large deciduous tree often grown as a specimen. Takes some time to establish and survives along the coast amongst other trees, but prefers salt-free air. In well-drained soil and sun it grows to 25m. In autumn the leaves turn golden-green.

Propagation – in autumn with seed.

SHRUBS

Cotinus coggygira, Rhus cotinus

Common name: smoke tree. A deciduous species that grows to 5m in sun or semi-shade and fertile, well-drained soil. The purple-leaved forms should be grown in full sun to ensure their best colour. Very decorative in any shrub boarder in autumn when its usually light-green foliage colours red and yellow and when, from February to April, fawnish-grey plume-like flowers appear.

Propagation – in summer by greenwood or softwood cuttings.

Daphne cneorum

Common name: garland flower. An evergreen with trailing branches that is low growing in sun or semi-shade and fertile well-drained soil to 25cm. Useful in a small shrub border. From October to December fragrant deep-pink flowers appear.

Propagation – summer by ripe seed and semi-ripe cuttings; selected forms only by cuttings.

Hypericum X inordorum, H. elatum

Common name: St John's Wort. Semi-evergreen and grows in sun or semi-shade to 1.2m. It is a good plant to grow on banks, though it does not tolerate dryness. Its deciduous habit allows grass to penetrate the area, which could encourage a weed problem. From November to February bright yellow flowers appear, succeeded by orange-red fruits.

Propagation – in autumn with ripe seed; in summer take softwood cuttings; selected forms only by cuttings.

Rosa chinensis

Common name: rose. A true deciduous shrub which is able to tolerate short dry periods and withstands wind well. In fact, the more air movement the better, as still, moist air encourages fungal diseases like blackspot and mildew. Roses grow in sun and moist but well-drained soil up to 1.5m. Being dormant in winter enables them to survive winter frosts well. Pruning roses involves removing the older wood to encourage the new growth, keeping the plant actively young. A winter application of rotted horse manure feeds their bursts of flowering as they build up strength to compete well with other growth. Roses make ideal shrubs for the wind garden where, planted amongst other shrubs, they survive happily and provide bright colour. Fragrantly scented white, red, apricot, golden-yellow, pink or pale lilac flowers that are decorative in a vase appear from November to April, succeeded by red or orange fruit.

Propagation – autumn or early winter by cuttings; summer by budding.

CULINARY HERBS

Anethum graveolens (annual)

Common name: dill. A herb that's slow growing in fertile, well-drained soil and sun to 1m. This plant suits cottage and herb gardens. It's good for pickling and has scented golden-yellow flowers that appear throughout the year.
Propagation – in spring with seed sown outdoors.

Borago officinalis

Common name: borage. A competitive, spreading, annual herb that grows in sun to 90cm high. It is adaptable to most situations from well-drained soil to soft garden conditions. From September to May, white, blue or pink flowers appear that are edible and good for salads.

Propagation – in spring with seed sown outdoors: self-seeds readily.

Chamaemelum nobile (perennial)

Common name: English chamomile. A spreading evergreen that prefers well-drained soil and is fast growing in sun to 10cm. This useful plant makes a nice herb tea and can also be used as a groundcover or for a lawn. From December to April fragrant white flowers appear.

Propagation – in autumn with seed; in spring by seed and division.

Levisticum officinale (herbaceous perennial), *Ligusticum levisticum*

Common name: lovage. Fast growing in sun and moist, slightly alkaline, well-drained soil to 2m. It adds a celery flavour to salads, and has antiseptic qualities when used medicinally in a bath. From December to February golden-yellow flowers appear.

Propagation – in late summer with seed.

Matricaria recutita (annual), *M. chamomilla*

Common name: German chamomile. Competitive and grows in well-drained soil and sun to 40cm. Because of its desire for lime soils, it competes with and succeeds grasses during dry periods and is often found on gravel roadsides. A double-flowered cultivar is used as a pot plant and in cottage gardens. From October to May white flowers with yellow centres appear.

Propagation – in autumn or spring with seed: self-seeds readily.

Melissa officinalis (perennial)

Common name: lemon balm. A competitive, spreading, semi-dormant herb that prefers moist conditions and fertile well-drained soil. In sun it grows to 1m and from December to May insignificant white or yellow flowers appear. Its green leaves make a refreshing herbal tea.

Propagation – spring by tip cuttings and seed: self-seeds readily.

Mentha piperita (perennial)

Common name: peppermint. A fragrant semi-dormant herb that prefers moist conditions and fertile well-drained soil. In sun it grows to 60cm and creeps through grass vegetation. The leaves make a refreshing herbal tea.

Propagation – in early spring by tip cuttings and division.

Satureja hortensis (annual)

Common name: summer savory. Competitive, prefers fertile, moist but well-drained soil and sun where it grows to 30cm. The leaves are used for seasoning meat and vegetables. From December to February fragrant pink flowers appear.

Propagation – in winter or spring with seed.

Satureja montana (perennial)

Common name: winter savory. A competitive, semi-evergreen that grows in sun and well-drained soil to 30cm. Used to flavour vegetables, especially beans, and eliminates strong odours of cooking cabbage and turnips. From December to February fragrant lavender-coloured flowers appear.

Propagation – winter or spring by seed; summer by softwood cuttings.

Thymus vulgaris (shrub)

Common name: thyme. Strongly scented and evergreen, or deciduous in cold areas. In well-drained soil and sun it is slow growing to 20cm and is used to season red meat, poultry and fish. Flavours vegetables and soups, can be added to herb tea and has antiseptic properties when used medicinally. From September to December purple-mauve flowers appear.

Propagation – in summer take semi-ripe or softwood cuttings.

GRASSES
Semiarundinaria fastuosa, Arundinaria fastuosa

Common name: narihira bamboo. Can be used as an evergreen hedge. In well-drained soil and sun or semi-shade it grows to 6m. It does take some time to establish but once it has, it holds its own and competes with other plants well.

Propagation – in spring or autumn with seed; in spring by division.

CLIMBERS
Hedera helix

Common name: ivy. A spreading, evergreen perennial that prefers well-drained alkaline soil and grows where sun is received for part of the day or in semi-shade. Can be used as a groundcover, although grass can outgrow it on the ground. It is best used to cover structures where it clings firmly

without any competition. It has decorative green and white leaves and golden-yellow flowers. The variegated green and white variety is not so frost hard.

Propagation – late summer by softwood cuttings and rooted layers.

Lathyrus odoratus

Common name: sweet pea. An annual; very fast growing to 2m in fertile, moist but well-drained soil and sun. When it grows in spring it smothers other plants and can get out of hand. From November to May fragrant red, orange, lavender-blue, salmon-pink or purple flowers appear that are decorative in a vase.

Propagation – early spring or early autumn with seed: soak before sowing.

GROUNDCOVERS
Acanthus mollis

Common name: bear's breeches. A competitive, spreading semi-evergreen perennial that is very fast growing in well-drained soil where sun is received for part of the day or in semi-shade. In frost-free areas, it remains evergreen throughout the year. Acanthus tolerates most conditions such as shade, poor soils, clay banks and even dry places. It grows up to 1.2m in the salt zone, even on the beach itself, although it appears battered in this location. Acanthus tends to cluster but needs room to grow robust large, glossy, dark-green leaves. Long thong-like roots wander freely through the surface soil. The plant is slow to start with, needing a good year to take hold in a new location but, once established, it is difficult to remove. Some may regard it as a weed but it has many advantages in the garden landscape. The plant soon forms bold clumps which tend to dominate weeds, and is extremely useful as a groundcover underneath trees, on banks and in difficult places where other plants struggle to survive. Mixed together with agapanthus it makes an ideal groundcover in almost any location and helps to reduce weed competition. During summer, from December to January, green and white flowers tinted with purple appear as a splendid display, contrasting beautifully against its glossy foliage.

Propagation – autumn or spring by seed and division; winter by root cuttings.

Myosotis sylvatica

Common name: forget-me-not. Competitive and spreading perennial that is grown as an annual in moist, well-drained soil, in areas that receive sun for part of the day or in semi-shade. It is a fast-growing groundcover good for the cottage garden in early spring as it naturalises where well situated. From June to November 30cm white, blue or pink flowers appear.

Propagation – in autumn with seed: self-seeds readily.

PERENNIALS
Artemisia stelleriana

Common name: artemisia. A rhizomatous evergreen that is slow growing in sun and well-drained soil to 50cm. Grown mainly as a cottage garden plant, it is suitable for exposed inland or seaside gardens. The foliage is silver in colour and, in summer, sprays of small yellow flower heads appear.

Propagation – summer by semi-ripe or softwood cuttings; spring or autumn by division.

Catananche caerulea (herbaceous)

Common name: Cupid's dart. Grows in well-drained soil and open sunlight to 60cm; compatible with most other cottage garden plants. From December to February purple-blue flowers appear that can be dried for floral decoration.

Propagation – autumn or spring by seed; in winter take root cuttings.

Echinacea purpurea (herbaceous), *Rudbeckia purpurea*

Common name: cone flower. Competitive and grows to 1.2m in well-drained soil and sun; is sometimes used as a medicinal herb. From January to April white, crimson-mauve or rosy-purple flowers appear that each last up to two months.

Propagation – winter to early spring by root cuttings and division.

Erigeron 'Quakeress' (herbaceous)

Common name: fleabane, midsummer aster. Grows well to 60cm in the front row of a mixed perennial border or on small banks in sun and well-drained soil. From December to February lilac-pink flowers with yellow centres appear

– they resemble Michaelmas daisies and are decorative in a vase.

Propagation – spring or autumn by seed and division; early summer take softwood cuttings.

Gypsophila paniculata

Common names: gauze flowers or baby's breath. A semi-deciduous plant that is slow growing in well-drained soil and sun to 60cm. The parent of different forms, the best of which is G. 'Bristol Fairy'. From November to January a veil of white or pink flowers appear that can be used fresh or dried for floral decoration.

Propagation – autumn or spring by seed; summer take softwood cuttings of side shoots; summer or autumn some double-flowered forms can be grafted with outdoor plants: in winter with greenhouse plants.

Heliopsis helianthoides var. scabra (herbaceous)

Common name: orange sunflower. Is easy to grow in sun and well-drained soil to 1.5m. Once established it holds its ground, provided that it is not shaded. The deep-yellow flowers that appear from March to May are very decorative as cut flowers.

Propagation – spring or autumn by seed and division.

Hesperis matronalis (herbaceous)

Common names: dame's violet or sweet rocket. Grows in well-drained soil and sun or semi-shade to 75cm. White, pink or violet flowers appear from January to April. These are very fragrant on humid evenings; good cut flowers.

Propagation – spring or autumn by seed and division; in spring take basal cuttings; in summer take softwood cuttings.

Kniphofia 'Blaze'

Common name: red hot poker. Competitive, semi-deciduous or evergreen and grows to 1.5m in well-drained soil where sun is received for part of the day. Can tolerate most dry situations; an excellent garden plant. From December to March 'Blaze' features coral-red flowers. Creamy-yellow flowers, pink-tinged and shaded pinkish-red to the tips appear on K. 'Jubilee' from December to February.

Propagation – spring by seed and division: selected forms by division only.

Lychnis viscaria (herbaceous)

Common name: campion. Grows competitively in fertile, well-drained soil and sun to 30cm. Suitable for the front of a border or a rock garden. From October to December lightly scented reddish-purple flowers appear.

Propagation – autumn or early spring by seed and division.

Papaver orientalis (herbaceous)

Common name: oriental poppy. Grows in moist but well-drained soil and sunlight or semi-shade to 75cm. There are a number of different varieties and hybrids of this species. From November to January double or single, orange-red, scarlet or cerise-pink flowers with black centres appear that are decorative in a vase.

Propagation – autumn or early spring by seed; in winter by root cuttings.

Silene vulgaris subsp. maritima, Silene cucubalus, S. inflata, S. latifolia

Common name: sea campion. Grows in well-drained soil and sun or semi-shade to 20cm, and is good for a rock garden. From October to December creamy-white flowers appear.

Propagation – spring or early autumn with seed; in spring take softwood cuttings.

Tanacetum coccineum, Chrysanthemum coccineum, Pyrethrum roseum

Common name: pyrethrum. Herbaceous and grows in fertile well-drained soil and open sunlight to 75cm. It is used as a natural deterrent to aphids and unwanted bugs. From October to December white, red or pink flowers appear that are decorative in a vase.

Propagation – in spring by division.

Tanacetum parthenium, Chrysanthemum parthenium, Matricaria parthenium

Common name: feverfew. Is used as a medicinal herb and grows to 75cm in well-drained soil and sun. From November to June white flowers appear.

Propagation – in spring by division.

BULBS

Allium moly

Common name: onion. Is spreading and fast growing to 35cm in fertile well-drained soil and sun. Adds interest to a rock garden or an herbaceous border. From December to February yellow flowers appear.

Propagation – in autumn with seed; in spring by division.

Muscari armeniacum

Common name: grape hyacinth. Dormant during summer and grows in fairly well-drained soil and sun or semi-shade to 25cm. This is a very attractive species for planter boxes or pots. From August to October fragrant white, blue or violet flowers appear; good as cut flowers.

Propagation – in autumn with seed; in spring by division.

Narcissus jonquilla

Common name: jonquil. Dormant during summer, and grows competitively to 30cm in well-drained soil and sun or semi-shade. Very decorative under trees in deciduous woodland areas. From August to November pale yellow flowers appear that, in a vase, fill a room with fragrance.

Propagation – in late summer or autumn with ripe seed; after flowering divide offsets of selected forms every 3-5 years.

Narcissus pseudonarcissus

Common name: Lent lily. Dormant during summer, and grows competitively in well-drained soil and sun or semi-shade to 30cm. It competes well with grass in pasture where it may naturalise, as it is poisonous to stock and not eaten by them. From September to October fragrant yellow flowers appear.

Propagation – in late summer or autumn with ripe seed; after flowering divide offsets of selected forms every 3-5 years.

ANNUALS

Chrysanthemum segetum

Common name: corn marigold. Grows in well-drained soil and sun to 50cm. A splendid summer bedding plant. From January to December fragrant yellow flowers appear that are decorative in a vase.

Propagation – in spring with seed sown directly in flower bed.

Eschscholzia californica

Common name: Californian poppy. Likes an open sunny position. Prefers dry gravel soils where grasses can't compete, such as river valleys and lakeshores. Flushes in spring with yellow and bright orange decorative flowers which open at sunrise and close at sunset.

Propagation – by seed.

Gypsophila elegans

Common names: baby's breath or chalk plant. Grows to 60cm in well-drained soil and sun. From November to January white or pink flowers appear that can be used fresh or dried for floral decoration.

Propagation – spring or autumn by seed; summer by softwood cuttings of side shoots.

Lychnis coronaria

Common name: rose campion. Competitively grows to 60cm in fertile, well-drained soil and sun. A delightful species that naturalises when well situated; even grows between rocks and stones or paving cracks. From October to December white, vivid cerise or pink flowers appear.

Propagation – autumn or early spring by division and seed: self-seeds readily.

Papaver nudicaule

Common name: Iceland poppy. Grows to 90cm as an annual in moist but well-drained soil and sun or semi-shade, but does not like to be transplanted once germinated. Lovely plant for colour in late winter; from August to September white, apricot, yellow or salmon-pink flowers appear that are decorative in a vase.

Propagation – in late summer with seed: self-seeds readily.

Papaver rhoeas

Common names: corn poppy or field poppy. Grows up to 1m in moist but well-drained soil and sun or semi-shade. Delightful summer bedding plants, as from December to January white, scarlet-red or pink flowers, without black markings, appear.

Propagation – in spring or autumn with seed: self-seeds readily.

Temperature drops to -15°C

Inland wind: light (*)
Coastal and salt wind: light (*)

PERENNIALS OR BIENNIALS

Angelica pachycarpa
Common name: angelica. A competitive plant used as an ornamental and sometimes culinary herb. It is fast growing to 60cm in moist but well-drained soil which receives sun for part of the day or in semi-shade. In frost-free areas its large glossy leaves continue growing through winter. From November to January greenish-white flowers appear.
Propagation – with ripe seed.

ANNUALS

Silene coeli-rosa, Agrostemma coeli-rosa, Lychnis coeli-rosa, Viscaria elegans
Common name: viscaria. Competitive and moderately fast growing in fertile, well-drained soil and sun or semi-shade. Makes an attractive groundcover, though grasses may invade it. From December to February, 50cm, white, blue, or pink flowers appear.
Propagation – in spring or early autumn with seed.

Temperature drops to -15°C

Inland wind: severe (***)
Coastal and salt wind: plants need complete shelter

TREES

Chamaecytisus palmensis, Cytisus proliferus
Common names: tagasaste or tree lucerne. A small, very fast-growing, competitive evergreen up to 5m. Though not recommended to be planted near the sea, it does grow in coastal localities in complete shelter from salt wind,and is often seen growing in waste places, river beds or hillsides where there is well-drained soil and open sunlight. It is a quick shelter plant against wind and is used in rural areas particularly as hedging and for a forage crop or for honey production. It also competes against gorse and adds to soil fertility as it is a legume. Other tree species can be inter-planted amongst tree lucerne for protection. From August to November white flowers appear.
Propagation – in autumn with seed; in summer take semi-ripe cuttings.

SHRUBS

Hebe cupressoides
Common name: whipcord hebe. An evergreen that is slow growing up to 2m in well-drained soil and sun. Grown for its decorative cypress-like, fine green foliage; attractive in a shrub border or rock garden. On mature plants tiny, pale lilac flowers appear as a dense mass from November to January.
Propagation – in summer take semi-ripe cuttings.

GRASSES

Aciphylla ferox (monocotyledon)
Common name: fierce Spaniard, spiky Spaniard. Grows naturally in alpine areas to 60cm and can be used in frosted climates.
Propagation – late summer or early spring by fresh seed.

Chionochloa flavescens (monocotyledon)
Maori name: haumata haumata. Common names: broad-leaved snow tussock or dwarf toetoe. A competitive, evergreen New Zealand native grass. It grows to 1m in most soils in situations where it is sunny for part of the day or in semi-shade, and survives dry seasons. The grass is wind-tolerant but does not like salt, growing naturally in sub-alpine scrub and grasslands. Attractive as a garden specimen and also in group plantings mixed with ornamental flaxes,

where the foliage colour and textures combine well. The lush dark-green leaves are paler on the underside; from December to February there are thick showy plumes of green flowers that develop into light-brown seed-heads.
Propagation – in spring by division; in spring or autumn with seed.

Chionochloa rubra spp. *cuprea* (monocotyledon)
Common name: red tussock. An evergreen New Zealand native grass that grows naturally in alpine areas in the snow zone, in peat soil types with sun; reaches 1–1.5m. It is brown-orange in summer and brightens to reddish-orange in winter. Now available commercially grown as spp. *cuprea*.
Propagation – in spring with seed; in spring or autumn by division.

Chionochloa pallens (monocotyledon)
Common name: mid-ribbed snow tussock. Grows to 1m tall in a well-drained moist soil; the leaves appear light green to yellowish. Grows naturally in frosted sub-alpine areas. Ideal in an alpine garden.
Propagation – by seed or division after flowering.

Chionochloa rigida (monocotyledon)
Common name: narrow-leafed snow tussock grass. Tawny green or gold, it tolerates dry conditions and grows to 1m tall. Flower stems can be 1.5m long. A South Island alpine grass that will endure freezing.
Propagation – by seed or division after flowering.

Festuca novae-zelandiae (monocotyledon)
Common name: fescue tussock, hard tussock. A native grass that grows to 60–70cm tall and will tolerate drought and exposure to wind. Found naturally as a high country grass with rigid, upright, pointed leaves. New green foliage intermingles with spent brown growth. Not used in coastal areas.
Propagation – by seed and division.

Uncinia egmontiana (monocotyledon)
Maori names: matau, matau ririki. Common names: hook sedge. An attractive native green grass that turns reddish brown in winter. Forms tussocks of 40cm tall in a well drained moist soil. Decorative foliage.
Propagation – by seed.

Temperature drops to -15°C

Inland wind: light (*)
Coastal and salt wind: plants need complete shelter

TREES

Syringa vulgaris
Common name: lilac. A small deciduous tree grown as an ornamental specimen in fertile well-drained soil and sun to 5m. This lovely tree favours a frosty climate and the fragrant white, pink or lavender flowers that occur from October to November are very ornamental in a vase.
Propagation – in summer by cuttings and grafting.

SHRUBS

Chaenomeles speciosa, C. maulei
Common name: japonica. Deciduous and grows in well-drained soil and sun to 2.5m. It is a hardy bush, enduring most situations, and from September to October red flowers appear.
Propagation – in autumn with seed; summer take softwood cuttings: selected forms by cuttings only.

Hamamelis mollis
Common name: witch hazel. Deciduous and grows to 4m in fertile, well-drained, peaty, acid soil and sun or semi-shade. From August to October fragrant orange-yellow or yellow flowers that are decorative in a vase appear on bare stems, and in autumn the leaves turn a purplish colour before they fall.
Propagation – autumn by seed; winter by grafting: late summer by budding; in summer by softwood cuttings: selected forms by softwood cuttings only.

List of species

Pieris japonica
Common name: lily of the valley. An evergreen that, in moist, peaty or acid soil and partial sun or shade, is slow growing to 1.75m. Forms a compact bush with soft, fine foliage. A great specimen plant; in November white-pink flowers appear.

Propagation – in summer take semi-ripe or soft-tip cuttings.

Potentilla fruticosa
Common name: finger bush. Deciduous and grows in well-drained soil and sun to 1m. From November to February yellow flowers appear, providing summer colour for the rock garden.

Propagation – in autumn with seed; in summer take softwood or greenwood cuttings.

Rhododendron luteum
Common name: azalea. Deciduous and slow growing to 1.5m where sun is received for part of the day or in shade, and in neutral to acid soil with very good drainage. A very good plant for woodland gardens. In August showy red or yellow flowers appear.

Propagation – in late summer by semi-ripe cuttings, layering and grafting.

Thuja occidentalis 'Rheingold' (conifer)
Common names: American arborvitae or white cedar. An aromatic, semi-prostrate evergreen that grows to 2m in any well-drained soil in sun or semi-shade. Very suitable for shrub border, heather, perennial or rock garden. Holds its shape well and is excellent for colour; it has golden-yellow foliage that turns golden-bronze in winter.

Propagation – late autumn to late winter: take cuttings from young plants or stratify seed.

Viburnum davidii
Common name: viburnum. An evergreen that grows in well-drained soil up to 1.2m where sun is received for part of the day or in semi-shade. Its dark-green leaves are useful in the shrub border or for foliage contrasts. From November to December small white flowers appear, succeeded by mid-blue berries.

Propagation – in autumn with seed; in summer by semi-ripe cuttings.

Viburnum opulus 'Sterile'
Common names: Guelder rose or snowball tree. Deciduous and slow growing to 4m in moist but well-drained soil and sun or semi-shade. Profuse, fragrant, hydrangea-like flowers that are green at first, then turn white, occur from November to December, followed by colourful autumn foliage; very decorative specimen.

Propagation – in autumn with seed; in summer take softwood cuttings.

Viburnum X burkwoodii
Common name: viburnum. Semi-evergreen and grows in moist but well-drained soil and sun or semi-shade to 2.5m. Useful for foliage contrasts as the older leaves assume rich orange-red and crimson tonings during late autumn and winter before they fall. From September to November fragrant pinkish-white flowers that fade to white appear.

Propagation – in autumn with seed; in summer by semi-ripe cuttings.

Weigela florida
Common name: apple blossom. Deciduous and grows in fertile, well-drained soil and open sunlight to 2.5m. It is used as a specimen or in cluster planting, and from September to November red or pink blossoms appear.

Propagation – in summer take softwood cuttings.

CULINARY HERBS
Carum carvi (biennial)
Common name: caraway. Competitive and grows to 90cm in well-drained soil and sun. From December to January white flowers appear, followed by seeds which add a rich flavour in baking and cooking.

Propagation – in spring or autumn with seed: self-seeds readily.

Pimpinella anisum (annual)
Common name: anise. Grows in fertile, well-drained soil and sun to 60cm. From December to January white flowers appear, followed by seeds with a penetrating aroma which are used to add culinary flavour.

Propagation – in spring with seed after last frost.

Rheum rhabarbarum (perennial)
Common name: rhubarb. Competitive and grows in moist but well-drained soil and sun or semi-shade. Has greenish-red leaves that spread out to 400mm, and reddish stems which are used to make tasty puddings. Has been used medicinally as a laxative for children.

Propagation – in spring or autumn by seed and division.

GROUNDCOVERS
Ajuga reptans
Common name: bugle. A semi-evergreen perennial which grows to 15cm in any soil where sun is received for part of the day or in shade. It makes a good groundcover but bigger weeds may invade it. Blue flowers appear at any time through the year.

Propagation – in spring by division.

Euphorbia polychroma, E. epithymoides
Common names: cushion euphorbia, milkweed, or spurge. This perennial grows to 50cm in fertile, moist but well-drained soil; useful filler in any sunny or semi-shaded border. From September to October its purple-green leaves turn bright sulphur-yellow; very colourful in spring.

Propagation – in spring or autumn with seed; in early spring or early autumn by division; in summer or spring take basal cuttings.

Iberis sempervirens
Common name: candytuft. A spreading evergreen sub-shrub that grows in well-drained soil and sun to 20cm; ideal for walls and rockeries. From September to November white flowers appear.

Propagation – in autumn with seed.

Mentha pulegium
Common name: pennyroyal. A fragrant, spreading evergreen perennial that grows to 30cm in fertile, moist but well-drained soil and sun. It is sometimes used as a medicinal herb and makes a pleasant addition to lawns; when walked on it gives off a rich peppermint scent. From November to May tiny purple flowers appear.

Propagation – early spring by tip cuttings, division and seed: self-seeds readily.

Viola odorata
Common name: sweet violet. A spreading, semi-evergreen, rhizomatous perennial that grows in moist, fertile, well-drained soil where sun is received for part of the day or in semi-shade. Forms a dense groundcover that competes well against larger plants. From July to October fragrant lavender, pink or violet flowers appear.

Propagation – spring by softwood cuttings; late summer by division; spring or autumn by separating runners and seed: self-seeds prolifically.

PERENNIALS
Anemone X hybrida (herbaceous), A. japonica
Common name: Japanese windflower. Slow growing to 1m in moist but well-drained soil and in either sun, semi-shade or shade. Suitable in woodland or wild gardens or for the herbaceous border. From February to April white, rose or pink flowers appear in either single or double forms that are decorative in a vase.

Propagation – in late summer with ripe seed; spring by division; in winter take root cuttings.

Aquilegia vulgaris (herbaceous)
Common name: granny bonnets. Slow growing to 1m in moist but well-drained soil where sun is received for part of the day or in semi-shade. Once established they reappear every year, making an ideal woodland or garden plant. From October to November white, red, blue, pink, or violet flowers appear.

Propagation – in spring or autumn with seed.

Aruncus dioicus (herbaceous), A. sylvester, Spiraea aruncus
Common name: goat's beard. Grows to 2m in fertile, moist but well-drained soil where sun is received for part of the day or in semi-shade. At home in

any wild or woodland garden near a pond or creek. From October to December creamy-white flowers appear that are decorative in a vase.

Propagation – in autumn with seed; in spring or autumn by division.

Aster amellus (herbaceous)
Common name: Italian aster. Grows to 50cm in sun or semi-shade in fertile, well-drained soil with adequate moisture. Have been used historically as a medicinal 'cure-all'. They flower for a long time and are good for cutting; from December to May daisy-like, yellow-centred, pink, lavender-blue, violet or purple flowers appear.

Propagation – spring by softwood cuttings; late autumn or spring by division.

Aster ericoides (herbaceous)
Common name: farewell summer. Grows to 75cm in sun or semi-shade in fertile, well-drained soil with adequate moisture. From March to May white, rosy-mauve, pale pink or lavender flowers appear. In the same garden conditions, Aster X frikartii grows to a similar height but flowers earlier; from January to May lavender-blue, daisy-like blooms with yellowish-green centres appear. All asters are good cut flowers.

Propagation – spring take softwood cuttings; in late autumn or spring by division.

Aster novae-belgii (herbaceous)
Common names: Easter daisy, Michaelmas daisy or New York daisy. Parent of many hybrids; grows in sun or semi-shade and fertile, well-drained soil with adequate moisture to 1m. Lovely for autumn colour, as from March to May lightly scented, white, rosy-red, mid-blue, pale blue, violet-blue, lavender-blue, creamy-pink, deep-pink or mauve-pink flowers appear that are decorative in a vase.

Propagation – spring take softwood cuttings; late autumn or spring by division.

Aster tongolensis (herbaceous)
Common names: Easter daisy or Michaelmas daisy. Grows in sun or semi-shade to 50cm in fertile, well-drained soil with adequate moisture; originally from China. From November to January pale-blue flowers with orange centres appear; decorative in a vase.

Propagation – in spring take softwood cuttings; in late autumn or spring by division.

Buphthalmum salicifolium (herbaceous)
Common name: yellow oxeye. Has a spreading habit and grows in poor, well-drained soil and sun to 60cm. From December to February yellow flowers appear; decorative in a vase.

Propagation – in spring or autumn with seed; in autumn by division: can be invasive.

Centaurea dealbata (herbaceous)
Common name: knapweed. Grows in any well-drained soil and sun to 1m. A very leafy plant useful in any mixed border. It has grey foliage and from November to January lilac-pink flowers appear; decorative in a vase.

Propagation – autumn, late winter or spring by seed and division.

Centaurea macrocephala (herbaceous)
Common name: globe centaury. A handsome plant that grows in any well-drained soil and sun to 1m. From November to January outstanding golden-yellow, thistle-like flowers appear that can be dried for floral decoration.

Propagation – autumn, late winter or spring by seed and division.

Chelone obliqua (herbaceous)
Common name: turtle-head. Grows to 1m in moist soils and areas that receive sun for part of the day or in semi-shade. A delicate addition to the cottage garden or herbaceous border. From December to January lilac-pink flowers appear; decorative in a vase.

Propagation – in autumn or spring by seed and division; in summer take soft-tip cuttings.

Coreopsis grandiflora (herbaceous)
Common names: calliopsis or tickseed. Very easy to grow to 75cm in fertile, well-drained soil and sun. Forms very satisfying strong clumps; from

October to April golden-yellow flowers in single or double form appear; decorative in a vase.

Propagation – in spring or summer take softwood cuttings.

Eryngium tripartitum (herbaceous)
Common name: sea holly. Grows in fertile, well-drained soil and sun to 1m; adds interest to a mixed or herbaceous borders. From December to April blue or violet-blue flowers appear that can be used fresh or dried for floral decoration.

Propagation – with ripe seed; in winter take root cuttings; in spring by division: selected forms by division only.

Filipendula rubra (herbaceous), F. venusta, Spiraea lobata
Common names: meadowsweet or Queen of the prairie. In moist or swampy soils and open sunlight or semi-shade grows to 1.8m. Ideal for around a pond. Has attractive fern-like foliage and from December to January, very long lasting, lacy, peach-pink flowers appear. F. vulgaris, dropwort or lace plant, also known as F. hexapetala or Spiraea filipendula, grows in moist soils and open sunlight or semi-shade to 60cm. This is the only filipendula that can tolerate some dryness. Suits a site that gets both very boggy and dry seasonally. From December to January ivory-white flowers appear; decorative in a vase.

Propagation – in spring with seed; from autumn to winter by division.

Gaura lindheimeri (herbaceous)
Common name: butterfly flower. Is competitive and grows in well-drained soil and sun to 1.2m. From November to April, for 2-3 months continuously, profuse soft-pink flowers appear; a great cottage garden plant.

Propagation – autumn or spring by seed; in summer by semi-ripe or softwood cuttings.

Geum X borisii (herbaceous)
Common name: avens. Semi-deciduous and grows in moist but well-drained soil and sun to 30cm. The flowering period can be extended by removing old or faded blooms. Has foliage like strawberry leaves, and from November to March colourful orange-red flowers appear; G. 'Lady Stratheden' blooms yellow.

Propagation – in autumn by seed or division.

Helenium autumnale (herbaceous)
Common name: sneezeweed. Grows easily in any well-drained soil and sun to 1.5m. The parent of many varieties that are all valuable in garden borders for their bright colours. From December to April crimson, coppery-orange or yellow flowers appear; decorative in a vase.

Propagation – autumn or spring by seed; in spring divide young off-shoots.

Helianthus X multiflorus (herbaceous)
Common names: little sunflower or perennial sunflower. Grows in fertile, well-drained soil and sun to 1m. Many spectacular cultivars are available for colourful displays from February to March when reddish-brown or yellow flowers appear; decorative in a vase or good for drying.

Propagation – in autumn or early spring by division.

Helleborus orientalis
Common name: winter rose. An evergreen that grows to 45cm in fertile, moist but well-drained soil, in semi-shade or where sun is received for part of the day. A handsome plant for the cottage garden; from August to October white, wine-red, greyish-pink or soft-pink flowers appear that are decorative in a vase.

Propagation – with ripe seed; in autumn or early spring by division.

Hosta spp. (herbaceous)
Common name: plantain lily. Grows to 75cm in fertile, moist but well-drained soil where it is sunny for part of the day or in shade. H. crispula makes a good groundcover under trees, forming neat clumps with large rounded leaves during summer. From December to January decorative variegated green and white leaves appear.

Propagation – in early spring by division.

Liatris spicata (herbaceous), L. callilepis
Common name: gay feather. In well-drained soil and open sunlight grows to 60cm. From March to May unusual white or lavender flowers opening from the top downwards appear; decorative in a vase.

Propagation – autumn or spring with seed; early spring by division.

Limonium latifolium
Common name: statice. Grows in well-drained soil and sun to 30cm. The misty lavender-blue flowers that appear from November to February add delicate colour to any garden and can be used fresh or dried for floral decoration.

Propagation – in autumn or early spring with seed; spring by division; in late winter take root cuttings.

Macleaya microcarpa (herbaceous)
Common name: plume poppy. Grows in fertile, well-drained soil and sun to 2m. Can be a prolific grower in the most favoured situation but surplus roots can easily be removed in winter if too invasive. From January to February bronzy-yellow or pink flowers appear.

Propagation – early spring by division; in winter take root cuttings.

Monarda didyma (herbaceous)
Common names: bee balm or bergamot. Grows to 1m in moist soil where it is sunny for part of the day or in semi-shade. Bergamot takes some time to establish. From December to March scented white, red, salmon-pink or purple flowers appear that are sometimes used medicinally.

Propagation – in spring with seed; late winter to early spring by division: selected forms by division only.

Nymphaea alba
Common name: water lily. Competitive, deciduous and grows in water in poor soil and open sunlight. Does not thrive in running water such as streams; needs still pond conditions. From November to March fragrant creamy-white flowers with golden centres appear.

Propagation – in spring or early summer with seed and by dividing young sprouting plants.

Paeonia officinalis (herbaceous)
Common name: peony. Slow growing; best suited to a cold winter climate; in fertile, moist but well-drained soil where sun is received for part of the day or in semi-shade reaches 60cm. From December to February scented white, crimson or pink flowers appear that are very decorative in a vase.

Propagation – in autumn or early spring by division of tubers; in autumn with seed: can take 3 years to germinate.

Phlomis russeliana, P. viscosa
Common name: Jerusalem sage. Grows in fertile, well-drained soil and sun to 1m. From November to December lightly scented yellow flowers appear; is spent by Christmas when the flowers should be cut back. An interesting and decorative plant for the cottage garden and the vase.

Propagation – in autumn with seed; in spring by division.

Physostegia virginiana (herbaceous)
Common names: false dragonhead or obedient plant. Grows to 1m in fertile, moist but well-drained soil and sun or semi-shade. If well positioned and left untouched in the garden can spread rapidly into a dense, showy mass of colour from February to April when white or pink flowers appear; decorative in a vase.

Propagation – spring by division and ripe seed: self-seeds readily.

Platycodon grandiflorus (herbaceous)
Common names: balloon flower or Chinese bellflower. Grows in sandy soil and sun to 60cm; tolerates dry conditions. Does not like either wet feet or transplanting. From November to February white or blue flowers appear; decorative in a vase.

Propagation – autumn or spring by seed; in spring by division; in summer by basal cuttings of non-flowering shoots with attached root.

Ranunculus acris 'Flore Pleno' (herbaceous)
Common names: double meadow buttercup, giant buttercup or yellow bachelor's buttons. Grows to 60cm in moist but well-drained soil and sun or semi-shade, and makes a very good spring bedding display. From September to November small yellow flowers appear; decorative in a vase.

Propagation – with ripe seed; in spring or autumn by division.

Rudbeckia laciniata (herbaceous)
Common name: cone flower. Grows in well-drained soil and sun to 2m. Makes a good backdrop for the summer garden. From January to March yellow flowers appear. *R. nitida* provides autumn colour with pale yellow flowers from March to April. Decorative in a vase.

Propagation – autumn or spring by seed and division; spring by cuttings.

Salvia X superba, S. nemorosa, S. virgata var. nemorosa
Common name: sage. Semi-deciduous, competitive and grows in fertile, well-drained soil and sun to 60cm. It is a great cottage garden plant; from March to June when most other plants are dormant, scented pale-blue flowers appear that are decorative in a vase.

Propagation – summer or spring by softwood cuttings; spring by division.

Scabiosa caucasica (herbaceous), S. stellata
Common name: pin-cushion flower. In fertile, alkaline, well-drained soil and sun grows to 60cm. From November to March white, violet-blue or lavender-blue flowers appear that can be used fresh; the seed pods can also be dried for floral decoration.

Propagation – autumn with seed; in summer take cuttings of young basal growth; spring by division.

Solidago canadensis (herbaceous)
Common name: goldenrod. In well-drained soil and sun grows to 1.5m. From February to May golden-yellow flowers appear that can be used fresh or dried for floral decoration.

Propagation – in autumn or spring by division.

X Solidaster luteus (herbaceous), X S. hybridus
Common name: solidaster. Grows to 60cm in well-drained soil and sun or semi-shade. The parent of many bright hybrids suitable for any mixed border. From March to May yellow flowers appear; a useful addition to autumn floral arrangements.

Propagation – in autumn or spring by division.

Thalictrum delavayi (herbaceous)
Common name: meadow rue. Is slow growing to 1.5m in moist but well-drained soil where it is sunny for part of the day or in semi-shade. It has soft, fern-like foliage and from December to January delicate but very attractive purple flowers.

Propagation – in autumn with ripe seed; in spring by division.

Veronica longifolia (herbaceous)
Common name: speedwell. Competitive and good for a wild garden. Grows in well-drained soil and sun to 1.2m. From December to February blue flowers appear; decorative in a vase.

Propagation – in autumn or spring with seed; in early spring or early autumn by division; in summer take softwood and semi-ripe cuttings.

Viola cornuta
Common name: horned violet. Evergreen and grows to 20cm in fertile, moist but well-drained soil in semi-shade or where sunny for part of the day. From October to April scented white, yellow, blue or lavender flowers appear that are decorative in a little vase.

Propagation – in autumn or spring with seed; late summer divide rhizomes; in spring take softwood cuttings.

BULBS
Crocus spp.
Common name: crocus. Slow growing, in well-drained soil where sun is received for part of the day or in semi-shade. Very attractive under trees in woodland locations. Tiny 10cm white, magenta-red, orange, yellow, blue, pink or purple flowers appear from August to October; decorative in a tiny vase.

Propagation – early autumn by seed and dividing corms where present.

Galanthus nivalis
Common name: snowdrop. Dormant during summer and grows to 15cm in moist, fertile soils where sun is received for part of the day, or shade. Lovely planted *en masse* under deciduous trees. From August to October white flowers appear; decorative in a vase.

Propagation – in spring, divide after flowering; in late summer or autumn divide dormant bulbs.

Lilium martagon

Common name: lily. Not so happy in a warmer climate where it should be semi-shaded; prefers a cool climate where it grows from 1-2m in fertile, well-drained soil and sun. The scented white, wine-red, pink or purplish-black flowers that appear from December to February are decorative in a vase.

Propagation – in spring or autumn with seed; in autumn with stem bulbs; in summer with bulb scales.

Tulipa spp.

Common name: tulip. Grows in well-drained soil and sun to 45cm. Vibrant bedding displays can be achieved, as flowering times are very reliable. From October to November white, red, apricot, yellow, lilac, pink or purple flowers appear; decorative in a vase.

Propagation – in spring or autumn with seed; in autumn by division of bulbs: selected forms by division only.

GRASSES

Uncinia uncinata (monocotyledon)

Maori names: kamu, matau-a-Maui. Common names: hook sedge. A dense native grass that grows to 40cm tall. It is grown for its decorative reddish-brown foliage in the open sun, or green in semi-shade; preferring a sheltered position. Seeds are dark brown and may cling to socks and skin.

Propagation – by seed.

ANNUALS

Centaurea cyanus

Common name: cornflower. Fast growing in any well-drained soil and sun to 1m. Naturalises in the garden. From December to February white, purple, rose-pink, blue or soft-pink flowers appear; decorative in a vase.

Propagation – autumn, late winter or spring with seed.

Consolida ambigua, C. ajacis, Delphinium consolida

Common name: larkspur. Easy to grow in fertile, well-drained soil and sun to 1.2m. From November to February white, blue, pink or purple flowers that look like delphiniums appear; can be used fresh or dried for floral decoration.

Propagation – in autumn or early spring with seed.

Iberis amara

Common name: candytuft. Fast growing in well-drained soil and sun to 30cm. Colourful edging for formal gardens, and good for rockeries. From September to November fragrant white flowers appear. *I. umbellata* produces white, pink or purple-pink flowers that look well in a vase.

Propagation – in autumn with seed.

Lunaria annua, L. biennis

Common name: honesty. Grows to 75cm in well-drained soil where sun is received for part of the day or in semi-shade. It is a good woodland plant, forming attractive groups. The white or purple flowers that appear from September to March can be used fresh, or the seed pods dried for floral decoration.

Propagation – with seed: self-seeds prolifically.

Primula flaccida, P. nutans

Common name: primula. A perennial that grows as an annual to 30cm in moist, peaty soil where sun is received for part of the day or in semi-shade. Ideal for under deciduous trees in woodland areas. Fragrant mid-blue or lavender flowers appear from August to December.

Propagation – spring, early summer or autumn with ripe seed.

Primula X *polyantha*

Common name: polyanthus. Grown as an annual to 30cm in fertile, moist but well-drained soil where sun is received for part of the day or in semi-shade. A good bedding plant that can last up to 3 years and flower right through winter in mild areas. From August to October scented white, red, yellow or pink flowers appear.

Propagation – spring, early summer or autumn with ripe seed.

Rudbeckia hirta

Common name: black-eyed-Susan. A perennial grown as an annual or biennial in well-drained soil and open sunlight to 1m. The parent of many

hybrids that are all good for adding rich colour to any garden. From January to April yellow, gold or orange flowers appear that are decorative in a vase.

Propagation – in autumn or spring by seed and division; in spring take cuttings.

Salvia horminum

Common name: sage. Prefers fertile, well-drained soil and sun or semi-shade where it grows to 50cm. Makes a great bedding plant en masse for ornamental colour. From March to April white, pink or purple flowers appear that can be used fresh or dried for floral decoration.

Propagation – in spring with seed sown outdoors.

Scabiosa atropurpurea

Common name: pin-cushion flower. Grows in fertile, alkaline, well-drained soil and sun to 1m. The scented white, dark-red, blue or pink blooms that appear from November to March can be used fresh or dried for floral decoration; cutting and dead-heading also prolongs flowering period.

Propagation – in spring with seed.

Viola tricolor

Common names: heartsease or wild pansy. A perennial grown as an annual in fertile, moist but well-drained soil and sun or semi-shade. It has been used as a medicinal herb, and from October to May scented, creamy-white, red, mustard and black, and yellow or violet flowers 15cm high appear.

Propagation – with ripe seed; late summer by division: selected forms by division only.

Viola X *wittrockiana*

Common name: pansy. A perennial grown as an annual to 20cm in fertile, moist but well-drained soil where sun is received for part of the day or in semi-shade. From October to February, scented, creamy-white, orange, yellow or violet flowers appear; invaluable for bedding colour and very cute in a small vase.

Propagation – in autumn or spring with seed; in spring take softwood cuttings; late summer by division: selected forms by division only.

Temperature drops to -15°C
Inland wind: plants need complete shelter
Coastal and salt wind: plants need complete shelter

PERENNIALS

Astilbe arendsii (herbaceous)

Common name: false spiraea. Easily grown to 1m in rich, moist soil where it is sunny for part of the day or in shade. Ideal in areas that are not too dry, in bogs or damp depressions or at the edge of a pond. From December to January white, dark-red, apricot, salmon-pink or lavender flowers appear that can be used fresh or dried for floral decoration.

Propagation – autumn by seed; late winter to spring or autumn by root division.

Campanula glomerata (herbaceous)

Common name: bellflower. Grows to 60cm in moist but well-drained soil where sun is received for part of the day or in semi-shade. They will flower over a longer season if, as soon as the individual flowers show signs of fading, they are removed from the stems. From December to February violet-blue flowers appear; decorative in a vase. *C. persicifolia* produces 1m high white or blue flowers that are also good for cutting.

Propagation – in autumn or spring with seed; in summer or spring take softwood or basal cuttings.

Delphinium elatum (herbaceous)

Common name: delphinium. Grows in fertile, well-drained soil and sun to 1.5m. Parent of many hybrids that make a wonderful display, and can have two sessions of flowering in one season if they are cut at the base of the stem before they seed. From November to February white, rose-pink, blue, bluish-pink or pale-lilac flowers appear; can be used fresh or dried for floral decoration.

Propagation – autumn or spring with seed; in spring by division and take basal cuttings of young shoots; selected forms by cuttings only.

Lythrum salicaria (herbaceous)
Common name: loosestrife. Reaches 1m in moist or wet soil where it is sunny for part of the day or in semi-shade; easy to transplant during winter. Ideal near any freshwater bog or in a wild garden. Several forms are derived from this species and through summer their rose-red, pink or rose-purple flowers create wonderful colourful displays; blooms can be used fresh or dried for floral decoration.

Propagation – in autumn or spring by seed and division: selected forms by division only.

BULBS
Iris reticulata
Common name: iris. Grows in moist, well-drained soil and sun to 30cm; good for any mixed flower border. From October to November scented blue or purple flowers appear that are very decorative in a vase. *I. xiphium* hybrids, Dutch or Spanish irises, grow to 80cm and display white, yellow, bronze, blue, deep-violet or purple flowers; also good for cutting.

Propagation – in autumn with seed; late summer by division of offsets or rhizomes: selected forms by division only.

ANNUALS
Alcea rosea, Althaea rosea
Common name: hollyhock. In well-drained soil and sun grows to 1.5m; often more successful close to a wall. From January to March many double and single varieties of creamy-white, red, salmon-pink or purple-mauve flowers appear; very decorative in a vase.

Propagation – in spring or late summer with seed.

Campanula medium
Common name: Canterbury bell. Grows to 1m as an annual in moist but well-drained soil and sun or semi-shade. When planting a border of proudly standing bells, they need to be spaced 30cm apart. From December to February enchanting displays of white, lavender-blue, pink or violet-blue flowers appear; decorative in a vase.

Propagation – in autumn or spring with seed; in summer or spring take softwood or basal cuttings.

Clarkia amoena, Godetia
Common names: farewell spring or satin flower. In well-drained soil and sun grows to 60cm. From December to February white, red, salmon-pink or lavender flowers appear; colourful bedding plants; last 2-3 weeks or more in a vase.

Propagation – in spring or early autumn with seed.

Helianthus annuus
Common name: sunflower. Is very fast growing in well-drained soil and sun to 2.5m. From January to March reddish-brown, bronze or yellow flowers appear. This stunning plant is also grown for its seeds from which oil is extracted; the seeds are also eaten whole.

Propagation – in autumn or early spring by division.

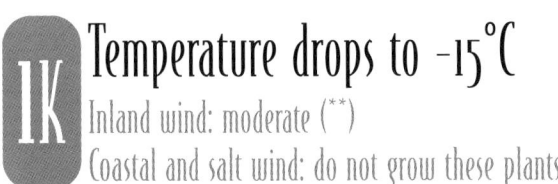

Temperature drops to -15°C
Inland wind: moderate (**)
Coastal and salt wind: do not grow these plants

TREES
Cedrus atlantica 'Glauca' (conifer)
Common name: blue atlas cedar. An evergreen, useful as a compact, large, handsome specimen tree or for shelter when it has attained its mature height which takes a full lifetime. In sun and most well-drained soils it is very slow growing to 20m, and has decorative, needle-like, silver blue-green leaves.

Propagation – late autumn to late winter: take cuttings from young plants or stratify seed.

Cedrus deodara (conifer)
Common name: Himalayan cedar. A relative of *C. atlantica,* with similar growth preferences but different in appearance. It has a symmetrical shape, with decorative, needle-like foliage of a faded green or grey-green colour. A handsome evergreen useful as a large specimen tree; becomes even more attractive with age. In sun and most well-drained soils it is slow growing to 30m. Like other cedars, is a welcome addition to shelter belts and cluster planting, especially in colder regions, where the winter foliage protects deciduous trees.

Propagation – late autumn to late winter: take cuttings from young plants or stratify seed.

Chamaecyparis lawsoniana 'Silver Queen' (conifer)
Common name: Lawson cypress. An evergreen useful as a specimen tree or for shelter and hedging. In sun and most well-drained soils it is slow growing to 8m. It has fragrant, very decorative silvery-green foliage.

Propagation – late autumn to late winter: take cuttings from young plants or stratify seed.

Chamaecyparis pisifera 'Boulevard' (conifer)
Common name: Sawara cypress. Another evergreen useful as a large specimen or for shelter. In sun and most well-drained soils it is slow growing to 30m. It also has fragrant, very decorative grey-blue foliage.

Propagation – late autumn to late winter: take cuttings from young plants or stratify seed.

Dacrycarpus dacrydioides (conifer), Podocarpus dacrydioides
Maori name: kahikatea. Common name: white pine. An evergreen used for shelter; slow growing to 36m in moist or wet soil where there is sun for part of the day. It has dark-green and bronze-coloured leaves.

Propagation – late autumn to late winter: take cuttings from young plants or stratify seed.

Eucalyptus leucoxylon
Common name: pink-flowering yellow gum. A competitive, large, aromatic, evergreen tree. It is fast growing to 12m in well-drained soil and sun. From June to November pink flowers appear.

Propagation – in spring or autumn with seed.

Larix decidua (conifer)
Common name: European larch. A large, deciduous tree grown as a specimen or for shelter and hedging. In sun and most well-drained soils it grows to 30m. Larix mingled with other conifers looks very attractive; the usually green leaves turn yellow-brown before they fall in autumn.

Propagation – with seed after stratification; between late autumn and late winter take cuttings from young plants.

Liquidamber styraciflua
Common name: sweet gum. A large, deciduous tree that grows to 30m in sun or semi-shade and fertile, moist but well-drained soil; a very decorative specimen. In autumn the usually glossy dark-green leaves colour orange, red and purple before they fall.

Propagation – in autumn with seed; in spring by budding.

Malus floribunda
Common name: crab apple. A deciduous specimen tree that grows to 5m in any but waterlogged soil and in sun or semi-shade. From September to November decorative red or pink flowers appear, followed by yellow crab apples.

Propagation – in mid-winter by grafting; in late summer by budding.

Metasequoia glyptostroboides (conifer)
Common name: redwood. A large, deciduous specimen tree that grows to 17m in sun and any well-drained soil. In autumn the usually soft green leaves turn yellow, pink and bronze-brown.

Propagation – late autumn to late winter: take cuttings from young plants or stratify seed.

Populus nigra
Common names: black poplar or Lombardy poplar. A large, competitive, deciduous tree used for shelter. In sun and moist but well-drained soil it is

fast growing to 25m; in autumn the green leaves turn bronze and golden-yellow before they drop.

Propagation – in winter take hardwood cuttings.

Prunus avium
Common name: sweet cherry. A large, deciduous, spreading specimen that grows in sun and any but waterlogged soil to 15m. From September to November scented white flowers appear.

P. serrulata 'Kanzan', Japanese flowering cherry, grows in the same way to 8m and produces scented, white or deep-pink flowers; decorative in a vase.

Propagation – autumn with seed; in winter by hardwood cuttings; from spring to autumn by grafting and budding: selected forms by grafting and budding only.

Salix alba var. vitellina
Common name: golden willow. Large, competitive, deciduous tree useful for shelter. In sun and any but very dry soil it grows to 25m. The usually green leaves turn orange-yellow and yellow before they fall in autumn.

Propagation – summer by semi-ripe cuttings; winter by hardwood cuttings.

SHRUBS
Cistus psilosepalus, C. hirsutus var. psilosepalus
Common name: sweet cistin. A small, competitive, spreading evergreen that grows to 1m in free-draining and sandy or loamy soil and sun. It is able to take strong wind and tolerates drought, competing reasonably well with other low growth such as grasses. From October to December sweet cistin is covered in an abundance of yellow-white flowers; a handsome ornamental for the wind garden.

Propagation – in autumn with seed; in summer take softwood or greenwood cuttings; hybrids and cultivars by cuttings only.

Cornus alba
Common name: red-barked dogwood. A deciduous shrub with young bright red shoots in winter and dark-green leaves that turn red or orange in autumn. It grows in sun or semi-shade, prefers fertile, well-drained soil and reaches an optimum height of 3m. From November to December creamy-white flowers appear, succeeded by blue-tinted white fruits.

Propagation – summer by softwood cuttings; in autumn or winter take hardwood cuttings.

Erica cinerea
Common name: bell heather. A dainty low-growing evergreen to 30cm. Favours free-draining acid soil, surviving dry summers reasonably well. Grows in semi-shade but prefers sun and is able to survive in windy terrain, provided other plant competition is not too aggressive; however, salt burns its foliage. The bush is soft and delicate and from December to February white, red or pink flowers appear that are decorative in a vase. A delight for the wind garden.

Propagation – in spring with seed; summer by cuttings, division and layering: selected forms by cuttings, division or layering only.

Prunus glandulosa 'Alba Plena', P. sinensis
Common name: white almond. Deciduous and grows to 1.5m in sun and any but waterlogged soil. From September to November scented white flowers appear. *P. triolba* 'Multiplex', double-flowering almond, grows to 4m and has scented deep-pink flowers; decorative in a vase.

Propagation – autumn with seed; winter by hardwood cuttings; spring to autumn by grafting and budding: selected forms by grafting and budding only.

PERENNIALS
Lobelia splendens (herbaceous), L. fulgens
Common name: lobelia. Grows to 1m in moist but well-drained soil and sun. Cannot tolerate dry conditions and quickly collapses if overshadowed by other plants. Leaves may be green or red-bronze, and from December to February white, red or salmon-pink flowers appear.

Propagation – in spring or autumn by seed and division: selected forms by division only.

ANNUALS
Anthriscus sylvestris
Common names: cow parsley, wild chervil. Competitive and fast-growing to 1m. This herb is especially useful in organic horticulture, used to nurture predatory insects with its nectar in early spring. Needs moisture in winter.

Propagation – seed crops in 6-8 weeks; will not transplant.

Temperature drops to -15°C
IL
Inland wind: light (*)
Coastal and salt wind: do not grow these plants

TREES
Acer palmatum
Common name: Japanese maple. Grows to 6m in sun or semi-shade and fertile, well-drained soil; parent of many other decorative forms. The usually green leaves of this attractive, small specimen tree colour brilliant yellow, orange and red in autumn. *A. platanoides*, Norway maple, is another decorative specimen that reaches 18m and has splendid autumn colour; the usually bright green leaves turn yellow and orange before they fall. In October clusters of yellow flowers appear.

Propagation – autumn with ripe seed; late winter to early spring by grafting; summer by budding: cultivars by grafting and budding only.

Betula pendula
Common name: silver birch. Large, deciduous specimen tree with silver-white coloured bark that grows to 25m in fertile, moist but well-drained soil and sun. Close plantings in groups look very attractive for parkland locations. From September to November yellow-green catkins appear, and in autumn the usually green leaves turn orange-yellow.

Propagation – early spring by softwood cuttings; late winter by grafting.

Dacrydium cupressinum (conifer)
Maori name: rimu. Common name: red pine. An evergreen specimen that is slow growing to 30m in any well-drained soil where sun is received for part of the day or in semi-shade. In winter the usually green leaves turn a bronze colour.

Propagation – late autumn to late winter: take cuttings from young plants or stratify seed.

Fagus sylvatica
Common name: European beech. A deciduous specimen reaching 20m and sometimes used for hedging. It grows in sun and any but waterlogged soil, though prefers limestone, not sandy, poorly-drained or saline sites. In autumn before they fall, the usually mid-green leaves turn to red, orange and yellow.

Propagation – autumn with seed; late summer by budding: selected forms by budding only.

Gleditsia triacanthos
Common name: honey locust. A large, deciduous specimen tree with a thorny trunk that grows in fertile, well-drained soil and sun to 30m; can tolerate some dry conditions. In autumn the usually glossy, fern-like, dark-green leaves turn yellow.

Propagation – in autumn with seed; late summer by budding: selected forms by budding only.

Rhododendron 'Cynthia'
Common name: rhododendron. An evergreen that is slow growing to 8m in shade or where sun is received for part of the day, and in neutral to acid soil with very good drainage. Plantings mixed with native bush look excellent, or can be used as a specimen. From September to December magenta-purple flowers appear.

Propagation – late summer by semi-ripe cuttings, layering and grafting.

Sorbus aucuparia
Common names: mountain ash or rowan. Large, deciduous specimen tree that grows in fertile, moist but well-drained soil and sun or semi-shade to 15m. Better suited to a cold winter climate where the foliage colourings are superior; in autumn the usually mid-green leaves turn red and yellow. From October to November white flowers appear, followed by bright red fruits.

Propagation – autumn with seed; summer by softwood cuttings and budding; in winter by grafting.

Taxodium distichum (conifer)
Common names: bald cypress or swamp cypress. Deciduous specimen tree that is slow growing to 30m in wet or waterlogged soil and sun. In autumn the usually green leaves turn reddish-brown.

Propagation – late autumn to late winter: take cuttings from young plants or stratify seed.

SHRUBS
Forsythia X *intermedia*
Common name: golden bell. Deciduous and is easily grown in fertile, well-drained soil and sun to 3m. Useful in the shrub border or in bold groupings. From September to October, before new summer leaves grow, yellow flowers appear that are decorative in a vase.

Propagation – in summer take softwood cuttings; in autumn or winter take hardwood cuttings.

Spiraea X *bumalda* 'Anthony Waterer'
Common name: spiraea. Deciduous and grows in fertile, well-drained but not over-dry soil and sun to 800cm. The young foliage is red, maturing to dark green; from November to March carmine-pink flowers appear that are decorative in a vase.

Propagation – in summer take softwood cuttings.

GROUNDCOVERS
Galeobdolon argentatum, Lamium galeobdolon, Lamiastrum galeobdolon
Common names: aluminium plant or dead nettle. A spreading, semi-evergreen perennial that grows to 30cm and carpets any well-drained soil where sun is received for part of the day or in shade. Useful in shrubberies, under trees or on banks; could be too invasive for small gardens or herbaceous borders. From December to May small white flowers appear.

Propagation – in winter by division of root runners.

PERENNIALS
Aconitum napellus (herbaceous)
Common name: monkshood. Grows to 1.5m in fertile, moist but well-drained soil with sun for part of the day or in semi-shade. Has been carefully used as a medicinal herb, as all parts are poisonous. From January to March violet-blue flowers appear that are delightful in bold groupings or in woodland areas. Blooms can be used fresh or dried for floral decoration.

Propagation – autumn by seed and division of root runners every 2-3 years.

Alchemilla mollis (herbaceous)
Common name: lady's mantle. Grows to 40cm in all but boggy soil where it is sunny for part of the day or in semi-shade. It is sometimes used as a medicinal herb, and from November to February bright greenish-yellow flowers appear.

Propagation – spring or autumn by seed and division.

Convallaria majalis (herbaceous)
Common name: lily of the valley. Reaches 15cm in moist, fertile soil in semi-shade or where sun is received for part of the day. From November to March scented white, lavender-pink or purple-mauve flowers appear.

Propagation – in autumn and after flowering by division of rhizomes.

Trollius ledebourii (herbaceous), *T. chinensis*
Common name: globe flower. Grows to 60cm in moist, clay soils where sun is received for part of the day or in shade. Brightens damp shady places with beautiful bright colours from October to March when golden-orange or orange-yellow flowers appear; decorative in a vase.

Propagation – spring or autumn with seed; early autumn or early spring by division.

ANNUALS
Nigella damascena
Common name: love-in-a-mist. In fertile, well-drained soil and sun grows to 60cm. From October to November white, magenta-red, deep-pink or purple flowers appear that are decorative in a vase. The flowers are followed by inflated, rounded, green seed pods that may be cut and dried for floral decoration.

Propagation – in autumn or early spring with seed.

Physalis alkekengi
Common name: winter cherry. A spreading perennial grown as an annual to 75cm in well-drained soil and sun or semi-shade. From December to January insignificant white flowers appear, followed by red, orange or yellow fruit that can be used fresh or dried for floral decoration.

Propagation – in spring or autumn with seed.

Saponaria vaccaria, Vaccaria hispanica
Common name: soapwort. Grows to 60cm in well-drained soil and sun; good for rock gardens, screes and banks. From December to January lightly scented white, pink or purple flowers appear that are decorative in a vase.
Propagation – in spring or autumn with seed.

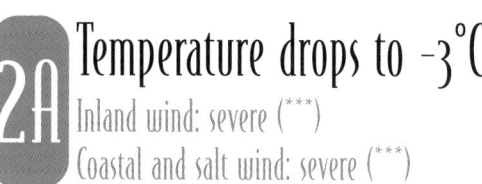

Temperature drops to -3°C
Inland wind: severe (***)
Coastal and salt wind: severe (***)

TREES
Araucaria heterophylla (conifer)
Common name: Norfolk Island pine. A competitive, evergreen specimen tree that grows to 30m in any free-draining soil and sun. It tolerates moderately dry conditions, but a frost of below −3°C will kill it. The tree grows from a central stem only and has a handsome, symmetrical shape, but does not provide shelter because of its open habit. Very tolerant of wind, it grows right up to the salt-water's edge and is often used for roadside plantings in public areas along coastlines. It is slow in the early phases of its life, but once established is strong in seasonal growth.

Propagation – late autumn to late winter: take cuttings from young plants or stratify seed.

SHRUBS
Agave americana
Common name: century plant. An evergreen xerophyte able to grow in deserts and regions of excess wind or salt wind. In well-drained soil and sun it survives competition from other plants reasonably well. The plant has thick fleshy leaves full of water and has very sharp spikes up to 2m long. This plant has an unusual life cycle; it takes at least 15 years to flower, at which point the large flower stem (inflorescene) appears suddenly in October, grows quickly to 4-5m in an exhaustive last effort to reproduce its own kind, flowers through the summer, then dies. The white to creamy-yellow flower stem is very dramatic and attracts interest as it often reaches into overhead power lines.

Propagation – in spring or summer with seed; after flowering when plant dies use offsets; young suckers transplant well.

Artemisia arborescens
Common name: hedge artemisia. A competitive, fast-growing evergreen reaching 1-2m in well-drained soil and sun. Artemisia is grown mainly for shelter, is useful for hedging and is very useful for cluster planting in seaside gardens. Prune the plant back hard every second autumn to avert a tendency to become leggy or straggly. The soft, fluffy, silver-grey foliage has a strong aromatic smell that deters plant-eating insects and can be used for floral decoration. From October to January, insignificant creamy-yellow flowers appear.

Propagation – in summer take by softwood or semi-ripe cuttings; in spring or autumn by division.

Brachyglottis compacta, Senecio compactus

Common name: Castlepoint groundsel. A compact, New Zealand native evergreen that grows to 1m in sun and well-drained soil. It withstands drought and tolerates the severest wind or salt winds. The shrub suffers from wet soils, becoming infected by a fungus that makes the leaves droop and gradually brown off. In summer, from November to February, it produces bright yellow, daisy-type flowers which contrast well with the dark-green foliage that is silver underneath. Winter pruning helps to keep it bushy.

Propagation – in late summer take semi-ripe cuttings.

Cassinia leptophylla

Maori name: tauhinu. Common name: cottonwood. A competitive, tough, densely branched New Zealand native evergreen with xerophytic adaptations such as reduced or very small leaves with tiny hairs on them. It grows from 2-5m in well-drained soil and sun; tolerates very dry conditions and is found in alpine or exposed coastal regions. In coastal locations with severe salt exposure, it is pruned naturally by wind, becoming a very useful, attractive, rounded, compact bush. When grown in a protected environment, it becomes straggly and looks untidy as it ages, and does not compete with aggressive plants. Therefore it is better used in exposed sites to which it is naturally adapted, and is a good filler for low cluster plantings. Another variety of cottonwood, *C. fulvida*, is also available. The only difference is its attractive yellow foliage. Both plants are very useful in situations of intense exposure and where decorative low shelter is required. Both varieties are aromatic. From November to February tiny, white, heather-like or daisy-like flowers appear.

Propagation – in summer take softwood cuttings.

Olearia albida

Maori name: tanguru. Common names: coastal daisy bush or tree daisy. A New Zealand native evergreen that grows in moist but well-drained soil and sun to 2-5m, surviving droughts well. It is a durable slow grower, competing steadily with other plants and well worth the time it takes to establish itself. Very hardy against salt-laden gales and therefore invaluable in severely exposed wind gardens. Leaves are light green, and their compact shape is retained with strength throughout the plant's life, making it a perfect hedge or wind break. From February to March small clusters of white daisy-like flowers appear.

Propagation – in summer take semi-ripe cuttings.

Olearia traversii

Common name: Chatham Island ake ake. Native to the Chatham Islands, this evergreen grows in sun and well-drained soil to 6m. Similar in its durability to *O. albida*, but not as handsome or as compact. It has darker-green, white-backed leaves, tough flexible branches, and sprouts again after severe salt burnings. It is useful in cluster plantings by providing shelter to other plants and can compete with gorse. From December to February greenish-white flowers appear.

Propagation – in summer take semi-ripe cuttings.

GRASSES

Aciphylla squarrosa (monocotyledon)

Maori Names: karamea, kurikuri. Common name: Spaniard grass or spear grass. A New Zealand native, reaching a height of up to 30cm. Found from arid zones to coastal cliffs, and likes scree slopes, where other plant competition struggles. The firm, spiky leaves are needle sharp and can inflict a painful stab. During the summer, long flowering spikes up to 1m high. Can be used in the rock garden, is tough, and will survive most exposed climates. A slow grower and is easily cultivated from seed.

Propagation – late summer or early spring by fresh seed.

Austrofestuca littoralis (monocotyledon), *Poa triodiodes*

Maori names: hinarepe, maatiatia, pouaka. Common name: sand tussock. Grows in sandy rocky places to 60cm. Tends to like colder places and is ideal for coastal gardens.

Propagation – by division or seed after flowering.

Cortaderia selloana 'Variegata' (monocotyledon)

Common name: yellow pampas grass. A competitive South American evergreen that is fast growing to 1.2m in well-drained soil and sun or semi-shade. This pampas is sometimes confused with *C. fulvida*. The differences between these two species must be understood. Unlike toetoe, which can tolerate severe frosts, yellow pampas cannot endure more than a light frost. Yellow pampas does not grow aggressively or become papery, and retains a tidy, permanent appearance. This plant is a wonderful addition to the wind garden as it produces bright-yellow, thick foliage and is strong against frequent salt wind. Can be used for cluster plantings, on mounds or in specimen plantings. From February to April 3m-high, silver-white flower plumes appear; can be used fresh or dried for floral decoration.

Propagation – in autumn or spring with seed; in spring by division: selected forms by division only.

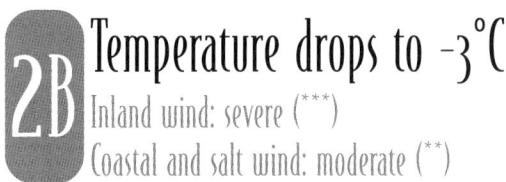

2B Temperature drops to -3°C
Inland wind: severe (***)
Coastal and salt wind: moderate (**)

TREES

Griselinia littoralis

Maori names: kaapuka, paraparauma or tapatapauma. Common name: broadleaf. A New Zealand native evergreen often seen growing in the wild in coastal regions. In well-drained soil and sun or semi-shade it grows from 4-9m. As a bush or a small tree, its main attraction is its compact shape and glossy, apple-green, leathery leaves. Though not a fast grower, it is able to withstand strong salt wind, but extreme saline conditions burn it back. It is valuable in the wind garden to provide shelter to other plants, and should be used in cluster plantings, hedging, mounds and shelter belts. In November tiny insignificant yellow-green flowers appear, followed by black fruit.

Propagation – spring or autumn by seed; summer by semi-ripe cuttings.

Myoporum insulare

Common names: Australian ngaio or boobialla. A competitive evergreen that is fast growing to 4m in well-drained soil and sun. Has an attractive shape derived from its branching frame, and although it has an open aspect, it is used for shelter. It has interesting, light-green, gland-dotted foliage, and from September to June tiny white flowers with purple spots in their throats appear, followed by fleshy purplish berries.

Propagation – spring by ripe seed; late summer by semi-ripe cuttings.

Myoporum laetum

Maori and common name: ngaio. A competitive, New Zealand native evergreen that is fast growing in well-drained soil and sun; reaches 12-15m. An excellent tree for coastal areas, standing up to most winds well. Severe, salt-laden gales burn the leaves but the tree is able to recover in a few months and produce new growth shaped by the wind. Very useful amongst larger cluster plantings. Is found naturally as far south as Kaikoura and is more common in coastal areas. Ngaio has interesting, light-green, gland-dotted leaves, and from July to April clusters of tiny, white flowers with purple dots appear followed by small, oblong, red-purple fruit.

Propagation – spring by ripe seed; late summer by semi-ripe cuttings.

SHRUBS

Corokia cotoneaster

Maori and common name: korokio. New Zealand native evergreen that grows to 1.75m in well-drained soil and sun. A slow grower and takes time to establish but is very useful as a low hedge, providing excellent shelter from severe wind or some salt wind. It responds very well to pruning but becomes straggly when left to itself. Also useful amongst cluster plantings. It has small dark-green leaves and from November to February fragrant, small, yellow flowers appear.

Propagation – in summer take softwood cuttings.

Hebe speciosa

Maori names: napuka or tiitiirangi. Common names: purple hebe or veronica. Competitive, evergreen shrub that grows in sun and well-drained soil up to 2m. This hebe can withstand the most severe inland winds and is useful in cluster plantings and shrub borders. Near the sea it thrives clumped together in mixed plantings where it shelters other plants. From September to February deep-red or purple-mauve flowers appear.

Propagation – in summer take semi-ripe cuttings.

Hebe townsonii
Common name: hebe. A competitive evergreen that grows up to 2.5m in well-drained soil and sun. Needs to be pruned every 2-3 years to maintain a good shape. Grows well on difficult banks; often seen wild along road edges. Very free-flowering from September to December; white flowers.

Propagation – in summer take semi-ripe cuttings.

Phormium cookianum subsp. hookeri 'Cream Delight' (monocotyledon)
Common name: flax. An evergreen flax that survives windy sites well and is slow growing to 50cm in most soils and sun or semi-shade. A superior, compact cultivar dominant over most low-growing weeds. It is a brighter but smaller version of 'Yellow Wave' that retains its colour well. The broad centre band of cream up to 4cm wide is its special feature. This is edged with a narrow band of dark green with cream stripings, with the margins of each leaf dark red.

Propagation – in winter or spring by division.

Phormium 'Sundowner' (monocotyledon)
Common name: flax. An erect evergreen flax that competes well against other plants and is sometimes used for hedging. The bronze leaves are striped with red and pink, although the striping varies and often the bronze is more dominant. When young, its foliage is more orange-bronze but it loses its orange tint as it matures. It prefers moist but well-drained soil and sun or semi-shade where it is fast growing to 2m. From November to December greenish purple-red flowers appear.

Propagation – in winter or spring by division.

Phormium 'Thumbelina' (monocotyledon)
Common name: dwarf flax. An evergreen that is slow growing in moist but well-drained soil and sun or semi-shade to only 15cm high. It has dark-red foliage and forms small ornamental clumps, although it is susceptible to plant competition and impractical for most wind gardens as grasses soon smother it.

Propagation – in winter or spring by division.

Phormium 'Yellow Wave' (monocotyledon)
Common name: flax. A competitive evergreen that grows to 2m in moist soil where sun is received for part of the day or in semi-shade. Tolerates wind but too much salt burns the tips of the leaves. Attractive in bold group plantings; a handsome specimen that contrasts with adjacent foliage. It has erect pendulous leaves of yellow and green, but with age it can revert to green foliage. When grown in shade, it loses some of the yellow in its green colouring. The leaves can become pitted with tiny red spots when grown in bright sunshine.

Propagation – in winter or spring by division.

GRASSES
Anemanthele lessoniana (monocotyledon), Oryzopsis lessoniana
Maori names: Hunangaamoho, toetoe hungaamoho. Common names: wind grass, gossamer grass. Grows reasonably fast to 30-40cm and is very good in dry areas. Likes an open sunny position, but will tolerate poor soils even under trees. It is a very attractive competitive grass with green foliage and red seed heads. This species is sometimes confused with the exotic marram grass *Ammophila arenaria*.

Propagation – self-seeds easily in summer.

Carex comans (monocotyledon)
Maori name: maurea. Common name: carex grass. An evergreen that grows to 45cm in any well-drained soil and sun. This grass can withstand frost to −5°C but cannot tolerate as much salt as *C. testacea* or *C. flagellifera*. It has attractive bronze-coloured foliage.

Propagation – in spring by division; in spring or autumn with seed.

Carex flagellifera (monocotyledon)
Maori names: maania, maanaia or maurea. Common names: frosted curl, Glen Murray tussock or tussock sedge. A native evergreen tussock. In any well-drained soil and sun it is low growing to 60cm and is able to survive salt-laden winds and drought as well as frosts to -5°C. The foliage is silver-green and looks handsome when contrasted with other coloured foliage. Other related varieties with similar habits are *C. fulvida* and *C. novae zealandiae*; both have brown-green foliage and are salt tolerant.

Propagation – in spring by division; in spring or autumn with seed.

Carex testacea (monocotyledon)
Common name: carex grass. Evergreen that grows in well-drained soil and sun to 30cm and can endure more salt than *C. comans*. This grass looks exceptionally handsome planted close together in very windy locations where the bold groups of colour contrast vividly as they sway with the wind; a must for any wind garden. It has olive-green and reddish-yellow foliage that turns orange in autumn, and from December to January brown flower spikelets appear.

Propagation – spring by seed and division; in autumn by division.

Carex trifida (monocotyledon)
Common names: tataki grass. Has a stout habit, growing to 60-80cm tall in open or semi-shaded situations. Likes moist soil and can tolerate some dryness as well. Will also grow in coastal areas.

Propagation – after flowering by division and seed.

Juncus maritimus var. australiensis (monocotyledon)
Maori names: wii, wiiwii, koopuungaawhaa. Common name: sea rush. Grows to 1m tall. Used for re-vegetation in wetland areas.

Propagation – by seed.

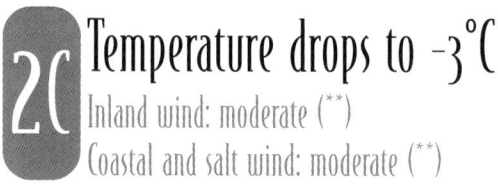

2C Temperature drops to -3°C
Inland wind: moderate (**)
Coastal and salt wind: moderate (**)

TREES
Banksia serrata
Common name: banksia. Is an evergreen specimen that grows to 9m in sun and well-drained sandy soil that is low in phosphates and nitrates. It is useful for hedging or cluster planting. From December to May reddish budded, cream flowers appear that are decorative in a vase.

Propagation – in early spring or autumn with seed.

Casuarina glauca
Common name: swamp oak. An evergreen better suited to coastal areas than *C. cunninghamiana* which, although fully frost hardy, is not as salt hard. The plant grows to 18m in sun and poor sandy soil, tolerating brackish salty water, poor drainage or drought. Swamp oak is grown for shelter and hedges as it takes regular clipping well. It has bluish-green weeping branchlets, and from March to May reddish-brown flowers appear in terminal spikes among the upper twigs.

Propagation – in spring with seed.

Phoenix canariensis
Common names: Canary Island date palm or Phoenix palm. An evergreen tree able to live in windy regions; slow growing, especially in its early life. Tall when matured, it grows in any well-drained soil and sun to 12m. Useful as an ornamental or in specimen plantings for its rather formal symmetrical shape. Feather-shaped, arching, green leaf-fronds grow from a central stem and have sharp spines. Bears clusters of tiny yellow flowers followed by orange fruits on female trees.

Propagation – spring at not less than 24°C with ripe seed; mid to late spring a small cluster of stems cut away from the parent plant.

SHRUBS

Callistemon citrinus
Common name: bottle brush. An Australian native evergreen that grows to 4m in well-drained soil and sun. The bush tolerates a light frost and any amount of wind, provided the salt content is not too severe. Good for cluster plantings. From November to March showy white, red, pink or purple-mauve flowers appear. The colour is provided by stamens, similar to the flowers of the pohutukawa.

Propagation – autumn by seed; summer or spring by semi-ripe cuttings.

Correa alba
Common name: Australian fuchsia. A compact evergreen that grows to 1.5m in moist but well-drained soil and sun or semi-shade. Can be used as coastal hedge. Close planting in groups helps it to grow better in a harsh environment. It has blue-green leaves and tiny, white, trumpet-shaped flowers that appear throughout the year.

Propagation – spring by seed; late summer by semi-ripe cuttings.

Elaeagnus pungens
Common name: wild olive. Competitive evergreen that grows to 3m in well-drained soil and sun or semi-shade. Although slow to begin with, once established it forms a compact bush good for hedging or cluster plantings. From March to May fragrant, creamy-white flowers appear.

Propagation – in autumn with seed; in summer take semi-ripe cuttings.

Escallonia rubra
Common name: red escallonia. A compact evergreen that grows in well-drained soil and sun to 4m. This shrub tolerates dry summers and makes a good hedge in windy areas, provided there is not too much salt in the air. Prune back every 3 years as it tends to become leggy if allowed to grow unchecked. The leaves are slightly sticky, and both flowers and foliage are aromatic. From October to May it is covered with tiny pink-red flower clusters.

Propagation – in summer take softwood cuttings.

Lavandula dentata
Common names: French lavender or toothed lavender. An evergreen that grows to 1m in well-drained soil and sun. Clipping improves its form; can be used as a hedge. Through winter and spring fragrant mid-blue flowers appear that can be used fresh or dried for floral decoration.

Propagation – in summer take semi-ripe cuttings.

Leucospermum cordifolium, L. nutans
Common name: nodding pincushion. An evergreen that is the parent of many hybrids, and grows to 2m in sun and well-drained soil low in phosphates and nitrates. The young plant needs protection from frost to establish itself; prefers a warm climate. From November to December vivid orange pincushion-shaped flowers appear that are decorative in a vase.

Propagation – in spring with seed.

Pachystegia insignis
Common name: Marlborough daisy. Native to coastal cliffs and rock faces in Marlborough. Slow to establish, it has very decorative large white daisy-like flowers.

Propagation – Easily raised from seed or from cuttings.

Phormium tenax (monocotyledon)
Maori names: harakeke or koorari. Common name: flax. Competitive, New Zealand native evergreen from which a number of cultivars have been produced. This flax is the taller species, growing from 2-3m, and is usually found in boggy or moist soil and sun or semi-shade. The leaves have dark-green margins on them and can be woven to make kete (open-weave baskets) which allow water to drain through; often used by Maori to carry seafood. From November to December dull reddish-brown flower spikes appear, followed by erect seed pods.

Propagation – in autumn by seed and division.

Phormium 'Dark Delight' (monocotyledon)
Common name: flax. An evergreen that is sometimes used for hedging. It prefers fertile soil and sun or semi-shade where it grows slowly in an erect form from 1-2m. It is competitive because of its height above grasses, and survives exposure, but this variety needs some shelter from extreme salt winds. To protect the very long drooping leaf ends, which lose some attractiveness from wind-bashing, it should be planted amongst other foliage. The deepest purple of the flaxes, becoming blackish-bronze with age. From November to December red flowers appear.

Propagation – in autumn by division.

Phormium tenax 'Purpureum' (monocotyledon)
Common name: flax. Competitive, taller, evergreen flax that forms a thick clump and is often used for hedging. It has red-bronze foliage that contrasts well with other plants. It grows in most soils and sun or semi-shade to 2.5m and is wind hard, accepting reasonably strong salt wind. Useful for cluster plantings or mounds, and mixes well with toetoe, creating an excellent wind shelter. From November to December purple-green flowers appear.

Propagation – in autumn by division.

Polygala myrtifolia 'Grandiflora'
Common name: sweet pea bush. A competitive evergreen that forms a dense bush and grows in fertile, moist but well-drained soil and sun to 2m. The shrub is hardy and able to live near the sea, provided it has some protection and is located in a sunny spot. Almost always in flower, the bush is a valuable ornamental contribution to cluster plantings, and as an individual specimen is a garden highlight. Numerous rich-purple, pea-like flowers appear all year round.

Propagation – spring by seed; late summer by semi-ripe cuttings.

Protea magnifica, P. barbigera
Common name: Queen protea. An evergreen that grows to 1.5-3m in sun and well-drained neutral to acid soil low in phosphates and nitrates. Varies in habit from low sprawling growth to bushy shrubs or erect small trees; can withstand frost to –8°C. One of the most spectacular proteas; from June to November creamy-white, rosy-red or soft-pink flowers with a black or pure white peak appear; decorative in a vase.

Propagation – spring or autumn with seed (germination is erratic); in summer take semi-ripe cuttings.

Westringia fruticosa, W. rosmariniformis
Common name: coast rosemary. An evergreen that grows in well-drained soil and sun to 1.5m; is able to survive coastal winds well and tolerates drought. Has small firm leaves and is compact in growth. A tidy plant, retaining its form, and is not aggressive in competition with other plants. A useful addition to exposed plantings. From October to February it produces a mass of tiny, very pale mauve-white flowers.

Propagation – in spring with seed; in summer take semi-ripe cuttings.

CULINARY HERBS

Rosmarinus officinalis
Common name: rosemary. An aromatic evergreen shrub that grows in well-drained soil and sun to 1.5m. Endurable, stands up to very strong winds with some salt content and dry summers in lightly frosted areas, and is sometimes used as hedging; grows well amongst other shrubs. A prostrate form, R. lavandulaceus or R. prostratus, is also available but is not as hardy and should be grown only in frost-free areas. Rosemary is slow growing to start with but is tenacious and succeeds against moderate competition from other plants such as grasses and spring weeds. The deep-green foliage is ornamental and can be used fresh or dried for flavouring meats and poultry. Has been used medicinally to stimulate hair growth. The blue flowers that appear from October to December attract bees.

Propagation – in summer take semi-ripe cuttings.

Temperature drops to -3°C
2D
Inland wind: severe (***)
Coastal and salt wind: light (*)

TREES

Coprosma robusta
Maori and common name: karamu. Grows to 5m in well-drained soil and sun. As an evergreen it is good for sheltering other plants in a cluster planting. Has brownish-green leaves.

Propagation – in spring with seed; in summer take semi-ripe cuttings.

SHRUBS

Grevillea rosmarinifolia
Common name: grevillea. A competitive evergreen that grows to 2m in sun and well-drained soil which should be rich in leaf-mould and somewhat gravelly. It also must be slightly acid and on the dryish side. An excess of phosphorus can make plants very unhappy. As the plant ages, its older foliage tends to die back, yet it still retains a dense head, combining well with other plants. Good in the wind garden as an ornamental or for cluster planting, and near the sea if sheltered from salt wind, as it tends to burn. From August to December grevillea is covered with tiny red, yellow or pink flowers.

Propagation – in spring with seed; in summer take semi-ripe cuttings.

Hebe hulkeana
Common name: New Zealand lilac. An evergreen that is slow growing up to 1m in sun and well-drained or rocky soil. Good for the small shrub, wind or rock garden. This is the largest flowered species of hebe, and parent of some good hybrids. From October to December decorative lilac-purple flowers appear.

Propagation – in summer take semi-ripe cuttings.

Leucadendron 'Safari Sunset'
Common name: leucadendron. A handsome evergreen that grows to 2.5m in sun and well-drained soil low in phosphate and nitrates. Makes a good hedge but should be pruned hard in spring. From autumn to spring flowers with cream centres surrounded by large deep-red bracts that turn golden-yellow with age appear.

Propagation – in spring with seed.

Pyracantha angustifolia
Common name: firethorn. A semi-evergreen that grows to 3m in well-drained soil and sun or semi-shade. A slow grower; grasses often grow through it, but it does stand up to competition and adverse wind conditions. It tolerates dry summers, withstands light frosts, but severe salt wind burns back the foliage. Best used for mass plantings, in shrub borders and mixed in with other shrubs. The spikes on its branches deter vandals. This is a decorative plant; it has green leaves, and from December to February white flower clusters appear, followed by bright orange berries.

Propagation – in summer take semi-ripe cuttings.

Spartium junceum
Common name: Spanish broom. Competitive, deciduous and fast growing in not too rich, well-drained soil and sun. Reaches 2-3m. A wonderful shrub that does very well in wind-blasted sites where other plants cannot survive. Strong salt winds burn the plant's branches which are green spindly stems thinly clad with small leaves. Very useful in the wind garden for cluster plantings and as a vibrant ornamental. Prune back every 2-3 years to regenerate the bush and to thicken its shape. It begins flowering in December, when the shrub is covered with fragrant, bright yellow, pea-like flowers, and continues through to May when most other plants have finished flowering.

Propagation – in autumn with seed.

GRASSES

Chionochloa flavicans (monocotyledon)
Common name: dwarf toetoe, tussock. A competitive and fast growing New Zealand native grass, lush green in colour, with thick showy plumes of flowers and seed-heads in the summer. It grows from 50cm-1m tall, and is wind tolerant and somewhat tolerant of salt. It does very well on exposed dry hillsides, but prefers reasonable topsoil. Attractive as a garden specimen, and also in group plantings mixed with ornamental flaxes, where the foliage colour and textures combine well. Flowers are more decorative and last longer than those of *C. flavescens*.

Propagation – by seed.

Temperature drops to -3°C
2E
Inland wind: moderate (**)
Coastal and salt wind: light (*)

TREES

Arbutus unedo
Common name: strawberry tree. An evergreen that grows in fertile, well-drained soil and sun to 9m. It is sometimes used for hedging or grown as a specimen. From February to August white flowers appear, followed by red crab-apple like fruit which attract birds.

Propagation – autumn by seed; late summer by semi-ripe cuttings.

Garrya elliptica
Common name: catkin bush. An evergreen that is slow growing in any poor soil and sun. Reaches 4-5m. The tree to begin with is green and inconspicuous but in time becomes solid and strong in its character. It is able to grow in reasonable exposure but its real value in the garden is in cluster plantings or as an ornamental specimen tree. From July to September it has unusual grey-green catkins (seed capsules) that droop downwards and can be used fresh or dried for floral decoration.

Propagation – in summer take semi-ripe cuttings.

Hoheria populnea
Maori names: houhere, houhi ongaonga or whauwhi. Common name: lacebark. New Zealand native evergreen that grows to 7m in fertile, well-drained soil and sun or semi-shade. Short lived in comparison with other trees, it has a life span of 10-20 years and has a tendency to die suddenly, possibly as a result of water stress. Lacebark is found throughout the New Zealand bush, preferring regular rainfall and a temperate climate. It is a good addition to cluster planting. From February to May spectacular clusters of white flowers appear.

Propagation – in autumn with seed; in summer take semi-ripe cuttings.

Ilex aquifolium
Common name: holly. An evergreen that is slow growing to 12m in fertile, well-drained soil which is sunny for part of the day or in shade. The variegated form should be grown in sun or semi-shade. It tolerates frost to −5°C and some strong wind, but is better suited as a specimen tree grown in shelter from strong salt wind. It is used for Christmas decorations in the northern hemisphere, as it has attractive dark-green leaves and during winter has bright red berries.

Propagation – spring with seed; late summer to early winter by semi-ripe cuttings.

Ilex cornuta
Common name: Chinese horned holly. An evergreen that is slow growing in fertile, well-drained soil where sun is received for part of the day or semi-shade; reaches 4m. The variegated form should be grown in open sunlight or semi-shade. It forms a neat compact bush and tolerates some strong wind, but is better suited as a specimen tree grown in shelter from strong salt wind. It is used for Christmas decorations in the southern hemisphere as it has attractive dark-green leaves and bright red berries in summer.

Propagation – in spring with seed; from late summer to early winter take semi-ripe cuttings.

Leptospermum ericoides, Kunzea ericoides
Maori name: kaanuka. Common name: white tea tree. Used for re-vegetation and bush planting. Grows in open sun or semi-shaded areas where the soil

is poor, can tolerate moderately dry conditions. Grows up to 3-4m, much taller than manuka.

Propagation – by seed.

Leptospermum scoparium

Maori names: kahikaatoa or manuka. Common name: tea tree. A competitive and spreading New Zealand native evergreen that is fast growing to 2-5m in well-drained soil and sun. Useful in the wind garden as an ornamental on dry banks, as shelter for other plants amongst cluster plantings or for hedging. It tolerates only light salt wind. It is used to establish vegetation in erosion-prone sites where poor soils have been leached. By simply laying down and pegging seeded branches upon the scarred earth the seeds germinate. Manuka is also very useful in allowing taller plants to succeed,as it eventually gives way to taller growth as light decreases. In the wild, manuka is one of the first plants to reappear once growth has been removed, especially in warmer areas where it can be a fire hazard in dry summers. It is difficult to remove and springs up where people have devastated the existing growth; it is similar in habit to gorse. In some areas, manuka is difficult to establish. One reason may be that its roots have a symbiotic relationship with a mycorrhizal fungi which may not be present. New, handsome single or double forms of manuka are available. From December to February white, red or pink flowers appear.

Propagation – in summer take semi-ripe cuttings.

Phebalium squameum

Common name: satinwood. A competitive evergreen that is fast growing in well-drained soil and open sunlight or semi-shade; reaches 3-10m. It has an erect linear shape, is able to survive droughts reasonably well and is easily transplanted in winter. Very useful for hedges or in mixed shelter plantings as it is able to take strong winds. It forms thick bushes when clipped, but if left alone it loses its compactness at the bottom, letting wind gusts penetrate. Satinwood does not like too much salt, as it tends to burn. It has silver-green leaves, and from September to November white flowers appear.

Propagation – spring by seed; early summer by soft-tip cuttings.

Pittosporum eugenioides

Maori name: tarata. Common name: lemonwood. A competitive New Zealand native evergreen that needs adequate moisture; grows to 10m in well-drained soil and sun or semi-shade. It makes an ideal hedge, taking 5 years to act as a solid wind-break. A compact specimen or shelter tree that tends to become drawn when competing with other aggressive growth. In the open, it grows into a neat rounded tree, dense with light-green foliage that has a pleasant lemon smell. Foliage burns off in strong salt-laden wind. From September to November yellow flowers appear.

Propagation – autumn or spring by seed; summer by semi-ripe cuttings.

Pittosporum tenuifolium

Maori and common name: kohuhu. An evergreen grown as a specimen or for shelter. It grows to 8m in moist but well-drained soil and sun or semi-shade. Similar in habit to *P. eugenioides* but its leaves are smaller; has black stems; and the plant is slightly less wind hard and not as fast growing. Several handsome forms have been derived from both these species. *P. tenuifolium*, like its relative, is burnt by strong salt wind from which it seldom recovers. It has light-green leaves, and from December to February tiny, fragrant, dark-purple flowers appear. *P. tenuifolium* 'Irene Patterson' is an evergreen grown as a specimen or for shelter. A handsome cultivar derived from *P. tenuifolium*, it is slow growing in moist but well-drained soil, and sun; reaches 10m. Like its relative, it is burnt by strong salt wind from which it seldom recovers. It has variegated green and white leaves, and from October to November tiny, fragrant, dark-purple flowers appear.

Propagation – autumn or spring by seed; summer by semi-ripe cuttings.

Pseudopanax crassifolius

Maori name: horoeka. Common name: lancewood. An evergreen native tree, it has a distinctive juvenile form with long, lance-like leaves. Grows in semi-shade on forest floors. Matures as a small tree with shorter and wider leaves than its juvenile form. A very decorative tree, useful in cluster plantings for its foliage.

Propagation – by seed in autumn or spring, or by semi-ripe cuttings in summer.

Sophora microphylla var. longicarinata

Maori and common name: kowhai. Semi-deciduous and slow growing to 5m in most moist soils and sun or semi-shade. It is grown as an ornamental specimen and is able to withstand some winds but only light salt wind. From July to October, hanging, deep golden-yellow flowers appear, and before they fall and carpet the ground several types of birds feed on their nectar. *S. tetraptera*, large-leaved kowhai, has the same flowering period. This tree is slow to start, beginning to show form after 5-7 years and then competes well with other growth; reaches 4-9m. This kowhai is welcome in any garden, blending amongst other trees and useful for cluster plantings or as a decorative specimen. Dwarf kowhai, *S. prostrata*, grows to 2m, has pale-lemon flowers in spring and is very decorative as a hedge or along paths or driveways.

Propagation – autumn with seed; summer take semi-evergreen and softwood cuttings.

SHRUBS

Abelia X grandiflora

Common name: abelia. A decorative evergreen that is fast growing to 2m in fertile, well-drained soil and sun or semi-shade. This shrub makes a dense handsome hedge or addition to cluster plantings. When clipped it recovers exceptionally well, sending out new growth. If left to itself, it tends to become leggy as it ages. Stands up to most winds except salt-laden winds which it can survive only in shelter of other plants. From January to April pinky-white or pink flowers appear.

Propagation – in summer take cuttings.

Beaufortia sparsa

Common names: gravel bottle brush or swamp bottle brush. Native to Western Australia, this evergreen grows in dry or swampy soil and sun to 2m. Tolerates heavy or wet conditions, but does better in freely drained soils. Wind tolerant but prefers shelter from excess salt. In summer and autumn showy male stamens appear as vermilion-coloured flowers.

Propagation – with seed; take half-ripe stem cuttings.

Calytrix alpestris, Lhotskya alpestris

Common name: fringe myrtle. An evergreen that grows in moist but well-drained sandy soil and sunlight to reach 1.5m. Useful in the shrub border but does not like being transplanted. From November to February white flowers appear. On *C. sullivanii*, Grampians fringe myrtle, pinky-white flowers appear.

Propagation – take cuttings.

Eriostemon myoporoides

Common name: wax flower. An attractive evergreen that reaches 1-2m in well-drained neutral to slightly acid soil and sun or semi-shade. Keeps a compact shape and grows reasonably well in wind. A welcome plant for the wind garden but does not like freezing temperatures. The foliage has an aromatic smell, and from September to November is covered in tiny, white, star-shaped flowers.

Propagation – autumn by scarified seed and semi-ripe tip cuttings.

Fatsia japonica, Aralia japonica, A. sieboldii

Common name: Japanese aralia. A competitive evergreen that grows to 3m in fertile, well-drained soil where sun is received for part of the day, in shade or semi-shade. Useful for growing under other big trees or as a pot or tub plant, as it has large, palm-like, dark-green leaves. From March to May appear white flowers that attract flies.

Propagation – autumn by seed; summer by semi-ripe cuttings or spring.

Hydrangea macrophylla
Common names: hortensia or lace cap. Deciduous and grows to 2m in fertile, moist but well-drained soil which is sunny for part of the day or in shade. Can withstand frost to approximately −10°C. Hydrangeas have two sorts of flowers: hortensias have tiny petals surrounding a cluster of stamens: and lace caps have large numbers of florets. While they do equally well in acid or alkaline soil, their colour is changeable, generally mauve-blue in acid soils and pink or red in alkaline soils. From November to March white, red, mauve-blue, pink or purple flowers appear.

Propagation − in summer take softwood cuttings.

Lavatera oblia 'Barnsley'
Common name: mallow. A competitive semi-evergreen that is easy to grow in well-drained soil and sun to 2m. Very decorative in a shrub border, as from December to February delicate pink flowers appear.

Propagation − in early spring or summer take softwood cuttings.

Leucospermum reflexum
Common name: sky-rocket pincushion. A handsome evergreen that grows from 2.5-4m in sun and well-drained soil low in phosphates and nitrates. The young plant needs protection from frost to establish itself; prefers a warm climate. From October to December orange-red flowers appear.

Propagation − in spring with seed.

Lophomyrtus bullata, Myrtus bullata
Maori and common name: ramarama. An evergreen that prefers to grow in the shelter of other plants, in moist but well-drained soil and sun or shade; reaches 4m. Responds to winter pruning, promoting strong spring growth. Has decorative, large, reddish-brown leaves, and from December to February white flowers appear, followed by red berries. While more spreading, *L. obcordata*, rohutu (previously *Myrtus obcordata*) is as useful for cut winter foliage. It has decorative, small, bronzy-purple leaves, and from December to February white flowers appear, followed by purple berries.

Propagation − in late summer take semi-ripe cuttings.

Myrtus communis
Common name: Greek myrtle. An evergreen that grows in fertile, well-drained soil and sun or semi-shade to 3m. Withstands frost to −8°C and can be clipped into a formal hedge or allowed to develop into an attractive but irregular-shaped bush. From November to January fragrant white flowers appear.

Propagation − in late summer take semi-ripe cuttings.

Nandina domestica 'Pygmaea'
Common names: heavenly bamboo or sacred bamboo. A semi-evergreen that makes a good container plant. It is slow growing in fertile, well-drained but not too dry soil and sun; reaches 1.75m. Lime-green leaves turn crimson-red and scarlet when planted in full sun. Panicles of small white flowers appear in January or February followed, in warm climates, by spherical red fruits.

Propagation − in summer with seed or take semi-ripe cuttings.

Olearia macrodonta
Maori names: arorangi, wharangikura. Common names: large toothed olearia. A coastal small tree or shrub that grows to 7m tall, preferring average soils and moisture. A native, it naturally occurs in lowland coastal bush. Ideal for cluster planting. Slow growing to begin with, but after the first two years is well established. Grown particularly for shelter and foliage.

Propagation − by semi-ripe cuttings in summer.

Phormium tenax 'Williamsii Variegatum' (monocotyledon)
Common name: flax. Prefers moist or boggy soil and sun or semi-shade where it grows from 1-2m. Although slow growing, it is a competitive evergreen in a situation that is exposed to some strong wind or light salt wind, and is sometimes used for hedging. It has green and cream, erect foliage useful for contrast against other foliage plants. From November to December greenish-yellow flowers appear.

Propagation − in winter or spring by division.

Photinia X fraseri 'Red Robin'
Common name: red robin. An evergreen that grows in sun or semi-shade and fertile, moist but well-drained soil up to 4m. The colourful foliage is red when young and turns glossy green as it ages. Useful for hedging and adds colour to a shrub border. In September and October broad heads of white flowers appear.

Propagation − in summer take semi-ripe cuttings.

Prostanthera incisa
Common name: Australian mint bush. A fragrant evergreen that grows in fertile, well-drained soil and sun or semi-shade to 1.2m. Has dense light-green foliage that has a strong, sweet, minty odour when crushed. From September to November lilac-coloured flowers appear.

Propagation − in spring with seed; in summer take semi-ripe cuttings.

Telopea speciosissima
Common name: New South Wales waratah. An evergreen specimen shrub that grows to 3m in sun and moist but well-drained neutral to acid soil. This plant needs winter sun but can endure a frost to −8°C. Becomes leggy if not picked or pruned heavily as soon as flowering ends. Spring is usually the peak flowering period when scarlet-red or crimson flowers appear; very decorative in a vase.

Propagation − in spring with seed; in winter by layering.

Thryptomene calycina
Common name: snowberry. An evergreen that grows to 1.5m in sun or semi-shade and lime-free, slightly acid, well-drained soil. From July to November white flowers appear. *T. saxicola* 'Rosea' grows in the same garden conditions to 1m and produces white or pink flowers. Both plants are good for a shrub border.

Propagation − autumn by very small cuttings: keep in a cool frame.

CULINARY HERBS
Anthriscus cerefolium
Common name: chervil. A competitive annual; grows to 60cm in well-drained soil where open sunlight is received for part of the day. This herb is only used fresh, adding flavour to salads, omelettes or herb butter. The white flowers that appear from December to February can be dried for floral decoration.

Propagation − in early spring with seed.

Salvia officinalis
Common name: sage. A semi-deciduous perennial; slow growing to 60cm in fertile, well-drained soil and sun. This plant has purplish-green leaves that can be added to herb teas, and are used fresh or dried added to meat, poultry or fish for seasoning. From March to April, fragrant blue flowers.

Propagation − in spring or summer take softwood cuttings; in spring by division.

CLIMBERS
Campsis X tagliabuana
Common name: trumpet vine. Semi-deciduous and grows in well-drained soil and sun up to 10m. In full sun and good situations it grows happily through other small shelter trees. From February to April red or orange-pink flowers appear.

Propagation − summer take semi-ripe cuttings; in winter by layering.

GROUNDCOVERS
Hypericum calycinum
Common names: Aaron's beard or rose of Sharon. An evergreen or semi-evergreen; grows to 80cm in fertile, well-drained soil that is not too dry; likes sun or semi-shade. An attractive bush that grows better as a ground creeper. It survives light frosts and in colder areas becomes deciduous or semi-deciduous. A useful ornamental for the wind garden, along path edges, dry banks, and mixed with other low-growing plants. From December to February it has showy yellow flowers.

Propagation − autumn with seed; in summer take softwood cuttings: selected forms by softwood cuttings only.

GRASSES
Carex buchananii (monocotyledon)
Common name: carex grass. An attractive reddish-brown moderately growing tussock. Leaves to 50-75cm tall, with a stiff and erect habit. Likes an average soil and will tolerate some dryness.

Propagation – after flowering, by division and seed.

PERENNIALS
Anthemis sancti-johannis
Common name: Roman chamomile. An evergreen that is easy and fast growing in well-drained soil and sun to 60cm. Makes a splendid display in a border, as from November until the first autumn frosts scented orange flowers appear that are decorative in a vase.

Propagation – late summer, autumn or spring by basal cuttings; spring by division.

Dendranthema indicum, D. morifolium, D. zawadskii
Chrysanthemum morifolium
Common name: chrysanthemum. Semi-evergreen and grows in fertile, well-drained soil and sun to 1.5m. Many cultivars are derived from the three original parents of the autumn-flowering chrysanthemum. Scented white, bronze, yellow, pink or lavender-coloured flowers appear from March to May; decorative in a vase.

Propagation – in spring by dividing basal growth and cuttings taken from plant material that is in active growth.

Dianthus barbatus
Common name: sweet william. A colourful bedding plant that is short lived; sometimes treated as an annual or biennial. It is slow growing to 50cm in well-drained, slightly alkaline soil and sun. The white, red or salmon-pink flowers that appear from October to November are decorative in a vase.

Propagation – in summer by cuttings and layering.

Felicia amelloides, Agathaea coelestis, Aster capensis
Common name: blue marguerite. A spreading evergreen that, in well-drained soil and sun, grows slowly to 60cm. Salt wind burns its foliage and it is better planted among other shrubs. From November to May blue flowers with bright yellow centres appear.

Propagation – in spring with seed; in summer or early autumn take greenwood cuttings.

Kniphofia praecox, K. zululandia
Common name: red hot poker. Competitive, semi-deciduous or evergreen plant which grows to 1.5m in well-drained soil where sun is received for part of the day. Stately plants adding interest and colour from June to September when red, orange-red or yellow, poker-like flowers appear.

Propagation – in spring by seed and division: selected forms by division only.

BULBS
Allium giganteum
Common name: onion. A spreading plant that is fast growing to 1.9m in fertile, well-drained soil and sun. This is the strongest-growing species and has ornamental foliage as well as fragrant purple-red flowers that appear from December to February; can be used fresh or dried for floral decoration.

Propagation – in autumn with seed; in early spring by division.

Anemone coronaria
Common name: windflower. This parent of many hybrids is dormant during summer and grows to 25cm in humus-rich, well-drained soil and sun or semi-shade. Very decorative in massed beds or borders where the mixed colours look attractive. White, red, blue, pink or violet flowers appear from September to November; excellent in a vase.

Propagation – in late summer with ripe seed; in spring by dividing tubers; in winter by root cuttings.

Nerine bowdenii
Common name: spider lily. Competitive and grows to 60cm in well-drained soil and sun. Bulbs should be set with the neck well above the ground. The red or deep-pink flowers that appear from February to April, when most other plants are spent from dry summer conditions, are decorative and remain in good condition in a vase for more than 10 days.

Propagation – with ripe seed; in autumn, and when leaves have died down, divide offsets.

Watsonia beatricis
Common name: watsonia. Competitive, spreading and fast growing to 1.2m in well-drained soil and sun. May be too invasive for a small garden; better suited to a wild garden. Parent of many colourful hybrids. Orange-red, red and pink flowers appear from December to April, and in milder climates in winter as well; decorative in a vase.

Propagation – in autumn with seed.

Zantedeschia aethiopica
Common names: arum lily or lily of the Nile. Competitive, spreading and grows to 1m in moist soil and sun or semi-shade; looks good in pasture, woodland or wild areas. The white flowers that appear from September to November are decorative in a vase.

Propagation – in winter, divide offsets.

2F Temperature drops to -3°C
Inland wind: light (*)
Coastal and salt wind: light (*)

TREES
Camellia japonica
Common name: camellia. An evergreen that cannot tolerate dry conditions. It grows to 7m where sun is received for part of the day or in shade, and in fertile, moist but well-drained neutral to acid soil. From June to October white, red or pink flowers appear. *C. sasanqua* grows to 3m in the same garden conditions and is good for hedging in warmer areas. From March to May lightly fragrant white, red or pink flowers appear.

Propagation – in late winter or early spring by grafting; in late summer take half-ripe cuttings; in mid-winter take hardwood cuttings.

SHRUBS
Convolvulus cneorum
Common name: convolvulus. A small evergreen with silvery foliage that grows in sun and most well-drained soils to 75cm. Endures light salt wind and, although it is slow in establishing, competes reasonably well with other growth. It is useful as a creeper under other taller plants in windy and coastal areas. From November to March pink-tinged buds appear, opening to white flowers.

Propagation – mid-spring by seed sown after last frost.

Phormium 'Goldspike' (monocotyledon)
Common name: flax. Although slow growing, this competitive, handsome, evergreen flax is sometimes used for hedging. Variegated green leaves have a broad band of yellow down each leaf edge. The plant is rigid and upright in growth and does not droop at the leaf ends, a dominant characteristic of all other flaxes. It creates a good focal point and is adaptable to most locations, but prefers fertile soil and sun or semi-shade where it grows to 2.5m. From November to December reddish-yellow flowers appear.

Propagation – in winter or spring by division.

Phormium 'Guardsman' (monocotyledon)
Common name: flax. Although slow growing, this is a competitive, handsome, evergreen flax in a situation that is exposed to light or salt wind; it is sometimes used for hedging. It prefers moist soil and open sunlight or semi-shade where it grows to 1.5m. The bronze leaves are striped with red and deep-pink, and from November to December reddish-purple flowers appear.
Propagation – in winter or spring by division.

GRASSES
Chionochloa flavescens (monocotyledon)
Maori name: haumata. Common names: broad-leaved snow tussock or dwarf toetoe. A competitive evergreen New Zealand native grass. It grows from 50cm-1m in most soils where it is sunny for part of the day or in semi-shade, and survives dry seasons. The grass is wind tolerant but does not like too much salt. Attractive as a garden specimen and also in group plantings mixed with ornamental flaxes, where the foliage colour and textures combine well. The lush green leaves are paler on their undersides; from December to February there are thick showy plumes of green flowers that develop into light-brown seed-heads.

Propagation – in spring by division; in spring or autumn with seed.

PERENNIALS
Cynara scolymus (herbaceous)
Common name: globe artichoke. Fast growing to 1-2m in fertile, well-drained soil and sun. From February to March the flowers, that appear towering above it, are a vegetable delicacy and can be eaten before they bloom. After the appearance of pale-blue flowers, that can also be dried for floral decoration, it dies off to re-emerge in late winter or early spring.

Propagation – in spring by seed and division.

Gunnera tinctoria (herbaceous), G. chilensis, G. scabra
Common names: Chilean rhubarb or elephant leaf. Competitive and very fast growing to 2m in wet soils where sun is received for part of the day; easily cultivated beside a stream or pond. Near the sea needs shelter from strong winds and can grow in cold areas where overhanging trees offer protection from heavy frost. It has very handsome, large green leaves about 1.2m across, and from October to November large cone-shaped spikes or panicles of greenish-yellow flowers appear, followed by green fruits tinted with red; very decorative and interesting.

Propagation – autumn or spring with seed; early spring by division.

BIENNIALS
Echium pininana
Common name: giant bugloss. Stunning flowers on stem trunk which can be 2-3m high. The stem trunk is without leaves but covered in small pink buds which open to light-blue flowers. Likes sunny, well-drained positions. Can fulfill its life cycle in 18 months, and self-seeds freely. Attractive in a shrub boarder and to create a wild-garden look.

Propagation – in spring and summer, by fresh seed or by green-wood or semi-ripe cuttings of side shoots.

Temperature drops to -3°C
Inland wind: moderate (**)
Coastal and salt wind: plants need complete shelter

TREES
Dodonaea viscosa
Maori and common name: ake ake. Competitive evergreen that grows in well-drained soil and sun or semi-shade from 2-3m. Has sticky, pale-green leaves, and from December to February clusters of green hop-like fruit appear. *D. viscosa* 'Purpurea' has sticky, copper-purple leaves and, from December to February, clusters of small reddish or purple seed capsules. Both forms tolerate dry summers and mature into handsome small trees, excellent for shelter and useful in cluster plantings. As hedges, a light trimming is taken kindly; however, heavy cutting results in collapse; they do not like being transplanted.

Propagation – in spring with seed; summer take semi-ripe cuttings.

GRASSES
Chionochloa conspicua (monocotyledon)
Maori names: hunangamoho, toetoe hunangamoho. One of the largest species of *Chionochloa*. Competitive, fast growing and forms a dense tussocks to a metre tall. Medium deep green colour with droopy flower plums on stalk 1.8m long. Prefers moist areas. Attractive in a shrub border.

Propagation – by seed.

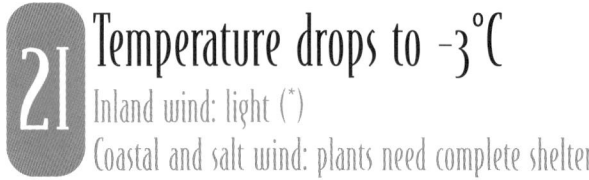

Temperature drops to -3°C
Inland wind: light (*)
Coastal and salt wind: plants need complete shelter

TREES
Aristotelia serrata
Maori name: makomako. Common name: wineberry. Evergreen, or deciduous in colder areas, and grows from 5-10m in fertile, well-drained soil and sun or semi-shade. Makes a good shelter tree; its leaves are heart-shaped, deeply serrated, bright green on the upper surface and paler underneath. In November clusters of rosy-pink flowers appear, followed by black berries.

Propagation – in summer take semi-ripe cuttings.

SHRUBS
Aucuba japonica
Common name: Japanese laurel. An evergreen that is slow growing to 2.75m in any but waterlogged soil where sun is received for part of the day or in semi-shade. Cultivated for its foliage; looks great mixed with other foliage plants in a shrub border, as it has decorative green or variegated green and gold leaves. In October small purplish flowers appear, followed by bright red berries.

Propagation – in summer take semi-ripe cuttings.

Berzelia lanuginosa
Common name: berzelia. An evergreen that grows in well-drained soil and sun to 2m; another impressive foliage shrub. It has green, feathery, conifer-like leaves, and from October to November panicles of pea-sized, creamy-white, button-like flowers appear that can be used fresh or dried for floral decoration.

Propagation – take small cuttings which root freely under glass.

Boronia heterophylla
Common name: Kalgan boronia. An evergreen that grows to 1.45m in fertile, well-drained but never very dry soil, and sun or shade. Boronia is also used as a medicinal herb and has a fragrance that can be smelt several metres away. From September to November pink flowers appear. *B. megastigma*, brown boronia, has brown flowers from August to November.

Propagation – in spring by seed and semi-ripe cuttings.

Chimonanthus praecox
Common name: wintersweet. Deciduous and grows in fertile, well-drained soil and sun to 2.5m. Held dear for the rich scent it brings to the garden from June to July when fragrant yellow flowers with purple centres appear on leafless branches; winter flowers are scarce.

Propagation – late spring or early summer with ripe seed; in summer take softwood cuttings: cultivars by cuttings only.

Choisya ternata
Common name: Mexican orange blossom. An evergreen that is slow growing to 2.75m in fertile, well-drained soil and sun. Can be used as a decorative specimen or for hedging. From November to December fragrant white flowers appear that attract bees.

Propagation – in late summer take semi-ripe cuttings.

Coprosma lucida
Maori names: karamuu, karanguu, patutiketike. Common names: glossy karamu. Good filler shrub for bush areas or shelter boarder. New Zealand evergreen, it grows to 2m in semi-shade and average soils.

Propagation – in autumn, by seed.

Daphne odora 'Rubra'
Common name: daphne. An evergreen that grows to 1.5m where sun is received for part of the day or in semi-shade, and in fertile, slightly acid,

peaty, well-drained but not over-dry soil. A specimen that lives for only 10-12 years but is worth cultivation, as every August to October very fragrant, dark-red flowers appear that, when cut, last in a vase of water for 2-3 weeks.

Propagation – in summer by fresh seed and semi-ripe cuttings: cultivars by cuttings only.

Phlomis fruticosa

Common name: Jerusalem sage. An evergreen that grows in well-drained soil and sun to 80cm; can withstand some dryness. From December to February unusual, interesting, lightly scented yellow flowers appear that are decorative in a vase.

Propagation – autumn with seed; in summer take softwood cuttings.

GRASSES

Carex secta (monocotyledon)

Maori names: puurei, maataa, makura, maaruu. Common names: niggerhead, sedge, swamp grass. Grows up to 1m in moist soils. Slow to start off with, but spreads itself in wet or boggy areas. Attractive yellow-green foliage.

Propagation – after flowering, by division and seed.

Libertia grandiflora (monocotyledon)

Maori name: miikoikoi. Common names: native iris or New Zealand satin flower. An evergreen that is not a true grass but is placed with them, as its foliage stands out decoratively amongst them. Grows to 75cm in well-drained soil where sun is received for part of the day or in semi-shade. From December to January white flowers appear, followed in autumn by golden-brown seed capsules useful for dried floral arrangements.

Propagation – spring or autumn with seed; in spring by division.

PERENNIALS

Alstroemeria aurea, A. aurantiaca

Common name: Peruvian lily. An evergreen or semi-evergreen tuber that is easy to cultivate and moderately fast growing in well-drained soil and open sunlight to 1m; naturalises on sloping banks. From November to February reddish-yellow or orange-yellow flowers with tiny maroon spots appear; decorative and last at least 10 days in a vase.

Propagation – in early spring by seed and division.

Dianella intermedia (monocotyledon)

Common names: flax lily or blueberry. An evergreen that grows to 1m in well-drained, neutral to acid soil where sun is received for part of the day or in semi-shade. A very decorative plant with orange, sword-like leaves; from October to November purplish-white flowers appear, followed by blue berries that ripen by February or March.

Propagation – spring or autumn by seed and division of offsets with roots.

Dianthus plumarius

Common name: garden pink. An evergreen that is slow growing to 30cm in well-drained, slightly alkaline soil and sun. Useful at the front of a border or in a rock garden. The scented white or pink flowers that appear from October to December are decorative in a vase.

Propagation – in summer by cuttings and layering.

Eremurus Shelford hybrids (herbaceous)

Common name: foxtail lily. Grows in well-drained soil and sun to 1.5m. Provides a fine display in any garden, but try not to lift them unnecessarily as the fleshy roots break easily. The white or salmon-pink, yellow, apricot and copper-toned flowers that appear from December to February are decorative in a vase.

Propagation – in autumn with seed; late winter to early spring or early autumn by division.

Eupatorium purpureum (herbaceous)

Common name: Joe-pye weed. Grows up to 2.5m in moist but well-drained soil and sun or semi-shade. Suitable for the back of an herbaceous border, as an established clump is very tall. From February to April rose-purple or purple flowers appear; decorative in a vase.

Propagation – spring with seed; early spring or autumn by division.

Euphorbia characias (herbaceous), E. characias subsp. characias, E. wulfenii, E. veneta

Common name: wulfen spurge. Competitive and spreading, growing to 1.25m in moist but well-drained soil and sun or semi-shade. A decorative plant often found as a garden escapee growing in wasteland areas of poor soils, droughts and wind. Stems are biennial, producing clustered blue-green leaves in contrast to long stems of pale yellowish-green flowers with purple centres that appear from June to September.

Propagation – spring or autumn with seed: in early spring or early autumn by division; in summer or spring take basal cuttings.

Francoa ramosa, F. glabrata

Common name: bridal wreath. An evergreen that is low growing in fertile, well-drained soil and sun or semi-shade. Easy to cultivate at the front of a mixed border; naturalises in the right situation. Can also be used as a tub or container plant. From December to February small white flowers appear along stems up to 1m high.

Propagation – in spring by seed and division.

Penstemon 'Susan'

Common name: beard tongue. Semi-evergreen and grows in fertile, well-drained soil and sun to 90cm; looks very attractive in any garden. Soft-pink flowers which deepen at the edges appear from October to February and are decorative in a vase.

Propagation – autumn or spring with seed; spring by division; in summer or early autumn take softwood or semi-ripe cuttings of non-flowering shoots: selected forms by cuttings only.

Verbena hastata

Common names: blue vervain, Indian hyssop or wild hyssop. Grows in well-drained soil and sun or semi-shade to 1.2m. Has been used as a medicinal herb. From December to April elegant, pale-blue or lilac flowers appear.

Propagation – autumn or spring by seed; summer or autumn by stem cuttings; late winter by division; spring by division of young shoots.

BULBS

Amaryllis belladonna

Common names: belladonna or naked lady. Dormant during summer; grows in well-drained soil and sun to 80cm. Neck of bulb should protrude well above the ground when planted. Flowering in the driest part of autumn, fragrant white, carmine-red or lavender-pink blooms provide a wonderful surprise along driveways or sunny banks from March to May; decorative in a vase.

Propagation – late spring or late summer by division: before growth begins.

Crinum X powellii

Common name: crinum. Semi-deciduous and grows in rich, well-drained soil and sun to 1m. Should be planted so that most of the bulb is out of the ground. From October to December lightly scented, trumpet-like, white or soft-pink flowers appear that are useful for cutting and especially treasured for the decoration of wedding celebrations.

Propagation – in spring by ripe seed and division of offsets.

Dierama pulcherrimum

Common name: angel's fishing rod. An evergreen that grows to 1.5m in sun and well-drained soil; must be kept moist during summer. Adds interest to any border. From December to February pretty, small, deep-pink flowers appear dangling on 1m long stems.

Propagation – autumn or spring with seed; in spring divide corms.

Hyacinthus orientalis

Common name: hyacinth. Deciduous in summer and slow growing to 20cm in well-drained soil and sun or semi-shade. Hyacinth lives for only 4 years; takes 3 years to reach full size and in the fourth year the parent bulb breaks up. The heavily scented, white, carmine-red, blue, pink or violet flowers that appear from August to October are decorative in a vase.

Propagation – in late summer or early autumn divide offsets.

Lilium Asiatic hybrids

Common name: Asiatic lily. Grows in fertile, well-drained soil and sun to 1.5m. Has a shortened life in warmer areas. The lightly scented white, orange or yellow flowers that appear from November to December are decorative in a vase.

Propagation – in spring or autumn with seed; in autumn with stem bulbs; in summer with bulb scales.

Lilium auratum

Common name: golden-rayed lily. Grows in well-drained, neutral to acid soil and in semi-shade to 1.5m. Very decorative in any garden. The scented white, carmine-red or yellow flowers that appear from December to February are decorative in a vase.

Propagation – in spring or autumn with seed; in autumn with stem bulbs; in summer with bulb scales.

Lilium longiflorum

Common names: Christmas lily or Easter lily. Grows in fertile, well-drained soil and sun to 1m. The scented, pure white flowers that appear from December to February are decorative in a vase.

Propagation – in spring or autumn with seed; in autumn with stem bulbs; in summer with bulb scales.

Lilium Oriental hybrids

Common name: Empress hybrid lily. Derived from *L. auratum* and *L. speciosum* from Japan. Grows well in warmer areas in fertile, well-drained soil and sun to 2m. The scented white, magenta-red, yellow, salmon-pink or pale-lilac flowers that appear from December to February are decorative in a vase.

Propagation – in spring or autumn with seed; in autumn with stem bulbs; in summer with bulb scales.

Lilium tigrinum, L. lancifolium

Common name: tiger lily. Grows in fertile, well-drained soil and sun to 1.5m. The scented orange-red, orange or yellow flowers spotted with purple that appear from January to March make a bold autumn display in any garden, and are used in Chinese herbal medicine for strengthening the heart. Good cut flowers.

Propagation – in spring or autumn with seed; in autumn with stem bulbs; in summer with bulb scales.

ANNUALS

Ageratum houstonianum

Common name: floss flower. The parent of many forms; grows to 30cm in sun and moist but well-drained soil, though flowering is very poor if the soil dries out. It can be moved at any time, even in bloom, and its many uses include bedding displays, cut flowers, edging and container work. The lightly scented, white, blue or lavender-mauve flowers appear from December to January.

Propagation – in spring with seed sown outdoors.

Ammi majus

Common names: bishopsweed or lace flower. Grows competitively in well-drained soil and sun to 1.5m and, in the right situation, tends to naturalise by re-seeding itself annually. Very suitable in a cottage garden. The lightly scented, lacy, white flowers that appear from November to March are decorative in a vase.

Propagation – in spring with seed.

Carthamus tinctorius

Common name: safflower. Fast growing to 1m in fertile, well-drained soil and sun. A strong orange-coloured dye is extracted from the plant. The orange-yellow flowers that appear from December to February are decorative in a vase.

Propagation – in spring with seed.

Oenothera biennis

Common name: evening primrose. Spreading; and in well-drained soil and sun it is fast growing to 1.5m. Naturally suits a wild garden. For many weeks from November to March fragrant yellow flowers appear.

Propagation – spring or autumn by division and seed: self-seeds readily.

2K Temperature drops to -3°C

Inland wind: moderate (**)
Coastal and salt wind: do not grow these plants

TREES

Prunus campanulata

Common name: Taiwan cherry. A spreading, deciduous specimen tree that grows in sun and any but waterlogged soil to 8m. One of the earliest specimens to flower; from August to September lightly scented, delicate, trumpet-shaped, magenta-red or deep-pink blooms appear.

Propagation – autumn with seed; winter by hardwood cuttings; spring to autumn by grafting and budding: selected forms by grafting and budding only.

Quercus palustris

Common name: pin oak. Deciduous and used as a specimen tree. It is slow growing to 18m in fertile, moist but well-drained soil and sun or semi-shade. In autumn its usually bright green leaves turn scarlet, orange-red and yellow-brown.

Propagation – autumn with seed; late winter by grafting: selected forms by grafting only.

SHRUBS

Cistus creticus, C. villosus, C. incanus

Common name: rock rose. A competitive evergreen that grows in well-drained soil and sun to 1.5m. A bushy aromatic shrub with protective hairs on the younger shoots, giving them a whitish appearance. The shrub favours warmer areas and survives only light frosts. From September to December attractive, paper-like, rose-pink or white and yellow flowers appear.

Propagation – autumn with seed; summer take softwood or greenwood cuttings; hybrids and cultivars by cuttings only.

CLIMBERS

Parthenocissus quinquefolia, Ampelopsis quinquefolia, Vitis quinquefolia

Common name: Virginia creeper. Deciduous and grows to 15m in fertile, well-drained soil and sun or shade; colours are more spectacular in a semi-shaded situation. In autumn its usually dull-green leaves turn crimson before they fall.

Propagation – summer take softwood or greenwood cuttings; early spring take hardwood cuttings.

2L Temperature drops to -3°C

Inland wind: light (*)
Coastal and salt wind: do not grow these plants

TREES

Hoheria angustifolia

Maori name: houhi-puruhi. Common Name: narrow-leaved lacebark. A large evergreen tree that is found in native bush. It is used for shelter when planted among other plants. In fertile, well-drained soil and sun or semi-shade it grows to an optimum of 10m. In March white flowers appear.

Propagation – autumn with seed; in summer take semi-ripe cuttings.

Magnolia campbellii var. mollicomata

Common name: magnolia. Deciduous and grows as a specimen to 20m in sun or in semi-shade, and fertile, well-drained soil. Magnolia prefers neutral to acid soil but grows in alkaline soil if deep and humus-rich. Dry sandy soil should be enriched with manure or leaf-mould before planting. From July to September fragrant lilac-pink flowers appear.

Propagation – summer take semi-ripe cuttings; winter by grafting.

Magnolia grandiflora
Common name: bull bay. Evergreen and moderately fast growing as a specimen to 10m in sun or semi-shade and in fertile, well-drained soil. Magnolia prefers neutral to acid soil but grows in alkaline soil if deep and humus-rich. Dry sandy soil should be enriched with manure or leaf-mould before planting. Once established this specimen becomes a very strong tree. From January to March fragrant white flowers appear.

Propagation – autumn with ripe seed; in winter by grafting; in summer take semi-ripe cuttings; selected forms only by grafting and taking semi-ripe cuttings.

Myrsine australis
Maori and common names: mapau or matipou. An evergreen that grows as a specimen to 6m in sun or shade and any fertile, well-drained soil other than a shallow lime type. Makes an excellent hedge, or good in cluster plantings. Young branches are reddish in colour and have smooth, pale-green or yellowish-green leaves. Insignificant flowers occur in summer.

Propagation – in summer take semi-ripe cuttings.

Nothofagus solandri
Maori name: tawhai rauriki. Common names: black beech or mountain beech. An evergreen that is slow growing to 30m in deep, fertile, moist but well-drained soil and sun. Grown as a specimen where there is plenty of space.

Propagation – in autumn with seed.

Phyllocladus trichomanoides (conifer)
Common name: celery-leafed pine. An evergreen that is slow growing to 8m in most soil types and sun; used for shelter.

Propagation – late autumn to late winter: take cuttings from young plants or stratify seed.

PERENNIALS
Cyclamen hederifolium, C. neapolitanum
Common name: cyclamen. Deciduous in summer and slow growing to 10cm in humus-rich, well-drained soil where sun is received for part of the day or in semi-shade. Lovely under large deciduous trees. From March to August white, carmine-red or pink flowers appear.

Propagation – in late summer or autumn with seed.

3A Areas that are frost-free
Inland wind: severe (***)
Coastal and salt wind: severe (***)

TREES
Coprosma repens, C. baueri
Maori names: angiangi, maamaangi, naupata or taupata. Common name: taupata. A New Zealand native evergreen that is fast growing in well-drained soil and sun; reaches 2-4m. It is aggressive in competition with other plants and is difficult to remove once established. This tree or shrub is possibly one of the most salt-hard plants found growing freely in coastal regions. As it is sculptured and pruned to a shape that indicates the prevailing wind, taupata is an excellent plant to analyse for wind behaviour in severely exposed localities. It follows with its form the shape of a hill as the wind is uplifted; can be seen growing on rocks along the seashore to the exact height and even the shape of those rocks, deflecting the wind around it. Taupata can also thread its way into drains where its roots spread about searching for water. Taupata fails as a thick hedge as its older foliage has a tendency to die, leaving gaps for wind. It is useful for shelter plantings along the coast, but a severe cutting-back is necessary every 2-3 years to keep it compact, or it will grow into brittle small trees. When left undisturbed for several years in sheltered locations it grows a taupata forest, providing excellent shelter from all winds. The glossy dark-green leaves are attractive, and from October to November dark-purple flowers appear. The plant has male and female trees. In early summer, the female is covered with numerous orange berries that are a food source for birds which naturally disperse the seed, causing it to spread.

Propagation – spring with seed; in summer take semi-ripe cuttings.

Metrosideros excelsa
Maori name: pohutukawa. Common name: New Zealand Christmas tree. A competitive New Zealand native evergreen that grows to 12-15m in well-drained soil and sun. A coastal tree often seen hanging from cliff edges on beaches and rocky foreshores, accepting abundant salt wind. The tree is unusual in that it has aerial roots which hang from its branches. They are fibrous mats of absorbent root tissue which collect moisture from evening humidity and rainfall, acting as a temporary water reserve. The tree grows tall and has strong branches supporting the top canopy. In the wind garden it can be used as a specimen, for shelter in cluster plantings or for hedging. From December to January it is covered in showy, bright red staminate or yellow flowers.

Propagation – in spring with seed; summer take semi-ripe cuttings.

Pittosporum crassifolium
Maori and common name: karo. A New Zealand native evergreen, one of the hardiest trees for windy areas. It is competitive in places where other plants fail, tolerating drought, wind and excess salt. Karo is usually seen in coastal regions, in well-drained rocky or poor soil and sun or semi-shade, where it grows from 4-5m. Responds to regular clipping, making it an excellent hedge or shelter tree, and should be used in exposed areas in cluster plantings. A slow grower with a non-aggressive habit but definitely durable. Karo takes 10-15 years to succeed gorse. The tree oozes a sticky latex from scale insects which suck the sap in young leaves, causing them to deform or blemish, but it survives this pest well. In moist areas it is often attacked by fungus, sooty mould, which lives off honey-dew produced by the scale insects. Karo looks similar to pohutukawa in shape but close observation distinguishes the differences. Karo has smooth bark and tiny rosy-purple flowers which appear from August to October.

Propagation – autumn or spring by seed; summer semi-ripe cuttings.

SHRUBS
Brachyglottis greyi, Senecio greyi
Common name: Cook Strait groundsel. A competitive New Zealand native evergreen that grows in well-drained soil and sun or semi-shade to 1-2m. It withstands strong salt wind and drought but suffers from wet soils, becoming infected by a fungus which makes the leaves droop and gradually brown off. Winter pruning helps to keep it bushy. From December to March bright yellow, daisy-type flowers appear, contrasting well with silver foliage.

Propagation – in late summer take semi-ripe cuttings.

Pseudopanax laetus, Neopanax laetum
Common name: five finger. An evergreen that grows to 3m in fertile, moist but well-drained soil and sun or semi-shade. Good as a coastal hedge amongst other trees,and takes pruning well. It has dark-green leaves, and in summer greenish-purple flowers appear.

Propagation – spring or autumn by seed; summer by semi-ripe cuttings.

GRASSES
Cortaderia splendens (monocotyledon)
Maori and common name: toetoe. Large and vigorous evergreen native grass. Will grow up to 6m tall when flowering. Occurs mainly in northern parts of New Zealand along coastal areas, in sand dunes, on rocks and cliff faces. Flowers in early December.

Propagation – by rhizome division or seed after flowering.

Desmoschoenus spiralis (monocotyledon)
Maori and common name: pingao. A sand tussock that grows on beaches. It has mixed yellow, orange, and green grass-like leaves which are stout, rigid, and hardy. The plant grows 60-90cm tall. Has a woody stem, which creeps along the ground, often for some distance. This plant is a good alternative to marram grass in the establishment of sand dunes. Pingao is now regarded as an endangered native species, a result of invading competition from marram grass and lupin, which are also used to stabilise

moving sand dunes. The leaves are popular for weaving kete and baskets.

Propagation – in spring or autumn by seed or in spring by rhizome division.

Spinifex sericeus (monocotyledon), S. hirsutus

Maori names: koowhangatara, raumoa, turikaakoa, wawatai. Common names: marram grass, silvery sand grass. A native grass that grows to 60cm tall from creeping underground stems. The foliage has a silvery appearance and is used to stabilise sand dunes. Likes well-drained sandy soils and full sun. The female form has attractive spiny seed heads. The exotic marram grass (*Ammophila arenaria*) looks similar but forms steeper sand dunes which are more prone to wind erosion. *S. sericeus* is a better choice for stabilising severely exposed sand dunes.

Propagation – by seed and division of rhizomes.

GROUNDCOVERS

Arctotis stoechadifolia, A. acaulis

Common name: Aurora daisy. An aggressive, spreading, evergreen creeper that is fast growing to 15cm in sun and well-drained sandy soil containing humus. Can be knocked back by light frosts but re-emerges and flowers again profusely in spring, though severe frost kills it completely as it is frost tender below 10°C. Very useful perennial on sun-drenched banks in windy areas. The plant is strong and able to compete amongst most other plants, provided it receives full sun. The flowers are on upright stems and open with the increase of sunlight, closing up again at dusk. There are several attractive-coloured varieties available. From November to March white, cream, yellow, orange, brick-red, plum or purple flowers appear.

Propagation – in winter by seed and division.

Gazania linearis

Common name: star daisy. A competitive, evergreen, perennial creeper that is low growing to 20cm in well-drained soil and sun. One of the original parents of the common gazania. Often seen in coastal gardens, as it tolerates droughts and is extremely wind and salt-hard, gazania is an asset to the wind garden. Gazania grows from a strong root and has rhizomatous stems from which linear leaves protrude. It is a good ground creeper that uses all available sun on dry banks, roadside verges, path edges and amongst rocks where they naturalise, becoming very colourful in spring or summer. Several different coloured varieties are derived from the parent clone. The bright flowers open with the sun and close when the sun goes. Under favourable conditions some flower throughout the year but otherwise from November to February in white, red, orange, yellow, pink or purple colours; sometimes flowers are striped.

Propagation – spring or summer by cuttings from shoots near the crown of the plants; late winter to early spring by seed and division.

Gazania rigens

Common name: black-eyed Susan. A competitive perennial creeper that is low growing to 15cm in well-drained soil and sun; an asset to the wind garden. Often seen in coastal gardens as it tolerates droughts and is extremely wind and salt-hard, with deciduous older leaves. Gazanias are good on dry banks, roadside verges, path edges and in rocky regions where they naturalise, becoming very colourful in summer and autumn. From January to May orange or yellow flowers appear.

Propagation – spring or summer by cuttings from shoots near the crown of the plants; late winter to early spring by seed and division.

Carpobrotus edulis, Mesembryanthemum edule

Common names: Hottentot fig or ice plant. A mat-forming, evergreen, xerophyte creeper that grows to 15cm in sun and well-drained sandy or rocky soil. A succulent with unbelievable tolerance of salt wind, drought, pollution and poor soils. In fact, it can survive for a few weeks in the sun without any soil at all. The plant smothers beach gravels, sand dunes, hangs down crib walls and dominates extremely difficult areas where other plants fail. The creeper needs full sun and is seldom found in areas where sunlight is absent. The plant looks handsome in its younger life, but the older foliage has a tendency to die off and can look messy as it allows grasses to grow through and live on its organic refuse. Very useful for quick cover to prevent wind erosion. From November to March pale yellow flowers appear that open with the sun and turn pinkish-orange with age.

Propagation – in spring or summer by seed and stem cuttings.

Disphyma australe

Maori names: horokaka, ngarangara or ruerueke. Common name: New Zealand ice plant. A coastal, native evergreen, spreading xerophyte that grows to 5cm in sun and well-drained sandy or rocky soil. A succulent able to grow right down to the saltwater's edge, it can live on rocks without any fresh water, and even survives submersion in sea water. Under these conditions the leaves redden and look like jellybeans. From October to March it produces abundant masses of lovely pink and white flowers 3-5cm in diameter.

Propagation – in spring with seed.

Osteospermum fruticosum

Common name: dimorphotheca. A prostrate evergreen perennial that is fast growing to 45cm in well-drained soil and sun. It has fleshy leaves, and flowers that open with the sun. Able to endure severe winds, recovering quickly from salt burn. Plant over dry sunny walls and banks, where it becomes a mass of flowers and forms a thick mat in exposed conditions. Lack of light makes it grow leggy. Both bright white and mauve flowers appear from August to January; they have dark centres, often lined on the lower surface and sometimes tinged with green.

Propagation – in summer take cuttings of non-flowering shoots.

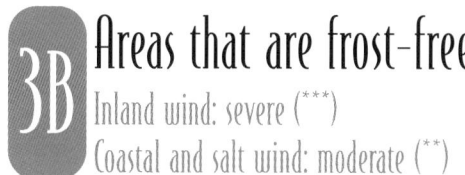

3B Areas that are frost-free
Inland wind: severe (***)
Coastal and salt wind: moderate (**)

TREES

Banksia integrifolia

Common name: coast banksia. An evergreen that grows to 10m in sun or semi-shade and well-drained soil low in phosphates and nitrates. A useful addition to cluster plantings or for shelter and is a steady grower. Able to survive a harsh environment but forms a better specimen in protected sunny areas with less salt. The bush has an open shape, typical of the protea family, and from March to August lime-yellow flowers appear.

Propagation – in early spring or autumn with seed.

Pseudopanax lessonii

Maori name: houpara. Common name: five finger. A competitive evergreen, native to New Zealand; grows in fertile, moist but well-drained soil and sun or semi-shade to 4-6m; commonly found amongst undergrowth in the bush. Five finger is an interesting tree, as it has a juvenile form when young and changes into a completely different form once matured – a process of metamorphosis. In nurseries, this plant often hybridises naturally with close relatives, and various cultivar forms occur regularly. Five finger is best used in the wind garden amongst cluster plantings where it fills gaps well or can be grown as a specimen. Frost tender below 5°C, it makes an excellent indoor plant. It has attractive rich-bronze leaves and several coloured forms are available, like *P.* 'Gold Splash' or *P.* 'Purpurea'.

Propagation – spring or autumn by seed; summer by semi-ripe cuttings.

SHRUBS

Aeonium arboreum, Sempervivum

Common name: stonecrop. An evergreen, xerophyte succulent that grows to 60cm in very well-drained soil and sun. It has a spreading or sprawling habit and grows well on steep, dry, sunny cliff faces where it competes easily with other plants; can be used successfully in window boxes. Frost tender below 2°C. It has bright green leaves and golden-yellow flowers which are very attractive, appearing from November to April on 2- to 3-year-old stems that die back after flowering.

Propagation – in summer with offsets.

Agapanthus praecox subsp. orientalis, A. orientalis

Common name: African lily. A competitive, evergreen native of South Africa that grows to 60cm in any well-drained soil and sun or semi-shade. It can survive a very light occasional frost in the shelter of other plants; near the sea, its leaf tips can burn from severe salty winds. It has thick roots that are used by the plant as food reserves to survive harsh seasons. Takes a good growing season or two to establish itself, forming thick clumps that can be divided. It does not spread on its own, occurring only where planted, and stands up to most other plant competition of similar height. *Agapanthus* has many ornamental uses as a groundcover or edging along paths as well as providing low shelter for other plants in the wind garden. From November to March white, blue or purple flowers appear on 1m long stems that are decorative in a vase.

Propagation – late winter to early spring by division and ripe seed: cultivars will not come true from seed.

Aloe arborescens
Common names: aloe or aloe vera. An evergreen xerophyte that grows to 1-2m in very well-drained soil, and sun. It is able to tolerate drought and salt wind. The succulent stores water in its leaves and is therefore frost tender below 5°C, but forms thick clumps and does well on dry sunny banks exposed to strong winds and salt. From August to November red flowers appear.

Propagation – spring or summer by seed, offsets and stem cuttings.

Argyranthemum frutescens, Chrysanthemum frutescens
Common name: marguerite daisy. Aggressive and spreading; deciduous in cold areas. It is fast growing to 1m in well-drained soil and sun, so provides good low-level shelter in windy locations; does very well in coastal areas provided it has protection from direct salt wind. To retain compact bushes prune the plant back hard in January after flowering. Several double-and single-bloom cultivars are available; the single white flowering marguerite daisy is a delightful escapee that is covered in flowers during spring and has found its home on the hillsides of Wellington amongst gorse. In warmer areas, plants are sometimes known to flower continuously throughout the year, but usually white, mauve or pink and yellow flowers appear from August to January; decorative in a vase.

Propagation – spring by cuttings from plant material in active growth and division of basal growth.

Beschorneria yuccoides
Common name: Mexican lily. An evergreen succulent that grows to 1m in well-drained soil and sun. Useful for rock gardens; can withstand dry conditions. It has grey-green leaves, and from December to February red flowers appear.

Propagation – in spring or summer by seed and division.

Coprosma acerosa
Maori names: tarakupenga, taatarahake or taataraheke. Common name: sand coprosma. An evergreen that grows to 2m in well-drained soil and sun, forming neat compact bushes. It has yellow-green leaves and tiny insignificant flowers that ripen from March to April, forming translucent, pale-blue berries. *C.* 'Coppershine' grows to 1.5m and has decorative greenish-brown, glossy leaves that colour up in winter.

Propagation – spring with seed; in summer take semi-ripe cuttings.

Furcraea foetida (Xerophyte)
Common name: furcraea. A perennial succulent with broad, sword-shaped leaves, it needs full sun and well-drained soil. In spring the flowers are very decorative: green, with white centres, on a pink spike up to 2m long.

Propagation – by bulbils when developed.

Hebe diosmifolia
Maori name: aute. Common name: hebe. An evergreen that grows to 1m in well-drained soil and sun; competes well with other low growth. This is one of the more ornamental hebes. It has compact light-green foliage, and from September to November light-mauve flowers appear.

Propagation – in summer take semi-ripe cuttings.

Hebe obtusata
Common name: northern koromiko. A small semi-prostrate evergreen that grows from 1-6m in well-drained soil and sun. It does not compete so well with other growth as it is a slow grower, but it is attractive in the wind garden. Small leaves form compact rounded bushes and from January to June small white or purple-mauve flowers appear.

Propagation – in summer take semi-ripe cuttings.

Protea neriifolia
Common name: oleander-leaved protea. An evergreen that grows to 3m in sun and fertile, well-drained, neutral to acid soil low in phosphates and nitrates. Good as a garden specimen or for picking, as from autumn through winter to spring creamy-white, red or salmon-pink flower bracts appear.

Propagation – summer take semi-ripe cuttings; spring or autumn with seed: germination is erratic.

Santolina chamaecyparissus
Common names: cotton lavender or sea lavender. An evergreen that is quick growing to 700cm-1m in poor, well-drained soil and sun. Able to endure salt wind and dry summers. Prune once a year to keep bushy. Does well on dry banks, crib walls or in a shrub border. Handsome, with silvery aromatic foliage, this plant produces bright yellow button-shaped flowers from October to December; decorative used fresh or dried for floral decoration.

Propagation – in summer take semi-ripe cuttings.

TRAILERS
Coprosma X kirkii
Common name: coprosma. A prostrate, evergreen shrub that grows to 40cm in well-drained soil and sun. It has small shiny green leaves and forms a compact trailing mat, good for covering walls.

Propagation – spring with seed; in summer take semi-ripe cuttings.

PERENNIALS
Osteospermum ecklonis
Common name: dimorphotheca. An aggressive evergreen that is fast growing to 1m in well-drained soil and sun. A shrubby mounded plant that has flowers opening with the sun. Able to endure severe winds but needs some shelter from the most severe salt wind. Plant over dry sunny walls and banks where it becomes a mass of flowers in the spring. From November to March daisy-like white flower heads appear, blue to violet beneath with dark purple-blue centres.

Propagation – in summer take cuttings of non-flowering shoots.

ANNUALS
Dorotheanthus bellidiformis,
Mesembryanthemum criniflorum
Common names: ice plant or Livingston daisy. Slow-growing succulent to 15cm in very well-drained soil and sun. This colourful plant loves baking heat; ideal for dry, sunny places and seaside gardens, as the flowers open only with the sun. From November to January white, red, crimson, apricot, yellow, buff, purple or pink flowers with a red eye appear.

Propagation – in autumn with seed: in cold areas in spring.

3C Areas that are frost-free
Inland wind: moderate (**)
Coastal and salt wind: moderate (**)

TREES
Corynocarpus laevigatus
Maori name: karaka. Common name: New Zealand laurel. A New Zealand native evergreen that is slow growing to 15m in moisture-retentive but well-drained soil and sun or semi-shade. A tree found in coastal bush areas that is able to survive difficult locations, but takes a few years to establish itself. It is used as a specimen or for shelter in cluster plantings amongst other large trees. It has glossy, dark-green or variegated leaves, and from December to February has small greenish flowers, followed in autumn and winter by fleshy, plum-like, orange fruits with poisonous kernels. Maori used to soak, then roast the kernels of karaka berries, which were eaten as a delicacy.

Propagation – in summer by semi-ripe cuttings and ripe seed.

Lagunaria patersonii

Common name: Norfolk Island hibiscus. A competitive evergreen that is fast growing to 15m in fertile, well-drained soil and sun. A semi-tropical which does well in northern regions, especially in coastal areas, where it accepts salt wind. The tree is pyramidal in its earlier growth but spreads as it ages. Useful in shelter plantings and competes well with other growth. It has grey-green leaves, and from December to February small bell-shaped, rosy-pink or mauve hibiscus-like flowers appear. Sharp hairs in seed pods can cause skin irritations.

Propagation – in spring with seed; summer take semi-ripe cuttings.

Leucadendron argenteum

Common name: silver tree. A competitive evergreen that is quick growing to 4-9m in sun and well-drained soil low in nitrates and phosphates; usually short lived, from 7-15 years. Tolerates strong, continuous wind with a reasonable salt content. Though able to resist droughts while young, lack of water to the mature tree often causes sudden death. Ideal for cluster plantings, as a specimen tree or for shelter belts. It has grey foliage, and from December to February insignificant flowers appear in silvery bracts.

Propagation – in spring with seed.

Meryta sinclairii

Maori or common name: puka. A New Zealand native evergreen that grows from 4-6m in well-drained soil with an adequate moisture content and sun or semi-shade. Puka is frost tender below 5°C and tolerates salt wind but prefers some shelter from strong winds. Its extra-large, glossy, bright green leaves and lush bold shape make it a spectacular specimen. Male and female trees occur separately, and from September to May greenish flowers appear.

Propagation – summer take semi-ripe cuttings; late summer with ripe seed: seed is short-lived.

SHRUBS

Echium candicans, E. fastuosum

Common name: pride of Madeira. A competitive evergreen that grows to 2.5m in sun and most well-drained soils including those which are rocky and sandy. It is a handsome ornamental for the wind garden and a wonderful coastal plant. The plant grows quickly to form a bush and has grey-green foliage and several long, upright, purple-blue inflorescences which begin to flower in early spring, lasting for 2 months and attracting butterflies and bees.

Propagation – spring or summer by greenwood or semi-ripe cuttings and ripe seed.

Nerium oleander

Common name: oleander. An evergreen that is fast growing to 2-4m in well-drained soil and sun. A subtropical shrub that cannot live in cold shadowy places; frost tender below 5°C. Able to stand up to most warm winds and droughts. Oleander is useful as an ornamental or amongst cluster plantings. A poisonous plant that is not eaten by insects or animals; it always looks healthy. From November to March white, bright pink, orange or red flowers appear.

Propagation – in spring with seed; summer take semi-ripe cuttings.

Protea cynaroides

Common name: king protea. An evergreen that grows to 1.5m in sun and well-drained neutral to acid soil low in nitrates and phosphates. Old bushes that become leggy or sprawling should be pruned heavily to promote vigorous new growth (not all proteas should be pruned this way). The largest flowered protea species. From June to November flowers appear, varying in colour from greenish-white through to silver-pinks, to deep-reds; spectacular for picking.

Propagation – in summer take semi-ripe cuttings; spring or autumn with seed: germination is erratic.

Senecio cineraria, Cineraria maritima

Common name: dusty miller. An evergreen that grows in well-drained soil and sun to 1m. Especially good for seaside gardens. It has grey foliage and from October to January golden-yellow flowers appear.

Propagation – in summer take semi-ripe cuttings.

TRAILERS

Rosmarinus lavandulaceus, R. prostratus

Common name: rosemary. A prostrate, aromatic evergreen that grows in well-drained soil and sun to 15cm. Endurable, but not as hardy as its relative. Stands up to strong winds with moderate salt content and dry summers. Rosemary is slow growing to start with, but is tenacious and succeeds against moderate competition from other plants. Grows well amongst other shrubs, and its deep-green foliage is ornamental. The blue flowers that appear from October to December attract bees.

Propagation – in summer take semi-ripe cuttings.

CLIMBERS

Tecomanthe speciosa

Common name: trumpet vine. A durable coastal climber with glossy deep green leaves. Forms a dense woody vine, but takes 8-10 years to produce clusters of very attractive cream-coloured flowers. Slow to establish but will take vigorously after the first two years and is very useful for covering pergolas and fences. Needs a good moist soil, and it will thrive in warm salt winds no less than 10°C.

Propagation – in spring seed or in summer by semi-ripe cuttings.

GROUNDCOVERS

Arthropodium cirratum (monocotyledon)

Maori name: rengarenga. Common names: renga lily or rock lily. An evergreen that grows to 1m in any well-drained soil and sun or shade. A handsome perennial plant found in exposed areas or coastal regions of the North Island and in Nelson and Marlborough. The leaves are flax-like but soft and fleshy, forming clumps. When shaded, grows lush and slightly taller to compete for light. Survives poor soils and dry Conditions, and can endure salt winds but not excessive salt spray. Can go through a stage of conditioning, which takes 5-6 months, where all the foliage may die back, but this is replaced within a season with new growth. New growth can burn off again and again, but over the seasons it hardens to exposure. Frost is its limiting factor and it is found in the South Island only in protected areas under trees. The roots were used by Maori for food but required prolonged cooking to make them palatable. The bases of the leaves and roots were used as a poultice for ulcers, tumours and abcesses; the sap is a sticky resin. From November to January white flowers appear clustered on stems. Rock lily is easily transplanted and raised from seed.

Propagation – in spring or autumn with seed; spring by division.

PERENNIALS

Euphorbia glauca (herbaceous)

Maori names: waiuuatua, waiuu-atua. Common name: shore spurge. Native evergreen with grey-blue leaves and purple flowers, it will grow up to 1m high in sand gravel and rocky situations. Tolerates dry conditions in open sunlight. Though it is rare, it is an attractive plant to use in coastal gravel gardens because of its foliage.

Propagation – in autumn or spring by seed or by rhizome division in winter.

Myosotidium hortensia

Maori name: kopakopa. Common name: Chatham Island forget-me-not. An evergreen that is slow growing to 60cm in fertile, moist soil where sun is received for part of the day or in semi-shade. One of New Zealand's more colourful perennials, it grows in peat, survives salt air and wind, but prefers to live amongst other foliage, under trees or grouped together with shrubs. A decorative plant with large, glossy green leaves. From September to November white or bright blue flowers appear in masses, sometimes with a mixture of pink on the same stem.

Propagation – summer or autumn with ripe seed; spring by division.

ANNUALS

Helipterum roseum, Acroclinium roseum

Common name: paper daisy. Moderately fast growing to 30cm in poor, very well-drained soil and sun. Suitable for rock gardens; can withstand dry conditions. The pink flowers that appear from December to March can be used fresh or dried for floral decoration.

Propagation – spring or summer with seed; in autumn take cuttings.

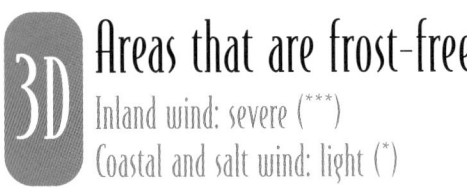

Areas that are frost-free
Inland wind: severe (***)
Coastal and salt wind: light (*)

TREES

Agonis juniperina
Common name: juniper myrtle. An evergreen that grows in moist but well-drained soil and open sunlight to 6m and is used as a handsome specimen. Can do with a spring trim to retain a good appearance. It is frost tender below 1°C. From March to November dainty sprays of white flowers appear that can be used fresh or dried for floral decoration.

Propagation — in spring with seed; summer take semi-ripe cuttings.

Buddleia salvifolia
Common name: butterfly bush. A competitive, South African evergreen that grows in well-drained soil and sun to 5m. A quick-growing bush, very useful as a specimen or hedge. Provides excellent shelter and is able to stand up to most winds with a moderate salt content; also able to endure moderate drought. This plant is a must for any shelter planting. Prune it back about every third year to keep it bushy. From June to September it has long clusters of mauve flowers with an orange eye whose fragrance can often be smelled some distance away; it attracts butterflies.

Propagation — in summer take semi-ripe cuttings.

Virgilia capensis, V. oroboides
Common name: Cape virgilia. A competitive evergreen that is fast growing in well-drained soil and sun to 7m. Reaches 3-4m in 2 years and endures strong winds, though salt wind burns the foliage. Resists considerable drought and competes well with most other vegetation. Can grow in shaded areas but tends to become drawn. Virgilia is short-lived, having a life span of up to 20 years, after which time it may blow over. Excellent plants for quick, reliable shelter and for cluster plantings or, in a position that does not interfere with light on other garden plants, for screening. In a large space can be an attractive ornamental. From November to March clusters of purple-mauve flowers appear.

Propagation — spring by seed: pre-soak in warm water for 24 hours.

Virgilia divaricata
Common name: virgilia. A competitive evergreen that is fast growing to 3-6m in well-drained soil and sun. Able to endure strong winds and considerable drought, and competes well with most other vegetation, though salt wind burns the foliage. Grows in shaded areas but tends to become drawn. Another virgilia with a life span of up to 20 years, after which time it may blow over. Excellent quick, reliable shelter. Good for cluster and shelter plantings and can be an attractive ornamental. From November to March clusters of bright pink flowers appear.

Propagation — spring by seed: pre-soak in warm water for 24 hours.

SHRUBS

Corokia buddleioides
Maori and common name: korokio. An evergreen that grows to 3m in fertile, well-drained soil and sun. It has glossy, dark-green leaves, and from September to December panicles of star-shaped, yellow flowers appear.

Propagation — in summer take softwood cuttings.

Euryops abrotanifolius
Common name: Paris daisy. A competitive evergreen that grows to 1m in well-drained soil and sun and can withstand a very light occasional frost. Prune back every second year after flowering, otherwise it grows too leggy. E. pectinatus, yellow marguerite, grows to 1.25m in the same conditions. From June to November yellow flowers appear, so both are useful for a bright winter display.

Propagation — in summer take softwood cuttings.

Melaleuca hypericifolia
Common name: paperbark. An evergreen that grows from 2-5m where sun is received for part of the day and in well-drained soil low in nitrogen. A coastal shrub that does well on exposed sites. Can be used in cluster plantings or as a specimen. From December to February it is covered with crimson-red flowers.

Propagation — spring with seed; in summer take semi-ripe cuttings.

Teucrium fruticans
Common name: shrubby germander. A competitive evergreen that grows from 1-2m in well-drained soil and sun. A wind-hard, compact, fragrant shrub that tolerates drought. Very useful for any wild wind garden, as it competes well with aggressive growth and fills gaps in the shrub border, but needs to be pruned back if it becomes leggy. Strong, salt winds burn it a little, but it can live by the sea provided there is some shelter. Makes a good hedge and is very useful amongst cluster plantings. It has silver-grey-green foliage that carries tiny blue or lavender flowers which attract bees.

Propagation — in summer take softwood or semi-ripe cuttings.

Areas that are frost-free
Inland wind: moderate (**)
Coastal and salt wind: light (*)

TREES

Agonis flexuosa
Common names: peppermint tree or willow myrtle. An aromatic evergreen that grows to 9m in moist but well-drained soil and sun. It is used for shelter but is frost tender below 5°C. From October to February insignificant white flowers appear.

Propagation — in spring with seed; in summer take semi-ripe cuttings.

Alectryon excelsus
Maori name: titoki. Common name: New Zealand ash. A spreading evergreen that grows in moisture-retentive soil and sun to 10m. It is used for shelter and makes an attractive specimen tree. Brown seed capsules split to reveal brilliant scarlet on the inside where black seeds take a year to ripen. From December to February cherry-red flowers appear; flowers and seed capsules may be present on a tree at the same time.

Propagation — in autumn with seed.

Eucalyptus ficifolia
Common name: scarlet-flowering gum. An aromatic evergreen that is moderately fast growing to 10m in well-drained soil and sun but is frost tender below 1°C. Used as a specimen, and from March to April white, red or pink flowers appear.

Propagation — in spring or autumn with seed.

Ficus macrophylla
Common name: Moreton Bay fig. An evergreen that grows to 30m in fertile, well-drained soil and sun or semi-shade. It is used for shelter but is frost tender below 8°C. It has dark-green leaves, and from December to February purplish, edible fruit appear.

Propagation — spring with seed; summer by leaf-bud or stem-tip cuttings and air-layering.

Jacaranda mimosifolia, J. ovalifolia
Common name: jacaranda. Deciduous and fast growing to 12m in fertile, well-drained soil and sun. It grows only in warm, humid, subtropical climates and is not found south of Raglan. Used as a specimen; can be seen lining streets in Sydney and Whangarei. Jacaranda is a must for any garden in warmer regions. From November to April mauve-blue, pea-shaped flowers appear.

Propagation — spring with seed; in summer take semi-ripe cuttings.

Racosperma baileyanum, Acacia baileyana
Common name: Cootamundra wattle. An aggressive, fast-growing and spreading, aromatic evergreen that grows in well-drained soil and sun to 6m. It is used for shelter, and in August yellow flowers appear that are decorative in a vase.

Propagation — in spring with scarified seed.

Racosperma verticillatum, Acacia verticillata
Common name: prickly Moses. An aggressive, aromatic evergreen that reaches 4-9m; fast growing in most well-drained soils and sun. It is used for shelter and hedging; withstands moderate drought and most winds but shows signs of salt burn in exposed coastal regions. A useful addition in shelter-belt planting but often needs staking to prevent it rocking in the wind. Hard pruning of the foliage helps root development. It is short lived, having a life expectancy under 20 years. The leaves are linear and rather thick; from September to November it produces fluffy yellow flowers.

Propagation – in spring with scarified seed.

SHRUBS

Adenandra uniflora, Diosma uniflora
Common names: China flower or enamel flower. An evergreen that is slow growing to 90cm in fertile, well-drained soil and sun. Diosma is a spectacular ornamental shrub; from October to November fragrant pinky-white flowers streaked with rose-pink or crimson appear.

Propagation – in spring with seed; autumn take semi-ripe cuttings.

Astartea fascicularis
Common name: astartea. An evergreen that is fast growing in moist soil and sun; reaches 3m. Useful as a background shelter shrub. The white or rose-pink flowers that appear all year round are decorative in a vase.

Propagation – in autumn take tip-cuttings.

Clianthus puniceus
Maori name: koowhai-ngutu-kaka. Common names: kaka beak or red kowhai. An evergreen or semi-evergreen that grows to 1.5m in well-drained soil and sun. From October to December red or pink flowers appear. *C. puniceus* 'Albus' has pure white flowers.

Propagation – in spring with seed; late summer take stem cuttings.

Coleonema album, Diosma ericoides
Common name: confetti bush. An evergreen that grows to 1m in sun or semi-shade and fertile, well-drained neutral to acid soil. From June to November fragrant white flowers appear.

Propagation – spring with seed; in summer take semi-ripe cuttings.

Coleonema pulchrum
Common name: breath of heaven. An evergreen that grows to 1.25m in sun or semi-shade and fertile, well-drained neutral to acid soil. Parent of other hybrids, including dwarf forms. Stands up to wind well and endures a light salt content; does not like long droughts. Survives competition from most plants reasonably well and is excellent both as an ornamental for the garden or in cluster plantings. Prune about every second year after flowering to keep bushy. A beautiful shrub with soft, fine, bright green foliage that bears numerous small pink flowers from October to November. *C.* 'Sunset Gold' has heath-like leaves that are yellow in spring, green in summer and gold in autumn, and from October to November flowers appear in various shades of pink.

Propagation – in spring with seed; in summer take semi-ripe cuttings.

Cytisus X spachianus, C. racemosus, Genista fragrans
Common name: broom. An evergreen that is fast growing to 3m in well-drained soil and sun. Stands up to wind well provided it is not top heavy; prune back to half size after flowering. Lives in coastal regions but its foliage burns easily. Useful as a filler amongst other trees and shrubs. Is also beneficial as a nitrogen fixer, improving the soil. From June to September it is covered in a profusion of sweetly scented, golden-yellow flowers that attract bees.

Propagation – in autumn with seed; in summer by semi-ripe cuttings, hybrids and cultivars by semi-ripe cuttings only in late summer.

Pomaderris apetala
Maori and common name: tainui. A competitive New Zealand native evergreen that grows from 3-4m in sun, and in gravelly, poor or sandstone soil with good drainage. Often seen growing on dry sunny banks; in warm sheltered regions it is found naturally in coastal bush. Becomes drawn and leggy when left, and is best included in cluster plantings with taller shrubs. From November to January pale green and white flowers appear. *P. kumeraho*,

golden tainui or gumdigger's soap (Maori name kuumarahou), has similar habits to *P. apetala* but grows to 2.5m and has golden-yellow flowers from September to October.

Propagation – late autumn by seed and slightly firm tip cuttings.

Salvia elegans, S. rutilans
Common name: pineapple sage. Semi-dormant; grows in fertile, well-drained soil and sun to 1m. This plant is great for winter colour and good in the cottage garden. From March to June scarlet-red flowers appear.

Propagation – in spring or summer take softwood cuttings.

Senna multiglandulosa, Cassia tomentosa
Common name: buttercup bush. A competitive evergreen that grows from 3-6m in well-drained soil and sun. An attractive bush, with an open shape and lush green leaves which fold in the evenings. Burns off from too much salt wind, and prefers warm, sunny locations. Useful in cluster plantings and as an ornamental. From January to June large clusters of yellow flowers appear.

Propagation – autumn by half-ripe cuttings and seed: self-seeds freely.

Serruria florida
Common name: blushing bride. An evergreen that grows in acid soil and sun to 1.5m, but is frost tender below 5°C. Needs pruning after flowering to ensure a bushy habit and increase the flowering stems for the next season. From June to September fluffy pink blooms, which make excellent cut flowers, appear.

Propagation – with seed: germinates in 2-3 weeks and flowers the following year.

Solanum laciniatum
Maori and common name: poroporo. A branching, competitive New Zealand native evergreen that is fast growing to 3m in fertile, well-drained soil and sun. This bush is cultivated to produce an ingredient used in contraceptive pills. Its aggressive nature makes it a useful short-lived ornamental for sheltering other plants in exposed sites. It has attractive foliage, and from September to April purple flowers with yellow centres appear.

Propagation – in spring with seed; summer take semi-ripe cuttings.

Tibouchina urvilleana, T. semidecandra
Common name: glory bush. An evergreen that grows to 3m in sun and fertile, well-drained neutral to acid soil. It is used as a specimen but is frost tender below 5°C. This is a great tree for the rear of a shrub garden, as it flowers when most other plants have finished. From February to July violet-blue flowers appear.

Propagation – late spring or summer by greenwood or semi-ripe cuttings.

CLIMBERS

Podranea ricasoliana, Pandorea ricasoliana, Tecoma ricasoliana
Common name: Port St John creeper. Competitive, moderately fast-growing evergreen; it survives cooler, temperate areas by losing most of its foliage in winter. Preferring warmer areas, such as Australia and the northern regions of New Zealand, it grows in fertile, well-drained soil and sun to over 4m, generally needing support such as wire netting. Reasonably wind hard, it grows and flowers along the coast but needs the protection of surrounding plants to avoid salt burn. It spreads by layering and scrambling on to other growth, but tends to be acceptable to other plants and is able to compete well. Produces large clusters of picturesque, bright pink flowers from December to May.

Propagation – in spring with seed; summer take semi-ripe cuttings.

Solanum jasminoides
Common names: jasmine nightshade or potato vine. Semi-evergreen which grows to 6m in well-drained soil and sun. Does well on trellis, fences and pergolas on windy sites and in courtyards, but burns from salt wind. Takes a few years to establish itself and needs some assistance by tying down new growth. White flowers appear all year round. A variegated cultivar that produces clusters of drooping white flowers is also available.

Propagation – in spring with seed; in summer take semi-ripe cuttings.

PERENNIALS
Anigozanthos 'Bush Gems'
Common name: kangaroo paw. An evergreen hybrid group that grows from 50cm-2m in well-drained soil and sun or semi-shade, and endures drought well. The interesting shape adds character to any garden. The bronzy-red, orange-yellow or deep-red flowers that appear from October to February can be used fresh or dried for floral decoration.

Propagation – in spring by division and ripe seed.

Pelargonium X *hortorum* hybrids
Common name: geranium. Aromatic evergreen that is fast growing to 1m in sandy soils where sun is received for part of the day or in semi-shade. Over the years geraniums have been hybridised to create new cultivars which all retain the same characteristics and are frost tender below 1°C. An excellent plant for window boxes, containers and windy places; they even endure light salt wind and cope reasonably well with dry conditions. From October to March vibrant displays of white, red, orange, salmon-pink or lavender flowers appear.

Propagation – from spring to autumn take softwood cuttings.

BULBS
Freesia alba, F. lactea, F. refracta var. *alba*
Common name: freesia. Dormant in summer; grows in well-drained soil and sun to 30cm. This freesia naturalises easily in warm areas. From October to November fragrant white flowers appear. *F.* 'Burtonii' produces scented white, orange-red, yellow, pink or purple flowers; decorative in a vase.

Propagation – in spring with seed; in autumn with offsets.

Narcissus 'Paper White Grandiflora', *N. papyraceus* 'Grandiflora'
Common name: paperwhites. Dormant in summer; grow competitively in well-drained soil and sun or semi-shade to 35cm. Can be useful in pots as well as the garden. The fragrant, pure white flowers that appear from August to November are decorative in a vase.

Propagation – late summer or autumn by ripe seed and division; after flowering divide offsets of selected forms every 3-5 years.

Nerine flexuosa 'Alba'
Common names: Guernsey lily or nerine. Competitive and grows in well-drained soil and sun to 50cm. White flowers appear from February to April, while *N. sarniensis* is good for autumn colour. It grows to 60cm and has orange flowers; decorative in a vase. Make sure the neck of nerine bulbs are well above ground when they are set.

Propagation – in autumn with ripe seed or when leaves have died down divide bulb offsets.

Watsonia bordonica, W. ardnerei, W. meriana, W. pyramidata
Common name: bugle lily. Competitive and grows in well-drained soil and sunlight to 1.5m; needs room to grow and naturalises in the right situation: corms are best left undisturbed to form clumps. Suitable for a wild garden but if found to be too invasive is easily pulled out. The parent of many colourful hybrids; the white, rose, apricot or pink flowers that appear from October to December are decorative in a vase.

Propagation – in autumn with seed.

Zantedeschia New Zealand Mixed Hybrids
Common name: calla lily. This perennial tuber grows in fertile, moist but well-drained soil and sun to 60cm. By planting bulbs over several weeks, a succession of blooms is ensured. The purple, rose-pink, yellow, lavender or soft-pink flowers that change colourings as they age appear from November to January and are decorative in a vase.

Propagation – in winter divide offsets.

ANNUALS
Ammobium alatum
Common name: winged everlasting. Spreading and fast growing to 1m in well-drained soil and sun; easily pulled out if too invasive. Naturalises in right situation, good for a cottage or wild garden, and can grow in sandy soil at the seaside. The white flowers that appear from November to February

can be used fresh or dried for floral decoration.

Propagation – in spring with seed.

Chrysanthemum carinatum, C. tricolor
Common name: painted daisy. Grows in well-drained soil and sun to 60cm. Brilliant for summer bedding colour, as from November to February white, scarlet, orange, yellow, mauve-pink or purple flowers appear; are decorative in a vase.

Propagation – in spring with seed.

Petunia X *hybrida*
Common name: petunia. A competitive perennial that is grown as an annual to 30cm in fertile well-drained soil and sun. This plant forms lovely colourful displays in massed beds or pots. From November to April white, red, blue, pink or purple flowers appear.

Propagation – early spring with seed sown outdoors or under glass.

Tagetes erecta
Common names: African marigold or Aztec marigold. Grows up to 1m in fertile, well-drained soil and sun; useful for edging or planters. The scented, cushiony, double creamy-white, orange or golden-yellow flowers that appear from January to April can be used fresh or dried for floral decoration.

Propagation – in spring with seed.

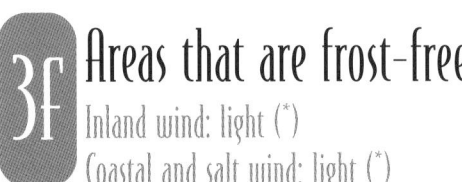

3F Areas that are frost-free
Inland wind: light (*)
Coastal and salt wind: light (*)

SHRUBS
Fuchsia boliviana, F. fulgens, F. magellanica
Common name: fuchsia. Deciduous or semi-deciduous and grows to 1m in fertile, moist but well-drained soil where sun is received for part of the day or in shade. From November to April a profusion of drooping flowers appear; a huge variety of colours is available, most common being red, orange, mauve, pink or purple and blue, often mixed together with white.

Propagation – take softwood cuttings in any season.

Podalyria calyptrata
Common name: sweet pea bush. A competitive evergreen that grows from 2-3m in fertile, well-drained soil and sun. The shrub has an open shape and is a handsome addition to the wind garden. It endures dry periods and competes well with other growth. Does not like too much salt wind and does much better when planted amongst taller shrubs in cluster plantings. From August to November mauve-pink, pea-like flowers appear.

Propagation – in spring with seed; summer take semi-ripe cuttings.

CLIMBERS
Pandorea jasminoides, Tecoma jasminoides
Common name: Australian bower plant. An attractive competitive evergreen that grows to 5m in moist soil and sun; ideal for gazebos, trellises and archways. From September to December creamy-white flowers with pink-flushed throats appear.

Propagation – spring with seed; summer by stem cuttings and layering.

Tecomaria capensis, Bignonia capensis, Tecoma capensis
Common name: Cape honeysuckle. A rambling evergreen shrub that is fast growing to 3m in fertile, well-drained soil and sun. Often used as a hedge but can smother other vegetation if not pruned. From December to March orange or red-orange flowers appear.

Propagation – spring with seed; in summer take semi-ripe cuttings.

ANNUALS
Helichrysum bracteatum
Common name: strawflower. Grows in well-drained soil and sun to 75cm; naturalises when left alone where other plant competition is moderate. The

white, red, orange, yellow, pink or purple flowers that appear from November to April can be used fresh or dried for floral decoration, hence its nickname, 'everlasting' flowers.

Propagation – in spring with seed.

Limonium sinuatum
Common names: sea lavender or statice. A perennial that is easy to grow as an annual in any garden in well-drained soil and sun. The 50cm high white, apricot, yellow, blue, pink or purple flowers that appear from November to February can be used fresh or dried for floral decoration.

Propagation – autumn or early spring with seed; in spring by division; late winter take root cuttings.

31 Areas that are frost-free
Inland wind: light (*)
Coastal and salt wind: plants need complete shelter

TREES
Brachyglottis repanda
Maori name: rangiora. Common name: bushman's friend. An evergreen used for shelter; grows to 3m in well-drained moist soil where sun is received for part of the day or in shade. It is an attractive bush with large green or purplish leaves; in November heads of tiny, heavily scented purple flowers appear.

Propagation – in late summer take semi-ripe cuttings.

Citrus limon, C. limonum
Common name: lemon tree. An evergreen that is slow growing to 7m in sun and nitrogen-rich, well-drained soil with plenty of water; frost tender below 5°C. Used as a specimen; white flowers appear all year round, followed by yellow fruit; fresh lemons are a must in every kitchen.

Propagation – autumn or spring with seed; varieties are budded on to suitable rootstock.

Clethra arborea
Common name: lily of the valley tree. An evergreen that grows to 8m in moist, peaty, acid soil where sun is received for part of the day or in semi-shade. Open-ground specimens over 1.3m are usually difficult to transplant, unless especially prepared several months before. A handsome plant that produces white flowers from February to April.

Propagation – in autumn with seed; in summer take softwood cuttings.

SHRUBS
Gomphocarpus physocarpus, Asclepias physocarpus
Common name: swan plant. Deciduous and grows in well-drained, humus-rich soil and sun to 2m. From December to February greenish-white flowers appear, attracting butterflies that often spin their cocoons on the plant.

Propagation – in spring by seed and tip cuttings.

Phylica pubescens
Common names: featherhead or flannel bush. An evergreen that grows to 1.2m in well-drained, moist soil and sun; decorative in a shrub border. Prune after flowering to preserve a good shape and prolong life. From June to August greenish-yellow, plume-like bracts fringed with buff-coloured hairs appear. A useful cut flower but bushes need replenishing every few years.

Propagation – with seed; autumn take cuttings of half-ripened shoots.

CULINARY HERBS
Ocimum basilicum
Common name: sweet basil. This annual grows to 60cm in well-drained, moist soil and sun. The leaves can be used fresh for flavouring or dried for later use, adding a spicy taste to all dishes that contain tomato.

Propagation – in late spring with seed.

GRASSES
Arundo donax var. versicolor
Common name: giant reed. This rhizomatous perennial is fast growing in well-drained soil and sun to 6m. Used to add interest and decoration to any hedge or at the back of a shrub border. It is herbaceous, dying back over winter, and has attractive variegated green and white foliage.

Propagation – in autumn or spring with seed; spring by division.

CREEPERS
Nierembergia hippomanica var. violacea, N. caerulea
Common name: cup-flower. This is an evergreen perennial that is fast growing to 20cm as an annual in well-drained moist soil and sun. Suitable for window boxes, rock gardens or for edging. From September to November white or violet-blue flowers appear.

Propagation – autumn with seed; spring by division; summer by semi-ripe cuttings.

CLIMBERS
Bougainvillea glabra
Common name: bougainvillea. Semi-evergreen and grows up to 3m in fertile, well-drained soil and sun. This plant loves the heat from baking sunshine and is frost tender below 10°C. It is slow to establish but wonderful from January to March when white, red or rose-pink flowers appear.

Propagation – summer take semi-ripe cuttings; when dormant take hardwood cuttings.

Gloriosa superba
Common names: climbing lily or glory lily. This tuber is deciduous and grows to 2m in rich, well-drained soil and sun. Clings to any suitable support like netting, old stumps or shrubs. Is frost tender below 8°C; attractive in pots in cold areas, with 3-6 tubers in a large pot. The red and yellow-orange flowers that appear from December to February are decorative in a vase.

Propagation – in spring by seed and division.

Hardenbergia violacea, H. monophylla
Common names: Australian lilac or sarsaparilla. An evergreen that grows in well-drained soil and sun but is frost tender below 7°C. Wanders through shrubs, and up and around verandahs, wire fences or trellises. From October to December pink or purple flowers appear.

Propagation – spring with pre-soaked seed; late summer or autumn by stem cuttings.

Jasminum azoricum
Common name: jasmine. A competitive evergreen that grows in fertile, moist but well-drained soil and sun. Covers wire or trellis fences and grows through hedging. From October to March fragrant white flowers appear.

Propagation – in summer take semi-ripe cuttings.

GROUNDCOVERS
Plectranthus oertendahlii
Common names: Brazilian coleus or prostrate coleus. A prostrate evergreen perennial that grows to 20cm in moist soil where sun is received for part of the day or in semi-shade; is frost tender below 10°C; can be grown in a hanging basket inside where the climate is cold. Has variegated red-green leaves backed with purple, and white-mauve flowers which bloom throughout the year.

Propagation – in spring or summer by stem cuttings and division.

PERENNIALS
Dianthus caryophyllus
Common name: carnation. Slow growing to 1m in fertile, well-drained soil and sun. Lovely in any garden border, as fragrant white, red, orange, yellow, pink or plum-coloured flowers appear from October to December; decorative in a vase.

Propagation – in summer by layering and cuttings.

Gerbera jamesonii (herbaceous)
Common names: African daisy, Barberton daisy, or Transvaal daisy. Grows in fertile, well-drained soil and sun or semi-shade to 60cm. Plant 60cm apart for groups, as they grow into large clumps; also suitable as individual pot

plants. The white, red, orange, yellow, pink or cerise flowers that appear from November to January are decorative in a vase.

Propagation – autumn or early spring with seed; late winter to early spring by division; in summer take cuttings from side shoots.

Limonium perezii
Common name: statice. A competitive, clump-forming evergreen that grows to 1m in well-drained soil and sun. Is frost tender below 7°C; can be grown as a pot plant in colder climates. The blue flowers that appear from November to February can be used fresh or dried for floral decoration.

Propagation – autumn or early spring with seed; in spring by division; in late winter take root cuttings.

Oxypetalum caeruleum (herbaceous), Tweedia caerulea
Common name: tweedia. Grows in well-drained soil and sun to 1m and is frost tender below 5°C. From December to March blue, star-shaped flowers appear that change colour with age and attract butterflies; decorative in a vase.

Propagation – in spring with seed.

Primula obconica (herbaceous)
Common name: primrose. Grows to 30cm in well-drained, gritty loam soil where sun is received for part of the day or in semi-shade, but is frost tender below 7°C. The scented white, red, blue or soft-pink flowers that appear from August to October are lovely in beds en masse, and in mixed borders, and are decorative in a vase.

Propagation – in spring with ripe seed; in early summer or autumn by division; during dormancy take root cuttings.

Salvia farinaceae (herbaceous)
Common names: mealy sage or silver sage. Competitive and grows in well-drained soil and sun to 1m. Attractive in beds and mixed borders for autumn colour contrast, as from March to April blue flowers appear.

Propagation – spring or summer by softwood cuttings; spring by division.

Salvia uliginosa (herbaceous)
Common name: bog sage. Grows in moist soil and sun to 1.5m. Valuable long-flowering plant for any border; from December to May very pretty, small blue flowers appear on tallish stems.

Propagation – spring or summer take softwood cuttings; in spring by division.

Trachelium caeruleum (herbaceous), Diosphaera
Common name: throatwort. Grows in fertile, very well-drained soil and sun to 90cm. Lovely in an herbaceous border. The bold white or blue flowers that appear from November to February are decorative used fresh or dried for floral decoration.

Propagation – with ripe seed.

BULBS

Gladiolus X hortulanus
Common name: gladioli. Grows in fertile, well-drained soil and sun to 1m, and provides splendid displays of colour for a mixed garden border. The white, red, orange, yellow, green, lilac, pink or purple flowers that appear from January to March are decorative in a vase.

Propagation – with seed and division of young cormlets.

Ixia maculata
Common name: African corn lily. Dormant during summer and grows in well-drained soil and sun to 90cm; very effective naturalised in wild gardens on banks or in lawns. The white, scarlet, orange, yellow, green, blue or purple flowers that appear from September to December are decorative in a vase.

Propagation – in autumn by seed and division of offsets.

Ornithogalum thyrsoides
Common names: chincherinchee or star of Bethlehem. Grows in well-drained soil and sun or semi-shade to 300mm. The white flowers that appear from November to January last for several weeks; when cut, and the stems rested in dye or ink, they absorb other colours; decorative in a vase.

Propagation – in spring by seed and division of offsets.

Polianthes tuberosa
Common name: tuberose. Grows in well-drained soil and sun to 60cm. The very heavily fragrant white flowers that appear from December to January are an exotic addition to any mixed border and are decorative in a vase.

Propagation – in spring clumps should be lifted and divided: bulb flowers only once but produces many side shoots: be sure to discard the old mother bulb, the only one with a hole.

Ranunculus asiaticus
Common name: Persian buttercup. Grows in well-drained, moist soil and sun or semi-shade to 55cm; valuable as a colourful bedding plant. The white, red, orange, yellow or pink flowers that appear from August to October are also decorative in a vase.

Propagation – with ripe seed; in spring or autumn by division.

ANNUALS

Antirrhinum majus
Common name: snapdragon. This perennial grows to 1m as an annual in rich, well-drained soil and sun; splendid in massed beds for colour. The white, red, orange, yellow or pink flowers that appear from January to December are excellent for cutting.

Propagation – in spring or early autumn with seed.

Begonia semperflorens
Common name: begonia. Competitive and grows to 30cm in well-drained soil where sun is received for part of the day or in semi-shade; frost tender below 13°C. Very versatile bedding plant for any garden border, edging and formal mass plantings. From November to April white or red flowers appear.

Propagation – in spring by seed and stem cuttings.

Celosia cristata
Common name: cockscomb, feather cockscomb or Prince of Wales feathers. Grows to 30-60cm in fertile, well-drained soil and sun; in December red, apricot, yellow or purple flowers appear, providing a blazing display of colour for any garden; decorative in a vase.

Propagation – in spring with seed.

Cosmos bipinnatus
Common name: Mexican aster. Fast growing to 60cm in moist but well-drained soil and sun. The lightly scented white, red, pink or mauve flowers that appear from January to May are decorative in a vase. C. sulphureus, yellow cosmos, has lightly scented orange and yellow flowers. These plants naturalise in the right situation and are ideal for the cottage or wild garden.

Propagation – spring or autumn by seed: self-seeds on right site.

Eustoma grandiflorum, Lisianthus russellianus
Common name: lisianthus. Grows in well-drained soil and sun to 60cm but is frost tender below 5°C; suitable for pots in cold climates. Lovely cottage garden plant that, from November to January, produces white, pink or dark-purple flowers which are very decorative in a vase.

Propagation – early autumn in frost-free areas with seed sown outdoors; late winter with seed sown under glass.

Gomphrena globosa
Common name: globe amaranth. Slow growing in fertile, well-drained soil and sun to 30cm; useful for bedding in any warm garden. The white, red, orange, soft-pink or purple flowers that appear from December to February can be used fresh or dried for floral decoration.

Propagation – in spring with seed.

Helipterum manglesii, Rhodanthe manglesii
Common name: paper daisy. Moderately fast growing to 30cm in poor, very well-drained soil and sun. The white, red or pink flowers that appear from November to February fade as they age, giving a multi-colour effect. Can be used fresh or dried for floral decoration.

Propagation – spring or summer with seed; in autumn take cuttings.

Pericallis X *hybrida, Cineraria* X *hybrida,*
Senecio X *hybridus, S. cruentus*
Common name: cineraria. A competitive perennial which grows as an annual from 50cm-1m in very well-drained soil where sun is received for part of the day or in semi-shade. Needs shelter from strong wind and is best grown amongst other plants. From October to December decorative white, red, pink, blue or purple flowers appear.

Propagation – in spring by division.

Phlox drummondii
Common names: annual phlox or pride of Texas. Slow growing to 40cm in fertile, well-drained, moist soil and sun or semi-shade. Can tolerate some dry conditions; colourful border or bedding plant. From November to March white, blue, pink or purple flowers appear.

Propagation – in spring with seed.

Primula malacoides
Common names: fairy primrose or primula. This perennial is the parent of many hybrids. It is easy to grow as an annual to 30cm in well-drained, gritty, loam soil where sun is received for part of the day or in semi-shade. A great colourful bedding plant, as from August to December lightly scented white, carmine-red, pink or purple flowers appear.

Propagation – in spring, early summer or autumn with ripe seed.

Psylliostachys suworowii, Limonium suworowii
Common names: Russian statice or statice pink pokers. Slow growing to 50cm in fertile, well-drained soil and sun. The lilac-rose flowers that appear from November to February are a stunning display for any flower bed and are decorative in a vase.

Propagation – in early spring with seed sown under glass.

Salvia splendens
Common name: sage. A perennial grown as an annual in fertile, well-drained soil and sun; reaches 30cm; beds for colour should be sown 20-30cm apart. From March to April white, scarlet, soft-pink or purple flowers appear.

Propagation – summer or spring take softwood cuttings; spring by division.

Schizanthus wisetoniensis
Common name: poor man's orchid. Fast growing in fertile, well-drained, moist soil and semi-shade to 45cm. Splendid bedding plant that does not like too much heat. From September to May white and gold, carmine-red, pink, purple or brown flowers appear.

Propagation – late summer or autumn with seed: plants flower late winter or spring.

Trachymene coerulea, Didiscus coeruleus
Common name: blue lace flower. Moderately fast growing to 50cm in fertile, well-drained soil and sun. The blue flowers that appear from December to March are attractive in a mixed border and decorative in a vase.

Propagation – in spring with seed.

Xeranthemum annuum
Common name: immortelle paper flower. Fast growing to 60-90cm in fertile, very well-drained soil and sun. Lovely displays of white, carmine-red, pink or purple flowers appear from November to February and can be used fresh or dried for floral decoration.

Propagation – in spring with seed sown outdoors.

Zinnia angustifolia, Z. linearis, Z. 'Little Star'
Common name: zinnia. Grows to 20cm in fertile, moist but well-drained soil and sun. Orange flowers appear from February to April. *Z. elegans* grows to 75cm and produces creamy-white, red, yellow, green, pink or purple flowers. Dead-heading regularly ensures prolonged flowering of both species. Useful for edging or bedding displays and decorative in a vase.

Propagation – early spring by seed sown directly in soil or under glass.

3J Areas that are frost-free
Inland wind: plants need complete shelter
Coastal and salt wind: plants need complete shelter

PERENNIALS
Cymbidium suave
Common name: orchid. An evergreen that needs warmth in winter; is slow growing to 30cm in well-drained bark and leaf-litter where sun is received for part of the day or in semi-shade. Adds an exotic atmosphere to woodlands when planted under trees in the right situation; commonly an indoor pot plant in colder climates. The red and green flowers that appear from May to September are decorative in a vase.

Propagation – divide orchid into sections of four or more pseudobulbs: cut the rhizomes in strategic places.

Dahlia excelsa (herbaceous), *D. imperialis*
Common name: tree dahlia. Competitive and fast growing to 4m in fertile, well-drained, moist soil and sun. A lush and interesting plant that, because of its size, is suitable at the back of a garden border. From February to April white or lavender-pink flowers appear.

Propagation – in spring by seed, division of tubers and basal shoot cuttings: stems cut to 60cm after flowering can be replanted.

Dahlia coccinea X *D. pinnata* (herbaceous),
D. rosea, D. variablis
Common name: dahlia. Competitive and grows to 1.2m in fertile, well-drained, moist soil and sun. Many decorative varieties are available. Tubers naturalise but prefer lifting every 2-3 years. Very suitable for a cottage garden; needs shelter. The scented white, red, orange, yellow, pink or purple flowers that appear from January to April are decorative in a vase.

Propagation – spring by seed, division of tubers and basal shoot cuttings.

Strelitzia reginae
Common name: bird of paradise flower. An evergreen that grows to 1m in fertile, well-drained soil and sun or semi-shade; frost tender below 10°C. Very colourful *en masse* in borders or wild gardens. The orange and blue flowers that appear from October to February are decorative in a vase.

Propagation – in spring by seed, division and young suckers.

BULBS
Hippeastrum equestre
Common name: amaryllis. Parent of many hybrids; grows in well-drained soil and sun or semi-shade to 60cm; suitable as a pot plant in cold climate. Make sure bulb neck is protruding from the ground when planted. From September to January white, red or soft-pink flowers appear.

Propagation – in spring with seed; autumn or spring by offsets: large-flowered hybrids by offsets only.

ANNUALS
Campanula pyramidalis
Common name: chimney bellflower. Grows to 2m as a biennial in well-drained, moist soil where sun is received for part of the day or in shade. Useful in a mixed border, and the white or blue flowers that appear from December to February are decorative in a vase.

Propagation – autumn or spring with seed; in summer or spring take softwood or basal cuttings.

3L Areas that are frost-free

Inland wind: light (*)
Coastal and salt wind: do not grow these plants

TREES

Agathis australis (conifer)
Maori and common name: kauri. An evergreen that is slow growing to 25m in most soil types and sun; thrives in warm, wet areas. An ornamental specimen of considerable beauty with its pyramidal shape.

Propagation – late autumn to late winter: take cuttings from young plants or stratify seed.

Albizia julibrissin
Common names: nemu tree, pink siris or silk tree. Deciduous and grows aggressively to 8m in sun and well-drained soil, preferably with added compost. Its soft green foliage folds up at night, and from November to January soft-pink, silk-like flowers appear; used as a decorative specimen tree.

Propagation – in autumn with seed.

Carmichaelia williamsii
Maori names: neinei, tarangahape, tawaro. Common name: New Zealand broom. A small tree that grows to 3-4m in open sunlight and good soils, but should not be grown in temperatures less than 10°C. Decorative flowers from October to November.

Propagation – in summer by semi-ripe cuttings or in autumn or spring by seed.

SHRUBS

Cuphea ignea, C. platycentra
Common name: cigarette flower. A decorative evergreen that is slow growing in fertile, well-drained soil and sun to 50cm; frost tender below 2°C. In colder climates from January to February red or orange flowers appear; in warmer areas it can bloom continuously.

Propagation – spring by seed; summer or spring by greenwood cuttings.

FERNS

Asplenium lucidum, A. oblongifolium
Maori names: huruhuru whenua or paranako. Common name: shining spleenwort. An evergreen that is slow growing to 1m in any moist soil where sun is received for part of the day or in semi-shade. It forms good clumps in woodland areas and has decorative green leaves but is frost tender below 2°C.

Propagation – in late summer with spores or bulbils where present.

Cyathea dealbata, Alsophila, Sphaeropteris
Maori name: ponga. Common name: silver fern. Evergreen and slow growing to 4m in humus-rich, moisture-retentive but well-drained soil where sun is received for part of the day or in semi-shade. It has very decorative green leaves, silver-grey underneath, which contrast with other green foliage.

Propagation – in spring with spores.

Dicksonia squarrosa
Maori name: wheki. Common name: tree fern. An evergreen that is slow growing to 4m in humus-rich, moist soil where sun is received for part of the day or in semi-shade. It has decorative green leaf fronds; lovely in a native garden.

Propagation – in summer with spores.

CLIMBERS

Jasminum mesnyi, J. primulinum
Common name: primrose jasmine. A competitive evergreen that grows to 3m in fertile, moist but well-drained soil and sun; most commonly found in northern areas where it can bloom all year round. In other areas from October to March fragrant yellow flowers appear.

Propagation – in summer take semi-ripe cuttings.

ANNUALS

Alonsoa warscewiczii
Common name: mask-flower. This perennial grows as an annual to 60cm in well-drained, rich soil and sun. Colourful en masse as a bedding plant, as from December to February scarlet or pink flowers appear.

Propagation – in spring with seed.

Amaranthus caudatus
Common name: love-lies-bleeding. Competitive and grows to 1.2m in fertile, well-drained soil and sun. The plant has green or red heart-shaped leaves and red flowers that appear from December to May. A. hybridus var. erythrostachys or A. hypochondriacus, Prince's feather, has purple-bronze leaves and, from February to April, white, red or pink flowers; both species can be used fresh or dried for floral decoration.

Propagation – in spring with seed.

Callistephus chinensis
Common name: China aster. Grows in fertile, well-drained soil and sun to 60cm. This plant has a short life, so sowing should be staggered over several weeks to provide continuous blooms into late summer. The lightly scented white, red, yellow, pale blue or rose-pink flowers that appear from February to April are decorative in a vase.

Propagation – in spring with seed sown under glass; in mid-spring with seed sown outdoors.

3m Areas that are frost-free

Inland wind: plants need complete shelter
Coastal and salt wind: do not grow these plants

FERNS

Asplenium bulbiferum
Maori names: manamana or mouku. Common name: hen-and-chickens fern. An evergreen that is slow growing in any moist soil and semi-shade to 30cm and is frost tender below 2°C. Grown as a pot plant in colder climates, it has decorative light-green leaves and is useful near ponds or on banks.

Propagation – in late summer with spores or bulbils which germinate on the leaves and drop off.

Marattia salicina
Maori name: para. Common name: king fern. An evergreen that is very slow growing to 50cm in any moist soil where sun is received for part of the day or in semi-shade; frost tender below 10°C. It is an endangered species in the wild; should be treasured as a very decorative fern whose large leaf fronds look lovely anywhere near water.

Propagation – by removing some small tuberous appendages from the main root and replanting in leaf mould.

GRASSES

Cyperus papyrus
Common names: paper reed or papyrus. An evergreen perennial rhizomatous sedge that grows to 5m in wet soil and sun or semi-shade. Good for swampy areas; naturalises easily in the right situation.

Propagation – autumn or spring by seed; spring by division: selected forms by division only.

Index

List of species